DESERT FLYER

DESERT FLYER

The Log and Journal of
FLYING OFFICER WILLIAM E. MARSH

Martyn R. Ford-Jones

Schiffer Military History
Atglen, PA

Dust jacket artwork by Steve Ferguson, Colorado Springs, CO.

HOLEY HURI
FltSgt Bill Marsh banks away from a probable victory over an Me 109 which he ran down on the perimeter of the enemy landing field. In seconds, his borrowed Mk.II, "Hurk NH-N," would take hits in the prop and nose cowling from the airdrome flak guns, resulting in a tense, but safe, run for home.

Book Design by Robert Biondi.

Copyright © 1997 by Martyn R. Ford-Jones.
Library of Congress Catalog Number: 97-67062.

Printed in China.
ISBN: 0-7643-0347-3

We are interested in hearing from authors with book ideas on related topics.

Published by Schiffer Publishing Ltd.
4880 Lower Valley Road
Atglen, PA 19310
Phone: (610) 593-1777
FAX: (610) 593-2002
E-mail: Schifferbk@aol.com.
Please write for a free catalog.
This book may be purchased from the publisher.
Please include $3.95 postage.
Try your bookstore first.

Contents

Acknowledgments

When Gil Marsh gave consent for me to peruse and edit his brother's journals into book form, I thought I could "go it alone." After all, the entries were written by Bill Marsh and the layout was similar to that in his journal. All I had to do was some research and a lot of typing; or so I thought.

However, even with a book of this nature, it is surprising how many people you can turn to for help along the way. Each contribution, however small, helping to pave the way through its preparation to eventual completion and publication.

To those who have helped me along the way, and to whom I offer my most sincere thanks are Jon Purday, nephew of Bill Marsh, who trusted a complete stranger with the journals and photographs compiled by his uncle, Victoria and Richard Hansen of Bushwood Books, Kew for their initial help and approaches to the publishers. June and Terry Watkins of Chelmsford, for the loan of material relating to the war in North Africa. Andrew Willis, of Swindon, for "battling" with and endeavoring to reproduce the photographs from the original (time worn) negatives.

Thanks are also extended to Derek Butler and Ian Small of the Commonwealth War Graves Commission, Mr Day of the Air Historical Branch, Ministry of Defense, the Staff of the Public Records Office and the Royal Air Force Museum, London, and editing team of the Ormskirk Advertiser Series Newspapers, Liverpool.

I would also like to say many thanks to Bob Biondi, Senior Editor at Schiffer Publishing Ltd., U.S.A., for his initial faith in the project, help with queries and continued guidance towards the completed work.

On the family side I must thank my wife Valerie, without whom things would not get done, and my youngest daughter, Alexandra, who has taken over responsibility for the telephone!

Acknowledgments

Finally, a very special and heart-felt thank you must be extended to my eldest daughter Emma, who spent a great deal of time re-typing the entire manuscript and photo-captions on to her computer, when my equipment was found to be alien to modern technology. Love you kid and thanks.

It is a tragedy that the person who unknowingly started all of this off was killed needlessly in 1944, Bill Marsh himself.

In reading his journals in depth, collating information from his Log and perusing his letters, I feel I have come to know William Marsh reasonably well. All I can say to him, through these pages is "Wherever you are, thanks Bill, and I hope Desert Flyer meets with your approval."

Introduction

Gilbert (Gil) Marsh is a modest and private man.

I already knew (from official records) the basic details of his exploits as a bomber pilot, when I was first introduced to him at a squadron reunion, at RAF Mildenhall, in May 1984.

Gil, who was badly injured by cannon fire from Ju 88 nightfighters, during an attack against Berlin, on 23rd August 1943, declined to assist me with information for a book I was preparing on No. XV Squadron.

The scars from that night, both physical and mental were, he said, still too painful to re-live. Nevertheless, over the following six months, Gil wrote down the details of that night.

Sentence by sentence, paragraph by paragraph, he slowly came to terms with his plight and put the pain behind him.

He sent the screed through the post, with a covering letter saying I was the first person to whom he had related this story.

Needless to say I felt both honored and privileged.

History was to repeat itself with regard to Gil's brother, William, or Bill as he was known to everyone, who was killed in 1944. The pain of losing a brother never totally goes away, and although Bill's name was mentioned in some of our later conversations, Gil never talked at length about him.

It was to be some twelve years since our original meeting that Bill's story emerged in detail.

Sitting with Gil and Amy Marsh, in the comfort of the lounge of their home at Aughton, near Ormskirk, Liverpool, the conversation turned to a large picture on the wall, of a Hawker Hurricane, Mark IIC, fighter/bomber. The type of aircraft flown by Bill.

William, like Gil, joined the Royal Air Force during World War Two. Unlike Gil, who was a bomber pilot over Europe, Bill was a fighter pilot and was a Desert Flyer. He flew Hurricane fighters and Hurri-bombers, during the North African campaign throughout 1942/43.

It was as he was replenishing our glasses with another shot of Glen Niven Whisky, to lubricate our throats, that Gil mentioned a journal, which Bill wrote whilst in the desert.

In all the years that I had known Gil, the existence of the journal had been unknown to me. I asked Gil about its fate and was even more surprised to learn that it had survived and was in his possession.

I readily accepted the invitation to peruse the journal and, turning its pages, realized the interest value of its contents. The day to day life of a Desert Flyer emerged from those pages, the majority of which were adorned with a photograph depicting the event recorded.

Remembering the response from Gil when I wanted to record his story, I tentatively asked him whether he had considered putting Bill's story into print. I was at first concerned by the seemingly long silence from Gil, who was apparently considering my comment. After some deliberation, he offered the journal into my safe keeping, with his consent to undertake the project.

The same feeling of honor and privilege I had experienced before was again invoked, not only had I recorded Gil's story, but now I was to do the same about the brother he had loved and lost.

Gil's physical injuries and scars are still with him, but out of the pain and suffering he endured came a friendship between two generations. To Gil, and Amy, I say thank you. Not only for your friendship, but also for allowing me to write to the story of William Marsh, the DESERT FLYER.

Desert Flyer is not a history of the struggle for supremacy in the North African Desert, although reference is made to some of the offensives fought there between March 1942 and June 1943.

It is an account of the life of one man who flew and fought with the Royal Air Force, against the German Luftwaffe and the Italian Regia Aeronautica, during those offensives.

An account of life as recorded at the time, on a day to day basis, by Sergeant (later Flying Officer) William "Bill" Marsh, of the flying, fighting and leisure activities that formed life in the desert in those dark days of war.

Circumstances in the desert did not always allow for entries to be made as they occurred, indeed some were made a day or two after the event. Likewise, news of occurrences in other locations often took time to filter through, and when it did (history informs us), it was not always totally correct.

Due to these circumstances, some of the entries in Bill Marsh's journal do not agree with "official" dates, which have now been accepted. However, this does not detract from the journal, but enhances it, especially when one considers the speed of retreats and advances during the aforementioned campaign, together with the primitive conditions endured.

It was whilst this book was in preparation that further journals came to light, together with a number of letters and many more photographs, allowing an insight to Bill Marsh's early years, including his training in Canada and life on his first squadron.

As far as can be ascertained, Bill started writing his journals on the 26th January 1941, the day he arrived in Canada, where he was to undertake further pilot training.

Initially, entries were small in content and took the form of a heading, whereas by the time he reached the North African Desert, the entries had increased to cover a whole page.

Unfortunately, some eight weeks before his death, in February 1944, Bill ceased to record any further details of his life in the desert; the reason for this being unknown. Did he have some form of premonition, or did he just get tired of writing? The answer will never be known. What is known however, is that he left behind an insight into the life of a DESERT FLYER.

Martyn R. Ford-Jones
Swindon, England
1997

CHAPTER ONE

The Fledgling Years

During March 1916, when the world had been at war for just over eighteen months, the officers and men of No.1 Squadron, Royal Australian Flying Corps, sailed from Melbourne. Their destination was Egypt, where they were to defend the Suez Canal. To enable them to carry out their duties they were, upon arrival in Egypt, to take over the aircraft and equipment from the British Royal Flying Corps, at Heliopolis. The Australian airmen were to fly above the desert sands in BE.2 airplanes.

During the same month, in England, Gertrude Alice Marsh, (nee Henesey) was to give birth to a baby boy who, in another world war, a generation later, was to follow in the footsteps of those young Australians. He was to fly a different type of airplane, but it was to be in the region of those same skies, and over the same sand; he was destined to become a Desert Flyer.

Known to everyone as Bill, William Ernest Marsh, was born on the 23rd March 1916, at Walton, near Liverpool. His mother came from Liverpool, whilst his father, William Arthur Robert Marsh, originated from Manchester. There was an eight year age gap between William and Gertrude. A daughter, Lilian, was born in August 1918 and another son, Gilbert (Gil) was to follow in January 1922. He too was destined to fly, but he would be a bomber pilot over Europe.

During the First World War, William senior served with the Royal Artillery, as an instructor, at Dungeness in Kent. In civilian life, after the war, he became General Manager of Waterworth Brothers, Wholesalers and Retailers, with a chain of 120 grocery shops in the north west of England.

Originally William and Gertrude, who had married during the early part of the war, lived in an apartment in Orrel Park, Walton, but in 1919 William senior moved the family to a house at No. 8 Stalmine Road.

Bill grew up in the Walton area, going to school there. First he attended the junior and primary school and later, from September 1926, Alsop High School for Boys, in Queen's Drive.

As a youngster, he loved sport. He enjoyed ice skating (in winter) at Sefton Meadow, was fond of swimming and cycling, and played football for the school team. He was a member of the First Football Eleven when it won the Senior Secondary School Shield. His Headmaster, Mr. F. B. Halford, M.A. thought of Bill as an outstanding athlete, and wrote as much on Bill's final school report.

When he left school, William Ernest Marsh had matriculated, with credit, in seven subjects, including Mathematics, French, Geography, History, Physics, Chemistry and English Literature. This last subject incorporated another of Bill's passions, reading. When not engaged in one of his sporting activities, Bill could be found with a book in his hand. His interests were far reaching, and he was known to have read as many as three books in one week, all on varying subjects.

That final school report, dated July 1932, also stated that W. E. Marsh was truthful, straightforward and reliable. It strongly recommended him for his intelligence and the fact that he was a good worker. It concluded with the comment that Bill would "do his best to give satisfaction in any position that he may obtain."

During the same year that Bill left school, his father purchased the Earl of Latham's shooting estate; the Earl having been declared bankrupt. The shooting estate, which consisted of 190 acres of woodland and 30 acres of arable farmland, was separated from the main park by a stone wall. Also on that part of the estate bought by William Marsh senior was a house called "Claytons", which was occupied by a tenant farmer who remained in residence, whilst the two Williams, father and son, built up a mushroom and nursery business on the remainder of the land.

Bill was fast becoming a young man, he had left school and had now acquired himself a 250cc Lee Enfield motorcycle, with a bullet-shaped sidecar. Whilst the motorcycle assisted Bill to get to and from work easily, the sidecar had an additional unexpected use. It enabled him to transport boxes of mushrooms home from the estate each evening and pass them to his father for sale through the Waterworth business.

The mushroom business began to expand and, by 1934, was known as Lathom Vale Nurseries. Furthermore, the tenant farmer who occupied "Claytons" had moved out, thus allowing William senior to move his family in.

The advantage of father and son living and working at the same location was obvious, but for Lilian and Gil the new family home had at least one disadvantage. It meant that this fifteen year old girl, and her twelve year old brother, now had to cycle five miles each way to and from school every day. The following year however, Lilian was to leave school and join the family business.

In 1937, due to various reasons, William and Gertrude's marriage ran into difficulties. It eventually broke-up and they went their separate ways. William stayed at "Claytons", where he now looked after the business full-time, having left Waterworths employment some time before. Gertrude moved out of "Claytons" and took up residence at No. 8 Hillcrest Road, Ormskirk, taking the rest of the family with her.

Bill's relationship with his father began to deteriorate and, at the same time that he moved house, both he and Lilian terminated their employment in the nurseries. Young Gil didn't have this problem, he was still at Ormskirk Grammar School.

However, Bill still needed to earn a wage. He tried various jobs, but could not find one which suited him, until finally he secured employment with Clucas Seeds, at Ormskirk.

With all his other pursuits, Bill had never shown anything other than a passing interest in airplanes and aviation, that is until he saw Sir Alan Cobham's "Flying Circus."

Alan Cobham, who had been a First World War pilot, was an aviation pioneer of the 1920s, who made many long distance flights, including those to Rangoon, Capetown and Australia.

He had started getting the public interested in flying as early as 1919, by giving "joy-rides" in Avro 504 aircraft, which were specially adapted for passenger carrying. Following his many flights across the British Empire Alan Cobham returned, to continue thrilling the public with displays of stunt flying and "joy-rides."

For four years, between 1932 and 1936, from April through to October Alan Cobham held a National Aviation Day Tour. He and his "Flying Circus" visited a number of towns and venues throughout Britain. Over this period, he gave in excess of 12,000 displays and took nearly a million passengers into the air; many for their first experience of flying.

Amongst those who took advantage of this opportunity were Bill, Lilian and Gil. When he heard the "Flying Circus" was going to be at the Aintree Racecourse, near his home, for the Grand National event, Bill made up his mind to go. Lilian and Gil did not want to be left out and so a day out was planned; a day which culminated with a flight over Liverpool.

The three youngsters marveled at seeing their part of the world from this vantage point. The streets they walked down and the fields they roamed and played in, were all visible to their eyes in one view. A memory which was never to be forgotten.

For both Bill and Gilbert, it was to be the first of many aviation related memories, for they had both been "bitten" by the flying bug.

However, not all their respective memories were destined to be happy ones, for as the decade of the 1930s grew towards its close, it was obvious to many in the free world that circumstances in Europe were edging towards another war with Germany.

When the war came, in September 1939, Bill knew where his duty lay. He also knew that, in order to carry out his duty, he would apply for pilot training with the Royal Air Force Volunteer Reserve.

Although he did not know it, he was about to follow in the footsteps of those young Australian airmen, and after training was to become a desert flyer.

Having made his application at the local recruitment center, Bill went home and waited for his call-up papers. He was eventually instructed to report to the Aircrew Receiving

Forming friendships. Ray Woodcraft, Bill Marsh, Bud Frearson (Killed July 42), Russell Frowde.

Center at Padgate, on 17th April 1940, where he spent a month, being kitted out and learning basic drill, before being transferred to RAF Marham, Station Headquarters, where he spent another month.

On 20th June, Bill was posted to No. 3 Initial Training Wing for basic training, first at Hastings, Sussex and then at Torquay in Devon, the unit moving to the West Country during the first week of July.

In Torquay, Bill was billeted in a fine hotel, situated on the high ground overlooking Torre Abbey Sands, with its beautiful views of the coastline and English Channel. Not that Bill and his fellow cadets had much time for sight-seeing.

Their day started at 05.45 hours, when reveille was sounded, and followed much the same routine as set out below:

Clean Rooms	06.00
Breakfast	06.45
1st Working Period	08.00
Cease Work	12.30
Lunch	12.45
2nd Working Period	14.30

L to R: Russell Frowde, Bud Frearson, Jim Rennolds, Ray Woodcraft, Bill Marsh, Ron Raynor. Bill Gregg (in uniform) sits on the beach.

Cease Work	17.45
Tea	17.45
Supper	19.30
Guard Mounting	20.00
Fire Party Parade	20.00
Roll Call	22.15
Lights Out	22.30

A sick parade was held at 08.30 each morning, and there were some minor variations to the Sunday timetable, which included Church Parade.

During this early period of his career, Bill did not keep a journal, but his interest in photography was taking shape and although he wrote little about his "exploits", training and surroundings, he did have a pictorial record of some of his fellow cadets. And of course, there were his letters home

Having passed his basic exams, Bill Marsh was posted on 28th October 1940 to No. 11 Elementary Flying Training School, at Perth in Scotland, where the basis of journal notes started to formulate.

Admittedly the majority of these notes related to the basic handling of an airplane, but the odd remarks were recorded.

An R.A.F. contingent marches past Torquay Harbor. Note the ship 'blocking' the harbor entrance.

Next stop Perth. L to R: unknown, unknown, Jim Rennolds, Bud Frearson, unknown, unknown, Bill Marsh, Bill Gregg, Unknown, Ray Woodcraft, unknown.

The initial training was carried out on De Havilland Tiger Moth bi-planes and began the moment that Bill and his fellow cadets arrived at the airfield, which was situated three and a half miles north east of the town.

By the end of the first day's training, Cadet Marsh had recorded the staggering total of three hours and ten minutes flying time. Albeit as a passenger with either Flight Lieutenant Reid or Flight Lieutenant Salisbury-Hughes, both of whom were to give the fledgling flyer instruction in the air.

On Saturday, 16th November 1940, having flown a training exercise with his instructor and landed the aircraft safely, Bill was allowed to take-off again, alone!! The moment he had waited for, to fly solo, had arrived. The excitement of the moment was mixed with joy, trepidation and no doubt a small amount of apprehension. He was on his own.

He taxied-out and went through the cockpit drills, before turning the aircraft into the wind and opening the throttle. The aircraft raced across the airfield gathering speed, before lifting into the air. Listening to the sound of his engine, watching his instruments and looking around him for other aircraft, the young pilot completed a circuit of the airfield and landed without mishap.

His first solo flight had lasted approximately ten minutes. However, two days later he was to repeat the exercise, on this occasion flying for one hour, twenty-five minutes.

Bill still had a lot to learn and of course it was not only flying; there were written exams which had to be taken into account, but he had taken that first important step and had obviously gained much confidence from it.

In an undated letter, to his mother, from Perth he wrote . . .

> . . .*thank Lil (Lilian his sister) for the pullover. I was up to 5,000' yesterday – above the clouds on the other side of Perth, doing steep turns for 40 minutes, all on my own. And, boy, was it cold! It took three cups of coffee and a sausage roll to thaw me out and my face still feels pale blue. . .*
>
> *In the same letter, he went on to write. . .*
>
> . . .*These courses are one long swot for exam after exam. We get about five weeks to cover a syllabus. . .and under 80% throughout is very poor.*

During his course Bill was taken off flying for medical reasons, a situation which he did not like, but knew he had to accept. He had developed a pain in one ear, and reported the fact to the Medical Officer, who tried to alleviate the problem with the use of glycerine drops. The M.O. also took Bill off flying duties until the problem had been overcome.

The following day the pain was worse, and seemed to be spreading around Bill's cheek. He could not sleep properly, and this of course was not helpful to the fact that he still had to

Some of the "boys" from Perth E.F.T.S. L to R: Permuth, Woolley, Connelly, Marsh, Burges, Braund, Potts, Hall, Giles, Parr.

take exams. It is known that during this time, apart from whatever else Bill might have done, he did manage to write one or two letters, but obviously did not pay much attention to what he was writing.

Two days later, as Bill was traveling into the airfield on the crew bus, the abscess in his ear burst, immediately reducing the swelling. That night Bill wrote to his mother, to let her know all was now well and explaining he had almost been arrested as an agent!

> *. . .Well, tonight I get in about 8.30 and the barrack warden says that the operator at the drome has rung up saying there was a telegram for Me So, after a lot of messing we get through and receiving same [the message] which reads, USE WARM SWEET ALMOND OIL*
>
> *Well he thought it was a [secret] code and would hardly believe it wasn't. And I was puzzled who had sent it as I wasn't sure whether I'd written to you this week. So decided it must have been Pa, who sent a long letter. . .and in answering I must have mentioned my ear being sore, but didn't say much more about it.*
>
> *. . .I think we'll leave ears alone now it's getting better.*

Chapter 1: The Fledgling Years

The flying training at Perth continued through to the end of the year, culminating on the 31st December 1940.

The first day of the New Year saw Bill Marsh, and those colleagues of his who had also passed the various flying tests and written exams, at the RAF Personnel Despatch Center in Winslow, Cheshire, awaiting a posting to Canada.

CHAPTER TWO

Canada

Leading Aircraftman Marsh left British shores on, or about, 7th January 1941, and sailed to Canada. The troopship crossed the Atlantic Ocean and made safe anchorage on the east coast of Newfoundland.

Bill and his colleagues were given time to recover from the sea crossing, and become acclimatized to the surroundings of a land many hundreds of miles from home.

Whilst others took things easy, Bill took the opportunity to venture out in the snow with his camera. His endeavors were rewarded with the sighting of a number of aircraft types which he had never seen before, including the landing of an American Boeing B.17 and a Liberator bomber.

Bill's ultimate destination in Canada was No.33 Service Flying Training School, at Carberry, near Winnipeg, Manitoba, where he arrived on Sunday 26th January.

Bill's first sighting of an American B.17, Flying Fortress, landing in Newfoundland, Canada.

Having landed the B.17 taxis to the parking ramp.

The main operations area at Carberry Airfield, Manitoba, Canada, as seen from a Harvard aircraft.

A Consolidated B.24 Liberator bomber also lands . . .

. . . and he too parks on the ramp.

Inside a hangar, a Boeing 247, a North American AT6 Harvard and the tail of an Anson.

As the new course was not officially due to start until the 2nd February, the airmen were given six days leave in which to settle in to their new environment; and get used to the change of climate.

Winter was not a good time to arrive in Canada, especially if you were a pilot-under-training. Not only was it very cold, but the snow and general conditions could affect the flying program. However, Bill was not concerned. It was a new venture and a new world, and he deemed to get his priorities right.

A few home comforts were required, one of which was, for Bill, a radio. Initially he experienced trouble getting a decent reception on it, that is until he hit upon the idea of connecting the aerial wire to the metal frame of his bed! The station, which he proudly noted in his journal was sponsored by National Electric, came through loud and clear.

The lectures commenced on Monday, 3rd February, at 08.15, with lessons on bomb sights and navigation (at this stage of their training it was assumed the men on this course were destined to become bomber aircrew), followed by link training during the afternoon. Flying started on Friday, 7th February.

The continuation of their flying training was to be carried out on the North American T-6 Texan, known in Britain as the Harvard. A large, formidable, two seat basic trainer, powered by a Pratt & Whitney engine, which sounded like an angry wasp when descending in a power dive.

Bill's first introduction to the Harvard came on Saturday 8th February when, accompanied by his instructor, Flying Officer Watson, Bill went up in Harvard 2718. The lesson, which lasted forty minutes was, according to his journal, carried out over the forced landing field!!

The next day Bill spent virtually the whole day learning to master the aircraft, which included a number of take-offs and landings, or as they are known in the RAF "circuits and bumps."

Wednesday, 12th February 1941

Received $17.70 for £4 [Exchanged]

The Canadian dollar was something new to Bill and his colleagues, and warranted some comment in his journal. He had exchanged some English money so as to enable him to go shopping in Winnipeg, where he purchased an electric iron for $3, and treated himself to a new Kodak Reflex camera for $7.60. The transaction being recorded by Bill at the end of the day.

The flying training continued, and two days after purchasing his new camera Bill flew solo for the first time. He felt it a day worth recording both on film and in his journal, even though the latter simply and modestly read, "1st solo in Harvard."

Bill was photographed wearing full flying kit, and standing on the mainplane of Harvard 2923, by his course colleague Ed Woolley. To complete the record, Bill photographed "Woolley", in similar attire, standing by a Harvard.

Snow permitting, further tests and examinations continued to be flown throughout February, with Bill flying a number of difference Harvard aircraft on a number of aerial exercises.

Towards the end of February, a break in the weather allowed Bill to photograph a visiting De Havilland Tiger Moth being prepared for a flight.

However, in mid-March, the weather nearly created a major catastrophe.

Saturday, 15th March 1941

Great fun with a blizzard
Waghorn last in with a Harvard.

Although a pupil by the name of Waghorn was fortunate enough to land at Carberry before the blizzard really hit, three Avro Anson pilots were not so lucky. The entry in Bill Marsh's journal continued . . .

. . .Brunning, Bowland and
Cockayne apparently flew
100 miles blind in Ansons.
All safe. . .

The following day, due to the airfield being unserviceable, no flying was carried out.

The weather improved over the next few days and allowed flying to recommence, but an incident occurred which could not be blamed on the elements.

ABOVE: Bill, in full flying kit, standing on the wing of Harvard, coded 2923, in which he made his first solo flight on type.

RIGHT: Ed 'Woolly' Woolley, who soloed the same day as Bill.

A visiting De Havilland Tiger Moth, coded 4257, is manhandled into position, by members of groundcrew.

The Moth is prepared for flight.

Tiger Moth, coded 4257, meets a Harvard (AT-6 Texan), at Carberry airfield.

LAC. Cockayne, LAC. "Brunn" Brunning and LAC Bill Marsh with a Canadian "admirer."

Thursday, 20th March 1941

Formation flying with P/O Richards.
Letter from Gil.

During the course of the morning, Bill was flying formation practice with Pilot Officer Richards. All was going well until Bill's aircraft endured a mid-air collision with a very large bird!

The engine cowling of the Harvard took most of the impact, which in turn did not do the bird much good, but Bill was obviously concerned as he added in his journal. . .

. . .[the impact] played hell with the cowling. . .

Having returned safely to Carberry, without further mishap, Bill found a letter from his younger brother awaiting him. Gil had written to say that he was going to join the Royal Air Force, and like his brother had applied for pilot training.

As the weather improved the snow melted turning parts of the airfield into a quagmire, creating new problems for its occupants.

Those pilots, like Russell Frowde who were training on the twin-engined Avro Ansons, found the dispersal area for their aircraft covered with large puddles and a sea of mud!

Leading Aircraftman Cripps, a pupil pilot, had the indignity of having to wade through the mud after a mishap with his aircraft.

Six AT-6 Harvards parked in the snow.

Melting snow turns the Anson dispersal area into a quagmire.

The recent had weather had created a backlog of work, which included much flying. Apart from the solo flights, there were a number of formation flying practices and cross-country exercises to be undertaken.

As always, Bill's camera was never very far from his reach and a number of air to air photographs were taken.

Whether Bill entrusted his camera to any of his fellow pupils is not known but some pictures of him, piloting Harvard aircraft, were also taken at this time

Presumably due to pressure of making up lost time on the course, Bill neglected his journal during the last two weeks of March. It was the unfortunate death of a fellow pupil that made him return to it.

Friday, 4th April 1941

Wesley died through crash. . .

Although the young men on the course had been flying for nearly six months, and obviously felt very confident about their respective abilities, they still had a lot to learn and digest.

This was brought home to them on 4th April when one of their number, carrying out night flying exercises, overshot his landing and went round again. On the second approach the aircraft flew into the ground at high speed. Bill continued the entry in his journal. . .

> *. . .[he] got too low. Assumed that he closed
> instead of opening up [the throttle]. . .*

Needless to say, in this case, the mistake was fatal, as was the next entry in Bill's journal, which was of a similar nature.

Saturday, 12th April 1941

*Lloyd crashed north of Petrel.
Very little left.*

LAC Lloyd had been engaged in practice flying when things went disastrously wrong. The pilot had either spun-in, or failed to leave sufficient height whilst carrying out low aerobatics.

Bill attended Lloyd's funeral, at Brandon, three days later.

Russell Frowde at the controls of
an Avro Anson.

The wireless operators' compartment of an Anson, looking towards the flight deck.

A second entry for the same day implied that Bill needed to be assured of his own confidence, capabilities and maybe mortality. Alternatively, the course instructors may have felt it necessary not to let the students dwell too long on recent events.

Saturday, 12th April 1941
(Second Entry)

Went up spinning with Bower, then [flew]
solo. [Climbed to] 7,000' and did a spin
3,000'. Came out easily.

Unfortunately, before the month was over, Bill Marsh recorded the loss of two more friends, who were flying together, on 19th April. They apparently failed to pull out of a dive and paid the ultimate price.

LAC Cripps returns, through a sea of mud, after ground looping his aircraft.

Another victim of the mud was this Anson, which lost part of its undercarriage.

The month of May brought forth a change of climate, both with regard to the weather and the general outlook on life.

On 1st May, Bill Marsh undertook a flying test for his pilot's badge. He flew a cross-country exercise, accompanied by Flight Lieutenant Lower, who assessed the former's abilities during the 278 mile trip. Bill later recorded in his journal, "PASSED."

The course was now nearing completion, and some consideration had to be given regarding the future career of each airman on the course.

On 10th May, Bill Marsh had a formal interview with the Group Captain, followed two days later by a night flying test with the Wing Commander. Unfortunately for Bill, things went horribly wrong.

Flying Harvard 2921, Bill took-off at 22.30 hours, with Wing Commander Morrison in the rear seat. All was well until the landing, when the aircraft went off the runway and ground looped. LAC Marsh was instructed to undertake two more landings, in another aircraft, before Wing Commander Morrison was satisfied.

The "sour taste" that Bill had incurred over his recent mishap whilst landing the Harvard was washed away by the alcohol he, and his colleagues, consumed following the presentation of their pilots "wings" on Thursday, 15th May 1941.

The following day saw the completion of the course, and with it came five days leave. Most of the guys were going to head for the delights that were on offer away from the military, but before they did they all got in some practice at a party, held in their honor, at the local Canadian Legion Hall.

Of the event, Bill wrote in his journal. . .

*. . .Celebration, I'll say, been
loading drink all night. . .*

33

Harvard Formation 1.

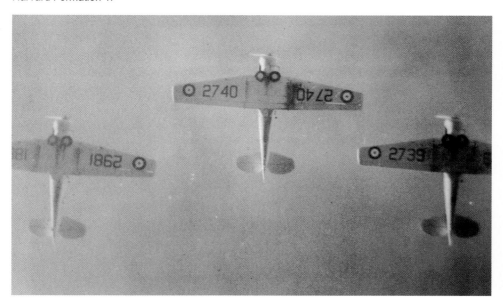

Harvard Formation 2.

Bill brings his Harvard in for a close-up shot.

Bill piloting Harvard, coded 3027.

Sergeant Birkbeck pilots Harvard, coded 2923, low over the Canadian prairie.

On Saturday, 17th May, Bill Marsh said good-bye to a number of the friends he had made during his time at Carberry, knowing that those who had undertaken the multi-engined flying course on Ansons would be leaving for Debert, Nova Scotia, on 22nd March.

Bill and Ed Woolley had other plans, and headed for the bright lights of Montreal, where they arrived late the following day. Naturally the camera went too!

Monday, 19th May 1941
(First Entry)

Went to Belmont Park. Great fun.

Away from the strains of the flying courses and exams, Bill set out to enjoy himself, and this he obviously did. He visited Belmont Park, where in the congenial atmosphere of the amusement park he relaxed. The testimony to his frame of mind being that he felt amply confident, in front of many people, to have a go at the "Try Your Strength Machine", and proudly recorded that he rang the bell; not once for FOUR times!!!

Monday, 19th May 1941
(Second Entry)

NPOEBZ OJHIU
TQFOU OJHIU XJUI FXOJDF QSJPS

Bill relaxed mood by the St. Lawrence Bridge, Montreal.

Ed Woolley at the St. Lawrence bridge, photographed by Bill during their sojourn there.

JO IFS GMBU. XFOU UIFSF FO
UBYJ. UIFO TIF QVU PO B AJQ-GSPDUFF
GSPDL BOE OPUIJOH FMTF. TPPO
HPU UN XPSL. 20/-. GVDLFE IFA
GPVS UJNFT UIBU OJHUI

With his ego in a state of high exhilaration, Bill was ready for anything and, when the delights that were on offer away from the military came later that Monday night, Bill did not falter.

His enjoyment of the evening was such that it was recorded in his journal, but mindful that he did not want prying eyes sharing his inner thoughts, he wrote the basic details of the second entry in code. Unfortunately the code he used is not too difficult to break and anybody interested enough could decipher it.

Leaving the delights of Montreal behind him, Bill boarded a train and headed east, towards the Atlantic coast.

On Wednesday 21st May 1941, Sergeant Bill Marsh reported to No. 1 Manning Depot, at Halifax, Nova Scotia, where he remained for nine days, prior to sailing to Iceland.

CHAPTER THREE

Iceland and Home

H.M.S. Derbyshire left Halifax at 12.00 hours, on 30th May 1941 bound for Iceland, via Sydney, on the north coast of Nova Scotia.

The weather was good and the sea was very calm, allowing the British ship to make good headway and reach its first port of call the following day. It lay at anchor, in Sydney harbor, for the remainder of the day, and throughout the following day, and waited for the protection of the second night before continuing its journey.

When darkness fell, H.M.S. Derbyshire weighed anchor and sailed out into the open sea, where she joined a convoy heading for Iceland.

The morning of 2nd June 1941 dawned bright and sunny, and although the sea still remained calm, the convoy sailed very slowly. A Bristol Beaufort, twin-engined fighter-bomber, flew above the convoy for a while, giving aerial escort.

Any members of the R.A.F. contingent on board His Majesty's ship who thought they were going to have a sunshine cruise to Iceland were disappointed when dawn broke on the morning of 3rd June. It was wet, cold and windy, and the sea was no longer calm. In fact, the weather sorted out many of the sea faring types from those who preferred dry land.

The sleeping arrangements on the ship, for the R.A.F. contingent, was in hammocks and after two days at sea Bill Marsh found he had somehow qualified as Sergeant Hammock Stower. It became his responsibility to ensure the hammocks were stowed away during the day, at lest those that were not being used by the airmen who could not take the tossing and pitching of the ship.

However, as the ship sailed on, it was not only the state of the sea which gave cause for concern.

The convoy sets course for Iceland.

Wednesday, 11th June 1941

*Still ploughing through this North
Atlantic; we were supposed, yesterday,
to have been in the same position as
a ship which was sunk by aircraft two days ago!*

The ever present threat of German submarines and long-range aircraft out in the North Atlantic was one which could not be dismissed lightly. However, such thoughts were pushed to the back of the mind as most people occupied themselves with other activities, as Bill revealed in a letter to his mother, dated 11th June 1941.

> *.". . .Having now been at sea for ten days on this H.M.S. Derbyshire,. . .one comes to wonder why anybody ever goes to sea without being pressed. The sailors, though, seem happy and contented enough, for the time they must be afloat does not depend on speed or number of journeys, whereas amongst the R.A.F. contingent, the sole hope is to reach home as soon as possible. So with the Australians and Canadians who are eager to see Britain and win the war.*
>
> *But we, for whom this is the second crossing, and infinitely the more pleasant of the two, have only one ambition – to get home*
>
> *Strangely enough, the first two days aboard ship are the only really boring ones. After them one develops a routine and can settle down to a hand of bridge etc. . ."*

Progress was slow and, although H.M.S. Derbyshire was expected to reach Reykjavik, Iceland on Saturday 14th June, it was not to be.

An entry, in Bill Marsh's journal, for the same day indicated the ever present threat that nearly prevented the ship from reaching its destination at all.

Saturday, 14th June 1941

Didn't reach Reykjavik.
Concert at night. Buck Ryan did [an]
imitation of [the] Weston Brothers
(British Music Hall Stars).
Heard some depth charges [and some]
slight activity about 8.00 p.m..
Rumored submarine attack.

Rumored submarine attack or not, when H.M.S. Derbyshire left the convoy at 10.00 hours the following morning, to proceed to Reykjavik, two British Corvettes stayed back and attacked a submarine, which was later reported to have been sunk.

Monday, 16th June 1941

Arrived Reykjavik

H.M.S. Derbyshire arrived at its destination without incident, much to the relief of many of the airmen on board. After all, if they had wanted to go to sea, they would have joined one of the naval services.

When the order came to disembark, they wasted no time in getting back onto terra-firma. They were met at the dockside by a fleet of army trucks, which were to convey them to Helgafell, which Bill found to be not to his liking. In fact, he summed it up in his journal in two words, "B. awful." Upon arrival at the transit camp, the airmen received a lecture from the commanding officer.

There wasn't much to do at the camp, and very few places to go for entertainment. In Bill's mind, the camp was as dreary (dull) as the weather.

However on his second day at the camp, Bill was surprised to meet an acquaintance from his short stay at RAF Marham, over a year ago.

It transpired that Sergeant P. Salt, who was a Leading Aircraftman when Bill first met him, had been promoted and was now an instructor. To Bill's even greater surprise, Sergeant Salt was actually going the opposite way, and heading for Canada, where he was to take up his appointment.

A Canadian pilot, with whom Bill had become friendly, unwittingly injected a shot of humor as they prepared to bed down that night, when he announced that he was scared to take his socks off in case he could not catch them the following morning!

Helgafell, which was not to Bill's liking.

Wednesday, 18th June 1941

Went into Allafoss. Pretty awful.

Bill's impression of the towns was equal to that of the desolate landscape that surrounded the transit camp. Under different circumstances he may well have found a natural beauty in the surrounding countryside, but like everybody else in the contingent he just wanted to get home.

A group of Australian airmen however found at least one advantage in the transit camps isolation, sheep! They managed to catch one and roast it on the stove in their billet hut! No doubt some poor Icelandic farmer spent hours, if not days, looking for a lost sheep.

Thursday, 19th June 1941

Sgt Salts' draft left for Canada.

With the departure for Canada of Sergeant Salt's group, Bill's contingent was instructed to be prepared to leave the camp at one hours notice. This led to much activity with airmen packing and repacking kitbags, including Bill, who was not sure as to how he was going to handle everything.

Saturday, 21st June 1941

Rumors of leaving.

Persistent rumors kept circulating that the contingent was about to leave, but in view of the inclement weather, Bill did not place much confidence in them.

His dislike for the climate, and his lack of enthusiasm towards Iceland, induced him to write in his journal. . .

. . .Weather consistently lousy.
What a Country!. . .

It seems the "luxuries" of life, whilst training in Canada. had made Bill forget the hardships of war. Little did he know at that time that he would face further hardships, whilst flying and fighting on another continent.

Sunday, 22nd June 1941

Heard today that Russia and Germany
have clashed at last, and that fighting
has broken out on two fronts.
On this lonely God forsaken island we
have lain nearly a week, and have long

Bill with the Icelandic tundra as a backdrop.

*exhausted reasonable possibilities for
recreation. But at last we are ordered to
parade at 16.45 hours tonight. So hope
is revived. We may yet be in England
before June is out.*

At 04.00 hours, on the morning of 22nd June 1941, the might of the German war machine fell upon Russia, signifying the start of Operation Barbarossa.

The German forces advanced rapidly across Russia's 1,800 mile long frontier, and gained complete tactical surprise from the Baltic to the Black Sea.

As the land forces smashed their way through the Russian armor, the Luftwaffe destroyed the Red Air Force, the majority of which was caught on the ground.

The initial victories gained were however to be short-lived, and the fighting that followed on this second front was ultimately to have a devastating effect for the Germans on the outcome of the war.

Monday, 23rd June 1941

*Almost certain to move today. [We] have
been here a complete week, with not a
single sunny day, dark clouds roll
perpetually across the sky line, blotting
out the mountain tops and swishing up the
valleys, [in] whatever direction the wind
may be blowing.*

*Monday, 23rd June 1941
(Second Entry)*

*Another day lying here waiting. At 10 pm
a lot of LACs came in – they are one of
the first drafts to go to the U.S.A. Got
a lot of gen (information) about conditions
at home*

Suddenly life did not seem so bad. One had not been placed here as a result of a penal offense, but found it really was a "staging post" for trainee personnel in transit to the American continent. Others were to endure the same discomfort and desolation of the island, but they had the advantage of imparting news to those who were about to move on.

Tuesday, 24th June 1941

*Up at 5 am and traveled down to
Reykjavik in open[-top] army and
RAF trucks, thick with cement [dust].
Aboard the H.M.T. Royal Ulsterman at
09.30 a.m. stowing baggage in [the]
hold. For which we received one of
the few cabins. Shared with George
Totlos, RAAF, and Dick Lawrie [who]
lodged. Sailed at 7.00 pm.*

Although he did not realize it at the time, Bill's experience as a baggage handler would prove useful when, at a later date, it was revealed that his younger brother was going overseas on a troopship.

Wednesday, 25th June 1941

*All day sailing along – pretty rough
but got roped in for a fatigue in the
hospital which just "cooked my goose",
as I'd had no breakfast.
A few of our "boys" from Carberry have
joined this boat at Reykjavik – Maskell,
Smith, Tuckson and Birkbeck.*

Bill, who had thus far managed to overcome the affliction of sea-sickness, succumbed when he was ordered to assist in the ship's hospital.

The rolling waves, tossing and pitching of the troopship and the sights he saw within the medical area, coupled with the fact that he had not eaten since the previous evening, all affected his stomach. Instead of assisting in the hospital, he finished up being assisted.

Thursday, 26th June 1941

*Sighted [a] large convey ahead and a
Whitley. Soon the Hebrides [were seen]
on the starboard beam at 6.00 pm.
Walking on the deck, somebody fired a
Vickers gun just above me*

There was great excitement aboard His Majesty's Troopship Royal Ulsterman as it drew nearer to the British Isles, giving those on board fresh topics of conversation.

First another convoy was sighted, escorted by a twin-engined Whitley bomber. It is not recorded whether a "trigger happy" sailor on watch, lacking in aircraft identification, mistook the RAF aircraft for a German bomber and opened fire. It is however recorded that a burst, from a Vickers machine gun, went off just above Bill Marsh's head!

Later in the day, the Hebrides were sighted. The RAF contingent knew they were nearly home, and looked forward to seeing "Old England" again. Whereas, for the airmen of the Dominion Air Forces it was the start of a new adventure; for some in the old homeland of their forefathers.

Friday, 27th June 1941

Reached Greenock

H.M.T Royal Ulsterman steamed up the Firth of Clyde, between the Isle of Arran and the west coast of Scotland, into the River Clyde, reaching the port of Greenock on 27th June.

The airmen on board the ship were obviously keen to get ashore, but as the vessel lay at anchor in the harbor all day, they had to wait until the following morning.

At 10.00 hours the next day, the RAF contingent were ordered to disembark from the ship and parade on the dockside, where they were addressed by an Air Commodore.

Following the Air Commodore's comments, the airmen were allowed a short period of free time before continuing their travels. Bill Marsh took the opportunity to send a telegram home to his family, to advise them of the fact he was back in England.

At 12.30 pm they boarded a train which took them south, via Carlisle, Lancaster, Preston (near Bill's family home!), Crewe, Stafford, Wolverhampton to Bournemouth on the south coast.

In the blackout of war torn Britain, the journey took sixteen hours, and they reached the south coast resort at 4.30 am on Sunday morning. Instead of the travel-weary airmen having to march through the streets to their billets, at the Wyche Hotel, a bus conveyed them from the railway station.

Tuesday, 1st July 1941

Kit Parade – drew new cap and tunic.
Met Jack Galyer, Acting Pilot Officer.

Having spent so much time sailing eastwards across the Atlantic, complete with a week's stay at the transit camp in Iceland, Bill Marsh was depressed to learn that A.P.O. Jack

Galyer had recently returned direct from Canada, aboard a Dutch ship, in just eight days!

Friday, 4th July 1941

Went on leave.

Three days after arriving on the south coast of England, British bureaucracy was about to become evident yet again, when Bill's contingent were given seven days leave.

The requisite train journey south had taken Bill through Preston, close to where his mother and sister lived. In order to see them, he now had to retrace over half his journey back north.

Being in the southern half of the Country, and believing he had time, Bill decided to go home via London; which meant he did not arrived in the north until Sunday, 6th July.

Needless to say, his family were very pleased to see him, but their pleasure was short lived when Bill received a telegram instructing him to report to O.T.U. at Usworth.

The home-coming of Sergeant Marsh, and the subsequent recall to his unit were reported by the local newspaper, the Ormskirk Advertiser, when they wrote:

> *AN ORMSKIRK SERGEANT-PILOT, One of the first batch of British airmen to get their wings under the training scheme in Canada is Sergeant-Pilot William E Marsh, elder son of Mrs Marsh, Hillcrest Road, Ormskirk, who joined the RAF just over a year ago. Sergeant-Pilot Marsh arrived in this country from Canada a fortnight ago and came on leave to his home in Ormskirk last Sunday, but was recalled at a few hours' notice to start operational training. He is twenty-five years of age and was educated at the Alsop High School.*

Thursday, 10th July 1941

Arrived Usworth

Having made his way via Durham, on the north-east side of England, Bill arrived at No.55 Operational Training Unit, where he reported for duty on Thursday 10th July.

The airfield at Usworth was situated just over three and a half miles to the west of Sunderland, and was situated in the fork of two railway lines; good as a landmark when flying. Apart from the coastline, which was not far to the east, another good landmark was the curve of the River Wear to the south east of the airfield.

It was at Usworth that Bill would receive the final stages of training, that would enable him to be declared combat ready by the instructors.

Initially he would undertake a period of flying in a Miles Magister, single-engined monoplane. Experience on this type would prepare him for the faster, heavier fighting machine named the Hawker Hurricane.

Saturday, 12th July 1941

First flight in a Magister

Lectures and ground exercises started a day before flying commenced, thus giving the pilots a chance to get back into the routine of learning.

Some may well have thought they were ready for operations but, as Bill found out, things were not that easy. After his first flight in the Magister, he wrote. . .

. . .Shocking approaches, all the knobs in the wrong places. . .

Monday, 14th July 1941

Gilbert joins R.A.F.

With his older brother now almost a fully-fledged fighter pilot, Gil Marsh answered the call to arms and joined the Royal Air Force.

He had enlisted six months earlier, but was instructed to return home and await his call-up papers. When they arrived, they ordered him to report to the Aircrew Receiving Center at Regent's Park, London, on Monday 14th July 1941.

Gil did not waste the intervening period. He had gone home and joined the Local Defense Force, or as it was later known, the Home Guard.

The Home Guard was made up of young men like Gil, awaiting call-up, and others who were classified as too old or infirm for active service.

On the training side, Gil had a lot to learn, but for Bill it was a question of relearning the cockpit layout of the Magister, which he obviously did as, four days later, he soloed in the aircraft.

It was on the same day, 16th July, that Bill also flew solo in a Hawker Hurricane; flying the aircraft for one hour and ten minutes.

Unfortunately, there were some who, even at this late stage in their training, were the victims of flying accidents. On 22nd July, a Magister with an instructor and pupil on board, flew into the North Sea, whilst on the following day Dick Lawrie, a friend of Bill's, crashed. In each case there were no survivors.

Gil Marsh practices his L.D.V. duties outside the garden shed.

Dick Lawrie, who was returning from a battle climbing exercise to 28,000', found his controls locked to the right. He could have baled out, but tried to land twice and spun-in into the ground on the second attempt.

On 25th July 1941 there was another accident, when a twin-engined Vickers Wellington bomber overshot the main runway, went through the perimeter fence and crashed onto the road outside the airfield.

Bill had come a long way since he first joined the Royal Air Force and all thought of the mushroom and nursery business he had run with his father had long since disappeared. He had no need at this stage of his life for stock taking, accounts and sales figures. His was now a life of aircraft, flying and training.

Bill was therefore somewhat displeased to receive letters from his father, which seemingly only contained "business" news. He had apparently written to his father on a number of occasions about this situation. In frustration Bill wrote to his mother on 31st July saying.
. .

> *. . .A letter from Pa saying he was glad to hear – can you believe this – that I am "doing my stuff" on Hurricanes. And requesting to be advised when I will be home any time So what? Otherwise strictly business accounts of [a] fire in Firswood and deals with Greenalls etc which, as I have told him, is almost Greek to me, who has a head full of airspeeds, boosts, cockpit drills, codes and procedures.*

The letter went on to inform his mother about an abortive trip to the firing range, which he recorded in his journal as "B. Awful." He wrote. . .

> *. . .Went today to do some air firing which is diving the plane at the target and firing the guns when in range. Also use drogues towed by Fairey Battles. But todays effort was washed out and all we did was to sit in a wet tent all afternoon. . .*

Saturday, 2nd August 1941

Gil to Torquay

Like his brother before him, AC2 Gil Marsh was sent to the coastal resort of Torquay, Devon, where he joined No.5 Initial Training Wing, for six weeks basic training.

As Gil Marsh was starting his training, brother Bill's training was coming to an end. The early weeks of August saw the latter undertaking a number of final flying exercises and tests, all of which culminated with Sergeant Bill Marsh being declared "Combat Ready."

CHAPTER FOUR

First Posting - No.605

Monday, 18th August 1941

Posted to Baginton, Coventry
Hurri. II. with 12 machine guns.

Bill Marsh left Usworth at 19.30 hours, on the evening of 18th August and, according to his journal, spent the night at Newcastle Station.

Traveling south via York and Birmingham, Bill made his way to Coventry, which he reached later the following evening. His ultimate destination being Baginton, the RAF base to the south of the city of Coventry.

He was in a state of excitement. Here he was on the eve of joining his first operational squadron which, by coincidence, was equipped with the aircraft he wanted to fly, the Hurricane MK.IIA, armed with twelve machine-guns!

The squadron to which Bill had been posted was No.605, an Auxiliary Air Force Squadron, which carried the name County of Warwick.

The Squadron was first formed in 1926, at Castle Bromwich as a day bomber unit, and it remained so until 1st January 1939, which it was redesignated a fighter squadron.

With the outbreak of war, the Squadron alternated between bases in the south of England and Scotland, until 7th September 1940, when No.605 was moved down to Croydon, south of London, for the closing stages of the Battle of Britain.

Further moves were made by the Squadron during early 1941, according to the role placed upon it. In February it went to Martlesham Heath, Suffolk for a rest period, followed by a move to Tern Hill, Shropshire, where various high altitude test were carried out.

On the 31st May, the Squadron moved yet again, this time to Baginton, where it was to commence intensive training for day and night operations. It was here, to Squadron Leader Gerry Edge, that Sergeant William "Bill" Marsh, RAFVR, reported for duty on 20th August 1941.

Wednesday, 20th August 1941

Baginton. No.605 Squadron.

It is not known from his journal whether Bill traveled to Baginton alone, or whether he had company. It is however recorded that, when he reported for duty, he was accompanied by four other pilots from No. 55 Operational Unit, with whom he had trained.

Although it did not really make any difference to Bill, the day he joined No.605, the Squadron took delivery of its first Hurricane MK.IIBs.

The established Squadron pilots took their "new" aircraft into the air and flew a total of twenty-five sorties, including cloud flying, formation flying and practice interceptions.

Tuesday, 26th August 1941

Leave – Torquay saw Gil

Having spent the first week settling in to his new surroundings, and flown a few familiarization flights over the local area, Bill was given a fortnights leave.

He first headed south to Torquay, where he had carried out his initial training, and where Gilbert was now going through the same process.

Gil had many questions and no doubt Bill, the fully trained fighter pilot, gave his younger brother the benefit of his experience. There was much news to be exchanged and a lot to talk about, and in all they spent four days together, before Bill headed north, on Saturday, 30th August, to see his family.

Although his relationship with his father was still slightly strained, Bill took time out to visit him on the Sunday, and impart all the news.

The following day was sister Lilian's birthday. The arrival of a telegram, recalling Bill immediately to his Squadron, marred the celebrations, but duty called. At least he had seen all his family.

During the final week of August, No.605 Squadron carried out an extensive training program, which included night flying, Army co-operation exercises and formation flying.

Aircraft were also placed at readiness during the day, in the event of a scramble being ordered. Such an occasion occurred on 30th August, when two sections of Hurricanes were scrambled at 08.40 hours, to intercept a Junkers Ju 88.

The enemy aircraft was attempting a reconnaissance mission over Birmingham, and

The first formal picture of Bill wearing his pilots' 'wings', taken at Torquay whilst visiting brother Gil.

was later recorded has having been attacked and damaged, whilst flying over the Irish Sea. It was reported, but not confirmed, that the enemy machine had forced landed in Eire.

Tuesday, 2nd September 1941

13.00 hours. Test with W/Cmdr Smith in Maggie. O.K.

Bill Marsh faced the daunting task of piloting a Miles Magister aircraft, affectionately known as a "Maggie", on a handling flight, with Wing Commander Smith, as his passenger.

Wing Commander Smith was testing Bill's ability to handle the aircraft, and his reaction to various situations whilst flying it. To Bill's relief he satisfied the Wing Commander's standards.

On the 2nd September the Squadron began to relocate to RAF Honiley, approximately seven miles to the west of Baginton. The ground staff moved first and, by the end of the next day, the Orderly Room and H.Q. Flight had settled in to their new quarters. The aircraft moved across at mid-day, on the 4th, leaving one of their number at Baginton for Station Defense.

Thursday, 11th September 1941

Now operational. Readiness until 9 p.m..

Sergeant Marsh, having been accepted as ready for combat, was made operational. However, although he spent the whole of the day at readiness, no operations were carried out.

Friday, 12th September 1941

1st Scramble 12.50. with Ron Noble
Friendly Fighter

At 12.45 hours, Blue Section, comprising of Sergeant Bill Marsh and Sergeant Ron Noble, were scrambled to intercept an incoming aircraft. Bill, piloting Hurricane BD740, raced across the airfield on his first scramble, accompanied by Ron Noble flying Hurricane BD763.

Having patrolled for thirty minutes Blue Section returned to base, where they reported the incoming aircraft as friendly.

It transpired later that the scramble was ordered for the benefit of the Air Officer Commanding, who was visiting the Squadron. The whole of the exercise had been pre-arranged!

During the evening the Officers of No.605 Squadron threw a cocktail and supper party, at the "Fleur de Lys" Inn, in the village of Lowsonford, five miles from the airfield.

Bill in the cockpit of a Hawker Hurricane of, No.605 Squadron, his first operational unit.

To ensure there would be enough food available (because of rationing in Britain), the Squadron Intelligence Officer spent the previous week visiting every shop in a fifty mile radius, acquiring various items of food.

The sixty-five sergeants who attended the evening, and for whom the party was being held, ensured the efforts of the officers were not waste, and really did justice to the food and drink supplied. Three particular revelers were found the following morning, suffering the effect of the night before, and had to be taken back to the airfield.

Saturday, 13th September 1941

Gil on embarkation leave. Got wire.

Young Gil Marsh, who had been posted to South Africa, for pilot training, was given two weeks embarkation leave, prior to going overseas.

He obviously wanted to see his family, including of course his brother to whom Gil sent a telegram.

Sunday, 14th September 1941

To Speke in Blenheim. P/O. Carlier. Home 6.00pm. Saw Gil.

Speke Airport, being only five miles south-east of Liverpool, was fairly close to the Marsh family home It was at this airfield, close to the north bank of the River Mersey, that Bill arrived, as a passenger, in a twin-engined Bristol Blenheim bomber. Exactly how he achieved this Bill does not record in his journal, but he did record that he was home by 18.00 hours.

Monday, 15th September 1941

Farewell to Gil.

Emotions ran high in the Marsh household on Monday, 15th September. Although Gil still had time to spend with the family, Bill had to get back to his Squadron.

The two brother said their good-byes, amid the promises of writing to each other, with each telling the other to look after himself and stay out of trouble.

Although at the time neither knew it, or even dare think about it, Monday 15th September 1941 was the last time they would ever be together. Face to face, hand to hand or embraced in a brotherly hug.

Waiting for the first mission.

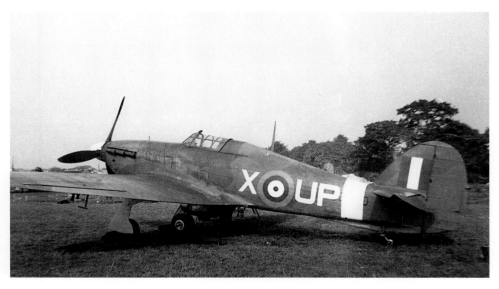

Bill's regular mount, Hawker Hurricane, Mk.IIB, serial BD740, coded UP-X, of No.605 (County of Warwick) Squadron, Royal Auxiliary Air Force.

A poor quality photograph of Bill Marsh piloting Hurricane, BD740, UP-X (in the background), flying in formation with Hurricane, BD760, coded UP-U, piloted by P/O. Carlier.

Tuesday, 16th September 1941

Arrived Honiley 11.00 hours.
Up with Allen – B. Awful.

Bill reported for duty, back at RAF Honiley at 11.00 hours, and was immediately detailed for practice during the afternoon.

He took-off, flying Hurricane BD740, as No. 2 to Pilot Officer Allen, who was piloting Hurricane BD739. They left the ground at 14.20 hours, in weather less than perfect, and undertook instrument calibration tests.

The flight lasted one and a half hours, during the course of which both pilots were subjected to poor visibility and unfavorable flying conditions. Bill Marsh was not a happy man and, having landed, summed up his feelings about the flight by writing only, "B. Awful" in his journal.

The weather conditions remained unstable for the next two weeks, which only enabled the Squadron to carry out the occasional formation flights or air tests.

The miserable weather also reflected the feelings of the Squadron members, who had been informed that they were to lose their Squadron Commander. Squadron Leader Gerry Edge was, to his men, a very popular commander and a brilliant leader. He was also the last of the original Auxiliary members of the Squadron, and with him would go the final link with the County of Warwick.

As a memento and a mark of the respect the officers had for him, Squadron Leader Edge was presented with a silver model of the Hawker Hurricane he flew. Apart from being inscribed with the aircraft's code UP-Z, it also carried the signatures of each of the officers. The presentation was made on the 25th September, the day before his departure. The new Commanding Officer, Flight Lieutenant Reid, who had arrived on the evening of the 15th September officially took over command of the Squadron on the 26th of the month.

Saturday, 27th September 1941

Letter from Gil.

As his older brother had done before him, Gil Marsh boarded a troopship and sailed to a foreign country, where he would undertake pilot training. Whereas Bill had gone to Canada, Gil was heading for Africa, and training as a bomber pilot.

Mindful of the hints and tips that Bill had imparted at their last meeting, Gil wrote to his brother. . .

> *. . .I now understand the reasons for trying to avoid the baggage party – needless to say I was unable to do so as we all had cards with numbers on – mine being 45 – the first 50 were called and put to work; through this we found ourselves in a part of the ship a long way from the cabins.*

Tuesday, 30th September 1941

Air Firing. A Sgt. pilot of No. 135 Squadron landed wheels up on the drome

The weather on the final day of the month allowed the Squadron to catch-up on some of the flying training, both during the day and night. Bill Marsh undertook three separate sorties during the day, which included formation flying and air to air firing.

Nine Hurricanes, including some from No. 135 Squadron, were detailed for night flying, one of which came to grief on landing. Sergeant Husband, of No. 135 Squadron, burst a tyre on landing, but emerged from the episode uninjured.

Friday, 3rd October 1941

Heard posted Egypt, end of month.

The Squadron received the news on Thursday, 2nd October, that it was going overseas, but no further details had been imparted.

By the following day, many of the pilots and members of the groundcrew thought they knew where the Squadron was headed, and many rumors abounded. The assured destinations ranged from Singapore, Leningrad, Cairo and Teheran. Most were in agreement that it would be Russia, but Bill felt sure the Squadron was headed for Egypt.

Saturday, 4th October 1941

45 minutes formation flying.
Ceiling 3000', visibility 400 yards.

No. 135 Squadron took over the responsibilities of dawn readiness from No.605, who had been declared non-operational the previous day. Although the latter Squadron did fly a forty-five minute practice formation, in appalling weather conditions.

Preparations for the move started with the inoculation of the pilots, who were informed that up to fourteen days leave was on offer.

Sunday, 5th October 1941 -
Monday, 6th October 1941.

To Sealand, packing Hurricanes. . .

The majority of Squadron members went on embarkation leave, but a few remained behind to ferry the Hurricanes to Sealand, near Chester, where the aircraft were to be prepared for their impending sea voyage. Bill Marsh was one of those held back for such duties which, due to the continuing inclement weather causing some of the aircraft to return to Honiley, took longer than expected.

Tuesday, 7th October 1941

. . .then home on leave.

Although some of the Squadron's Hurricanes had still not been delivered to Sealand, due to the weather conditions, Bill was allowed home on leave.

However, the next day, the weather relented enough to allow the Hurricanes to reach Sealand, where they too were packed-up prior to shipment.

Having been kept in existence by a skeleton staff for the previous two weeks, the Squadron began to reassemble at Honiley, on the 22nd October, when the officers and men returned from leave.

The Squadron's eventual destination was by this time known to a selected few, but to the uninitiated it was still open to conjecture. It was however known that a party would soon be in the offering, and on this point everybody was proven correct.

A farewell party was held on the evening of 23rd October, at which Sir Lindsay Everard, an Honorary Air Commodore of No. 605 Squadron, and Group Captain Lord Willoughby-de-Broke were guests of honor.

The following day, at 11.00 hours, a farewell parade was held. The officers and other ranks of the Squadron were inspected by Lord Willoughby-de-Broke and Sir Lindsay, who took the salute at the march past. The former was later reported to have commented that the march past could not have been bettered by the Brigade of Guards on Birdcage Walk (the Duke of Wellington Barracks) near Buckingham Palace.

The atmosphere continued to be one of uncertainty, due to the fact that the departure date for the Squadron's overseas move had still not been announced.

The Squadron had acquired a number of long-range Hurricanes, fitted with extra fuel tanks, which they were using for practice flying to keep themselves busy.

Sunday, 26th October 1941

30 minutes flying long-range Hurricane (2c)

A considerable amount of time was logged on practice flying sessions by members of the Squadron, including Bill Marsh who flew a thirty minute slot.

Flying was however curtailed in the mid-afternoon, in preparation for an official visit. The Squadron was prepared and its dispersal area tidied-up. Even the Hurricane pranged on the airfield by a pilot from No. 135 Squadron was cleared away; albeit just before the visitor arrived.

At 15.40 hours, the Air Officer Commanding arrived for a short visit, during which time he addressed a few words to the pilots.

On 27th October, a number of the Officers were granted forty-eight hours leave, whilst preparations were made for an immediate departure on 2nd November. The day after the Officers went, the airmen were granted the same concession, with the proviso that they returned to Unit by 13.00 hours on the 1st November.

Bill Marsh had returned to Honiley by 20.00 hours on the evening of 29th October where, like his fellow pilots who had also been recalled to base, he prepared himself and his kit for the impending move. This came the following day, when Bill and his colleagues, led by Squadron Leader Reid, set off for Rugby railway station. Having caught the 14.40 hours train, with very little time to spare, the pilots all settled down for the long journey north.

Friday, 31st October 1941

Arrived Abbotsinch 01.00 hours
Went aboard H.M.S. Argus at Gourock.

CHAPTER FIVE

The Sinking of the Ark Royal

Saturday, 1st November 1941

Left Gourock on H.M.S. Argus

Nineteen weeks after disembarking from a troopship on the River Clyde, having spent six months on foreign shores, Sergeant Bill Marsh found himself retracing his own steps.

The first day of November found him on board H.M.S. Argus, a Fleet Air Arm aircraft carrier, which was about to slip her moorings and sail down the River Clyde, and out into the Firth of Clyde.

Once again he was heading for foreign shores but unlike on the previous occasion, fate was to dictate that he would never return.

As H.M.S. Argus sailed out of the Clyde estuary and into the open sea, Bill watched the receding coastline; unaware that this would be the last glimpse of his homeland.

Sunday, 2nd November 1941

Swordfish came down in sea.

On the first day out H.M.S. Argus lost one of her aircraft, when a single-engined Fairey Swordfish, torpedo bomber, biplane crashed into the sea off Northern Ireland. The three crew members, consisting of pilot, observer and air gunner were all rescued safely.

The rest of the voyage was without incident, apart from the rumor of an enemy submarine being reportedly sunk on the evening of the 3rd November.

Apart from taking a turn on Aircraft Watch, Bill passed the time playing cards with his squadron colleagues, occasionally recording in his journal the sum of his winnings.

At 22.00 hours, on the evening of 7th November, excitement broke out amongst the airman, when word spread that Gibraltar was in sight. An hour later the ship docked, and was moored alongside another British aircraft carrier, the Ark Royal.

Saturday, 8th November 1941

Ashore. Whoopee

The short, but to the point, entry in Bill's journal summed-up his feelings (and no doubt those of most of his friends) about getting back onto dry land. For a pilot, whose place was in the sky, he seemed to be spending an awful lot of time on the sea!

The airmen were given shore leave as from 13.00 hours, and Bill headed for the Canadian Engineers Mess, where he had heard a drinking binge was in session!

The alcoholic intake of a certain sergeant pilot is not recorded, but Bill was sober enough to impart to his journal that he returned to the ship by lorry.

Shore leave was granted again the following day, and Bill spent the time in a more subdued activity, by visiting a cinema. The whole scene being quieter than the previous day, Bill returned to the ship, where he kept himself busy preparing for the next stage of the voyage.

The crew of H.M.S. Argus were also busy, and had spent their day preparing for her departure, at 01.00 hours, on the morning of the 10th November.

Under the cover of darkness, the Argus, accompanied by the other carrier, H.M.S. Ark Royal, the battleship H.M.S. Malaya, the cruiser H.M.S. Hermoine and seven destroyers edged out of the harbor and steamed away from Gibraltar.

Tuesday, 11th November 1941

Should have sent Hurricanes off.

A number of Hawker Hurricane fighters should have been dispatched from the Argus, enroute to Malta, but the weather conditions prevented the operation taking place.

Wednesday, 12th November 1941

11 Hurricanes took-off. No.5 off port side, but got away o.k.

At 10.00 hours, six Hurricane fighters took-off from the deck of H.M.S. Argus, followed twenty minutes later by a further five similar machines. All got airborne safely, except for No. 5 which, during take-off, veered off the port side of the flight deck but recovered and staggered into the air.

There were no dramas aboard the Ark Royal, as twenty-eight aircraft were dispatched from her deck. Each fighter dipped momentarily as it left the end of the flight deck, but climbed up to gain both airspeed and altitude.

The fighter formation was enroute to Malta, and was to be escorted there by twin-engined Bristol Blenheim fighter/bombers.

Thursday, 13th November 1941

Returning to Gib. Heard that all aircraft arrived safely at Malta.

The day had dawned fine and clear, with no hint of trouble, but for reasons unknown to Bill Marsh the convoy was returning to Gibraltar. He was aware it had turned-about but thought little of it, rumors would start to circulate and he would soon find out what was going on.

However, for the sailors on the Ark Royal, it might have had a different connotation, the date was after all the 13th and sea going types were said to be superstitious. Some may have even recalled that the Ark Royal was launched on 13th April 1937.

There was a lot of practice activity going on as the convoy cut through the water, and Bill had secured himself a vantage point from which to watch the display.

As H.M.S. Malaya fired off practice salvos, aircraft were flying on and off Ark Royal's deck.

During the afternoon, just as the Rock of Gibraltar came into view, twelve aircraft flew off the Ark's deck. Fourteen other machines circled above waiting to land.

From his vantage point on H.M.S. Argus, which was sailing on the port quarter and approximately 200 hours astern of the Ark Royal, Bill watched as the circling aircraft returned to the deck of the carrier ahead.

At 15.41 hours, just after the penultimate aircraft (the 13th machine) had landed, the Ark Royal was struck by a torpedo, on the starboard side. As the ship shuddered under the impact, and took on an immediate list to the starboard, a number of the aircraft on her deck were seen to be thrown into the air, whilst others slid down towards the water.

In his journal, Bill Marsh recorded that two more torpedoes streaked through the water heading for the carrier, but both missed their target.

The Ark Royal was cutting through the water at a reported 18 knots when she was struck by the "tinfish", which speed only endeavored to increase the damage sustained.

The aircraft carrier H.M.S. Ark Royal, photographed from H.M.S. Argus.

Various actions were taken on board the ship in order to try and counteract the list, but such was the angle of the tilt that it was almost impossible for the crew to stand upright.

The Captain realized he had no choice but to give the order to abandon ship, retaining only the essential personnel required to try and get her back to port.

Over one thousand five hundred officers and men were eventually taken off the stricken carrier, in an exercise which was not without its own moments of danger. As the list increased, parts of the Ark Royal's superstructure, coupled with the swell of the sea, created restrictions which intermittently prevented the destroyers from getting in close to take off the crew.

A stern view of Ark Royal, with a Fairey Swordfish patrolling above right.

Aircraft circle Ark Royal waiting to land on.

The aircraft on the deck of the carrier slid as Ark Royal develops a list to starboard.

Efforts were made to prevent the list from getting worse and, for a short while, the reduced crew were successful in their action. However, their battle was lost when the power failed, the lights went out and the engines stopped.

Just after 19.30 hours, a line was cast and a tug took the Ark Royal in tow. A second tug also gave assistance enabling the carrier to move forward at a speed of two knots.

Further problems were encountered below deck through the night, and into the early hours of the morning of the 14th November. By 03.00 hours, the list of the ship was 24.5 degrees; one hour later this had increased by a further 2.5 degrees.

Realizing all attempts to save the ship were futile, the towing lines were abandoned, and the remainder of the crew were taken off the destroyer; no easy task as the carrier was now at an angle of 35 degrees.

There was nothing to do now other than watch the final moments of this once fine ship. She dipped another 10 degrees and floated for a while, with her flight deck partially submerged, before turning over and slowly sinking. Her final memorial being an expanding oil slick on the surface of the sea. The Ark Royal's death being recorded at 06.13 hours.

Friday, 14th November 1941

Ark Royal sank [a] few miles out of Gib. 600 of [her] crew aboard Argus now.

Although Bill had taken a number of photographs of the Ark Royal immediately after she had been hit by the torpedo, from his "perch" on the Argus, he did not witness the final end of this stricken carrier.

With nothing left to be done, H.M.S. Argus turned towards the Rock and steamed into a busier than ever Gibraltar harbor, where the 600 members of the Ark Royal's crew she was carrying were taken ashore. Later in the day the R.A.F. contingent, including Bill, were granted an unexpected shore leave.

Sergeant Marsh went into town, where he met a group of friends, who were on a stopover whilst flying Vickers Wellington bombers out to Cairo, where they were to join the Middle East Air Force. He was able to catch-up on all the news, as well as imparting details of the event he had recently witnessed.

Sunday, 16th November 1941

Moved to North Front Aerodrome

Not being able to continue his journey Bill was, along with some of his contingent, a spare entity. He would have to remain at Gibraltar until a new posting was received.

On Sunday, 16th November, he was instructed to report to North Front airfield, where his "accommodation" consisted of a palliase (thin straw filled mattress) stretched out over eight petrol cans! He didn't think much of the food either.

Bill's time was initially spent playing chess with the Blenheim crews, and swapping flying stories. However, on 22nd November he found himself listening to two stories with which he could not compete.

Saturday, 22nd November 1941

*Met two sergeant pilots, a Czech
and a New Zealander, who were shot
down in Spits (Spitfires) over
Northern France three months ago.
They made their way through France
and Spain to Gib, where they are
waiting for a passage home*

Another pastime for Bill Marsh was to watch others fly.

Sunday, 23rd November 1941

Watched L.R. Hurricanes practice.

On his ninth day at North Front airfield, Bill went down to the fight line to watch the practice flights of the long-range Hurricanes. It was almost with some smugness that he later wrote in his journal. . .

. . .S/L T. nearly pranged – Twice. . .

It was unfortunate that one particular pilot nearly crashed his aircraft twice during the same practice period, for Bill was not the only one watching. The Air Officer Commanding and Lord Gort were also watching.

Tuesday, 25th November 1941

Watched No.258 Squadron flying.

Bill, again, took himself down to the flight line to watch the practice flying session being undertaken by No.258 Squadron.

Unfortunately for him, and No.258, the session came to an abrupt end when one of its aircraft taxiing out for take-off tipped-up onto its propeller.

Wednesday, 26th November 1941

Duty pilot.

The first real job Bill was given since his arrival at North Front airfield, was that of Duty Pilot, and the day was not to pass without some excitement.

A state of alarm was induced, when a twin-engined Bristol Bombay transport aircraft signaled a Mayday call, advising the airfield control that it was short of fuel.

The fact the aircraft was out over the sea heightened the tension, which grew when the Bombay became two and a half hours overdue.

It was later learned that the aircraft had in fact ditched into the bay, off Algeciras, to the west of Gibraltar, and that some of the crew had been "apprehended" by the Spaniards.

Later in the day a flight of six Bristol Beaufighters aircraft landed safely at North Front. As Duty Pilot, Bill was informed that another flight was expected, and was excited at the prospect that his friend Ray Woodcraft may be with them.

The sea claimed another victim on 27th November, when a Vickers Wellington bomber crashed into the water, a half a mile out, after a night take-off. The rear gunner was the only member of the crew to perish in the accident.

Saturday, 29th November 1941

Solo. 33 minutes. Hurricane.

Not having flown for four weeks, Bill was delighted to be given the opportunity of piloting a long-range Hurricane. The nature of the flight was to carry out radio-telephony tests, or as they were more commonly called, "radio checks." The flight only lasted 33 minutes, but in that time he flew round the Rock and along the straits. Feeling pretty pleased with himself, he made a perfect landing at dusk.

Sunday, 30th November 1941

Seven Beaus arrived

The expected second flight of Beaufighter aircraft arrived at North Front airfield, minus one of their number. Eight machines had taken-off, but one was reported lost at sea during the flight! However, the story was to have a happy ending, much to the relief of Bill Marsh.

The missing Beaufighter was last reported spiraling down from 12,000', towards the sea, just off the Portuguese coast. Fortunately the pilot regained control of the spinning aircraft just above sea level, and was therefore able to maintain level flight. By flying over-land, across Portugal and Spain, the "lost" Beaufighter landed at North Front two hours late. It is not recorded who was the happier when the aircraft landed, the crew of the Beaufighter, Ray Woodcraft and his Belgian pilot Yves Tedesco, or Bill Marsh. It is re-corded however that the three friends spent that evening at the Grand Hotel, celebrating!

Tuesday, 2nd December 1941

Duty Pilot

For the second time in a week Bill was detailed as Duty Pilot and, as with his previous period of duty, there was to be some excitement.

A Hawker Hurricane from No.258 Squadron was forced to land at C. Spartel, on the North African coast. The pilot, Pilot Officer Jaffene, was taken prisoner.

On receiving the news that the Hurricane had gone down, two similar aircraft each piloted by an Australian pilot, were dispatched to locate the downed Hurricane and destroy it with cannon fire.

Sunday, 7th December 1941

Ray and Ted left.

Their stay at Gibraltar over, Ray Woodcraft and Yves Tedesco prepared themselves and their aircraft for the long flight to Malta.

They took-off at 08.00 hours, accompanied by two nightfighter Beaufighters, one of which returned to Gibraltar shortly after take-off.

Being mindful of the traumatic episode Ray and Yves experienced during their in-bound flight, Bill was very much relieved to hear later that his friends had reached their destination without incident.

Saturday, 13th December 1941

Wimpey crashed in harbor

At 22.30 hours, another Vickers Wellington bomber attempting a night take-off crashed into Gibraltar Harbor seconds after leaving the ground.

The bomber, commonly known in the RAF as a "Wimpey" (after the character in the Popeye cartoons) had taken-off with its flaps down, and therefore failed to gain height.

Although it had come down in the sea, the aircraft burst into flames on impact, killing five of the seven men on board.

Sergeant Marsh was ordered, along with others, to attend the combined funeral service two days later.

Friday, 19th December 1941

Hudson caught fire.

A Lockheed Hudson, taking-off at 07.30 hours for an anti-submarine patrol, swung during its take-off run. The incident caused the aircraft to burst into flames, but not before the crew had managed to escape from the wreckage. A short while later the depth charges, with which the aircraft had been armed, blew up.

On Saturday, 20th December, Bill boarded the Athene moored in Gibraltar harbor. He was to spend three days aboard the ship before she finally cast-off, at 18.00 hours on the evening of the 23rd December, and set sail for West Africa.

Thursday, 25th December 1941

XMAS?

The calendar told him that it was Christmas Day, but Bill did not feel in a festive mood. He had, as they say, "drawn the short straw" and found he was on aircraft watch for the majority of the day; and night.

The watch periods were carried out on a four hour shift basis, commencing for Bill at midnight on Christmas Eve until 08.00 hours Christmas morning. His second shift started at 12.30 hours until 16.00, followed by another stint between 20.00 hours and midnight! What a Christmas!

The ship sailed passed Dakar during the night of 27th/28th December, and reach Freetown at 18.00 hours on the 29th December.

Although the Athene lay at anchor in the harbor for the next 38 hours, no shore leave was granted. However, during this period an oil tanker went alongside and refueled the ship, whilst a lighter (a large barge) took off two ambulances.

The Athene recommenced her journey to Takoradi at 08.00 hours on the morning of the 31st December, arriving at her destination three days later.

Saturday, 3rd January 1942

Arrived Takoradi. Ashore 2 p.m..

The Christmas and New Year celebrations came Bill's way after the Athene had docked at Takoradi, when Christmas lunch was served to those men who had missed it the week before.

Sergeant Marsh left the ship at 14.00 hours and reported to the Pan American Airways base, where he and his luggage were weighed. Feelings of annoyance and frustration arose when Bill and his fellow travelers were ordered, by the watching customs, to split and open their luggage. This infringement brought forth much sweating and swearing from those who had not long before partaken of a convivial lunch.

The Pan Am Douglas DC-3 aircraft took-off from Takoradi, piloted by Captain King, at 08.00 hours on the morning of 6th January, bound for Wadi Saidna.

Apart from Bill there were eight other airmen on board the DC-3, including Arthur Brown and Stan Goodwin, both ex No.242 Squadron, Bill Lockwood and Ron Jones, both ex No.604 Squadron and Malcolm Husband, ex 135 Squadron.

Its route took the aircraft north east to Kano, where it landed at 12.30 and lunch was taken. Ninety minutes later it took-off again and headed east to Maiduguri, where an overnight stop was made.

The Pan Am travelers at Maiduquiri, 7 January 1942 (standing left to right): Sergeant Bill Marsh, No.605 Sqdn, Sergeant Ron Jones, No.605 Sqdn, Joe Hutton, Malcolm Husband, Colonel ? , British Army. Ricky Wright, No.605 Sqdn. (kneeling left to right) Art Brown, ex.No.242 Sqdn, P/O. Bill Lockwood, No.605 Squadron, Stan Goodwin, No.73 Sqdn.

The following morning the Douglas took-off at 04.35 hours and continued on to Fort Lamy, which it reached one hour later.

After a short stop of twenty-five minutes, the aircraft was back in the air heading for El Odeid, approximately two hundred miles south west of Khartoum, where it arrived at 16.00 hours. The final destination of Wadi Saidna was reached one and a half hours later, at 17.30 hours.

Bill continued his journey, to RAF Khartoum, by truck, the following morning, reporting for duty there at midday.

Friday, 9th January 1942

Mk.1 Hurricane. 30 minutes

Bill got the opportunity to get in some flying time on his first full day at RAF Khartoum airfield, when he took up a Hurricane for thirty minutes. During the time he was in the air, Bill flew around the local area and "beat up" the Nile.

Two days later, Sergeant Marsh's flying career very nearly came to a premature end, whilst continuing his journey across Africa.

Monday, 12th January 1942

By truck to Wadi Saidna

Receiving orders to depart for Port Sudan (on the west bank of the Red Sea), Bill left RAF Khartoum and was driven by truck to Wadi Saidna, where an aircraft was waiting for him.

Bristol Blenheim, MK.IV, serial Z9671, piloted by Sergeant Mike Fitzherbert, took-off at 14.50 hours, with Sergeant Marsh occupying the gunners turret, situated amidships on the top of the fuselage.

The flight was without incident until 17.27 hours, when the Blenheim was approximately seventy-five miles from Port Sudan, and it became necessary to force-land the aircraft at Gebeit.

Mike Fitzherbert put the aircraft down, but it was written-off in the ensuing crash. However, all those on board escaped without injury, including Bill Marsh.

The journey to Port Sudan, home of No.117 Maintenance Unit, was continued the following day, when seven airmen and their luggage all clambered aboard a Plymouth automobile.

Having reached their allotted destination, the seven airmen were issued with further orders. Sergeants Wright, Lockwood and Hutton were posted to No.232 Squadron, whilst Sergeants Ridewell and Jones were to be held as reserves.

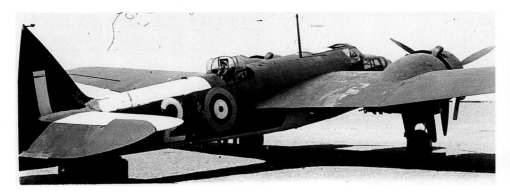

Bristol Blenheim Mk.IV, serial Z9671, coded 2, at Wadi Saidna.

Sergeant Marsh and Sergeant Goodwin were informed that they would rejoin their Squadrons!

Effectively Bill didn't have a Squadron to join. His Unit had become non-operational prior to being posted overseas.

A detachment from No.605 Squadron had gone to Malta, whilst others were posted to the Far East. To add to the confusion, equipment, records and documentation appertaining to No.605 Squadron were lost when the Ark Royal was sunk.

Some of Bill Marsh's personal and service effects, including his flying log book, were lost when the carrier went down.

The view from the turret looking aft, as the Blenheim takes-off.

Saturday, 17th January 1941

Flew [a] Kittyhawk. 30 minutes

Five days after his crash landing in the Blenheim, Bill had another dice with death. On this occasion though it was his own inexperience that caused the problem.

Sergeant Marsh had been given permission to take up a Curtiss Kittyhawk, powered by an Allison engine, for a short flight.

Unfortunately he had never flown this type of aircraft before, and was therefore not conversant with its landing procedures.

The flight went well, and without incident, but things went wrong as he landed. Touching down at 100 m.p.h., Bill applied pressure to what he thought was the rudder bar. The tail-end of the aircraft came up and continued its arc, thus turning Kittyhawk, Mk.I., AK816, onto its back.

Apart from hurting his pride, Bill sustained a sprained back and a cut forehead. He was taken to the station sick quarters, where it was deemed he would he confined to bed for one week.

His first duty on leaving hospital, on 23rd January, was to file an accident report.

There was no Court of Inquiry however. The Officer Commanding deduced that due to Bill's inexperience on that type of aircraft, the latter had unwittingly applied pressure to the wheel brakes, which resulted in the Kittyhawk flipping over.

Bill and his accommodation, at Port Sudan.

Monday, 26th January 1942

Preparing to go to Cairo. Drew a suit of blue and received a large kit deficiency list.

In the usual British Service manner that everything had to be accounted for, even in wartime, when Bill Marsh arrived at Port Sudan his kit was checked.

Prior to his departure, on 27th January, Bill was issued with a certificate which stated that 993910 SGT. Marsh, W.E. had arrived at No.117 M.U. with the following items of kit:-

1 Topee (sun helmet)	1 Flying Topee
2 Pairs Stockings (socks)	1 Pair Shorts (tropical)
1 Tunic (tropical)	1 Field Service Cap
1 Kit Bag	1 Pair Shoes
3 Shirts (khaki)	1 Pair Slacks (trousers)
1 Water Bottle	1 Towel
1 Great Coat	1 Tie
1 Kit Bag (Universal)	1 Life Jacket
1 Parachute	1 Helmet (flying) & Equipment
1 Revolver, Pouch and Belt	

Wearing a suit of blue (an RAF Uniform), Bill awaits transport from Port Sudan.

The document, which was signed by the Adjutant, went on to state that the remainder of Bill's kit had been lost due to enemy action.

Wednesday, 28th January 1942

Arrived Atbara

Having made his way across to Atbara, situated on the River Nile, north of Khartoum, Bill caught a train to Wadi Halfa, where he arrived at 20.30 hours the following evening.

At 09.00 hours, on the morning of 30th January, Bill continued his journey by taking a boat up the Nile to Shollal. From there he took another train via Aswan, Luxor to Cairo, where he arrived at 07.30 hours, on the morning of the 1st February.

He took a room at the Commonwealth Hotel in Cairo, where he was amazed to find a number of former friends from training days, and the more recent past. Amongst the group was Jimmy Hair, whom he had last seen at No.55 O.T.U. Whereas Bill had joined No.605 Squadron, Jimmy Hair had spent the last five months in North Africa, flying Curtiss Tomahawks. Amongst the more recent acquaintances Bill met were Art Brown, Stan Goodwin and Malcolm Husband, three of his fellow travelers on the Pan Am DC-3!

Tuesday, 10th February 1942

Almaza – tent with Blenheim boys.

After spending a week in Cairo, Bill reported to the Transit Camp at Almaza, where the accommodation left a lot to be desired. The comfort of the Commonwealth Hotel was exchanged for the dubious luxury of a tent, which he had to share with the crew of a Blenheim aircraft.

Friday, 13th February 1942

Gil's first solo, Tiger Moth.

The two brothers, now on the same Continent, but separated by many hundreds of miles, still managed to keep up to date with each other's news. Thus, it was recorded in Bill's journal that his younger brother had made his first solo, on Friday 13th February!

Gil Marsh was now at No.26 Elementary Flying Training School, at Gwelo, Rhodesia, where he was learning to fly in De Havilland Tiger Moth aircraft.

On the recorded morning, after a fifty-five minutes dual flight in Tiger Moth T9724 Gil Marsh was sent off to fly his first solo which lasted ten minutes.

During his stay at the Transit Camp, Bill met his old C.O. Squadron Leader Reid, who

Brother Gil, the young aviator, in flying mood.

had gone with the No.605 Squadron detachment out to Malta, during the final months of 1941.

Reid, who had been wounded, did not talk much about the conditions on the Island, and had been invalided home via Almaza, Khartoum and Takoradi.

Sunday, 15th February 1942

Bilbeis. Air Firing School.

A week long air firing refresher course took place at Bilbeis, north-east of Cairo, between 15th and 21st February.

The School used Hurricane Mk.I aircraft which Bill was happy about, bearing in mind his last encounter with a fighter aircraft. Unlike one of his colleagues, who flew into a drogue cable during one of the exercises. Fortunately for the pilot, he was uninjured and able to land his aircraft safely.

On completion of the course, Bill returned to Almaza, where he stayed for a further five days before, again, moving on.

Thursday, 26th February 1942

Transit Camp – Sidi Haneish. O.K.

The airfield at Bileis, north-east of Cairo, where Bill spent a week flying Hurricanes, on the air firing refresher course.

Sergeant Marsh had left Almaza at 16.00 hours the previous afternoon, and headed west to Sidi Haneish Transit Camp, situated mid-way between Fuka and Mersah Matruh.

His first impression of the camp was one of satisfaction, although Bill was not going to be there long enough to enjoy any comforts it may have had.

On 28th February, two days after his arrival, Sergeant Marsh was posted yet again, but this time he was going to a Squadron; No.274.

No.274 Squadron operations tent, with the Unit number "written" in stones.

CHAPTER SIX

The Western Desert

Tuesday, 3rd March 1942

Sector recce'

Sergeant Bill Marsh became operational with No.274 Squadron four days after his arrival on the unit, when he took to the air, in Hurricane MK.IIB, Z5064, for an interception patrol.

As part of a four aircraft formation, he took-off at 08.15 hours, to locate and intercept an enemy aircraft reported in the area. However, nothing was seen and all the aircraft returned to base.

Later in the day, flying the same aircraft, Bill Marsh took-off again, this time to fly to Gambut 2, where he and five other pilots were to be held at readiness. Bill's frustration of an uneventful first operation was to be repeated when the detachment was ordered to return to base, where they landed at 17.30 hours.

During the afternoon of the 4th March the weather changed and it started to rain. The downpour grounded all aircraft and prevented further operations, not only for the rest of the day, but throughout the following two days.

Thursday, 5th March 1942

Wild and windy – to fly as No. 2
to F/Lt. Moriarty in "K."

Profile of a Desert Flyer

Sergeant Marsh was to have flown a mission, as No. 2 with Flight Lieutenant Pat Moriarty, but the inclement weather "scrubbed" all aerial activity. The rain also flooded a number of tents, including that used by the newly arrived pilot.

The bad weather did however give Bill the opportunity to meet some of his colleagues, as they spent the time sitting around chatting. Amongst those in the group were Flight Lieutenants Pat Moriarty and "Bags" Playford. Also present were Sergeants Hamish Dodds, Roy Macfarlane, Edward Eagle and Jack Neil from Canada.

Orders were received by the Squadron, during the course of the afternoon of 6th March, to prepare for a move to Gambut Main, on Sunday 8th.

Saturday, 7th March 1942

*SCRAMBLED to 10,000' at 13.00 hours.
Got off late and lost others – Stooged
over El Adem for 30 minutes and then
returned to base. Ropy landing, but o.k.*

During the course of the afternoon, ten Hurricanes were scrambled in pairs to intercept, reported in-coming hostile, enemy aircraft. However, nothing was reported and all aircraft landed safely.

It is not recorded why Bill Marsh was late taking-off, or how he came to lose contact with the rest of the flight, but he was lucky not to have encountered enemy aircraft. A

Sergeant Jack Neil, RCAF.

"rookie" desert flyer would have been an easy target for a more experienced German or Italian fighter pilot.

Sunday, 8th March 1942

*Shot up by 109s at 13.00 hours. Six planes
hit on ground – one on circuit hit with cannon
shell and force-landed on drome. No 109s hit !
F/Lt. Playford put (Hurricane) "Y" on its nose.*

On Sunday, 8th March, the Luftwaffe paid No.274 Squadron a visit, whilst some of the latter's aircraft were out on patrol.

At 12.45 hours, five Hurricanes from No.274 had taken-off for an interception patrol over Tobruk and El Adem. Whilst they were away, nine Me 109Fs roared over the landing ground firing at anything in their sights. Two ground strafing runs were made, which resulted in six Hurricanes sustaining damage.

During the course of No.274's sortie, Sergeant Persse had become separated from the patrol and had made his own way back to base. Unfortunately for him, four of the Me 109's struck as he was making his landing approach. As he was about to touch-down the first Messerschmitt 109 opened fire from a range of approximately 100 yards. Bullets whizzed around his aircraft, but missed their target. Two of the other 109s then tried their luck with better results, compelling Sergeant Charles Persse, RAAF, to force-land his aircraft, but not before he had been wounded in the leg.

Squadron scramble, where Bill was not the only one late away!

During the course of the same afternoon, "B" Flight moved its aircraft to the Landing Ground at Gambut Main as ordered. "A" Flight joined them at 12.00 hours the following day.

Flight Lieutenant Playford's Hurricane succumbed to an area of soft sand, whilst touching-down on the rain sodden landing ground. The undercarriage dug-in and the tailplane rose up into the air.

One of the six Hawker Hurricanes, which sustained damage during the ground strafing attack by Me 109s. Note the Squadron code letters NH on the fuselage.

A battered twin-fin tail assembly from a Me 110, bearing numerous bullet holes, is prepared for unloading outside the mess tent at Gambut.

The tailplane, prior to being inverted for use as a squadron bar. The Commanding Officer's car indicates his presence at the mess tent.

Monday, 9th March 1942

A Kittyhawk shot down in flames near drome
Moved to Gambut Main and put up tents, after
Jack Neil tipped (Hurricane) "R" on its nose
whilst taxiing.

"B" Flight, having flown to Gambut main the previous day, were on readiness throughout the day. They were joined at midday by "A" Flight and between them they undertook no less than twenty-four scrambles, but all to no avail as no hostile aircraft were sighted or intercepted.

Saturday, 14th March 1942

Took Pilot Officer Graves to Gambut Main. Landing
Ground bombed by 109's just before we landed, and
D.A.s [Delayed Action bombs] going off as we taxied in.
Binge at night – Mick Thompson returned and W/C
Linnard posted to H.Q.M.E.

Operations for No.274 Squadron began during the morning, when five Hurricanes were scrambled in order to patrol over their Base. These however were recalled shortly after take-off.

Later in the morning, at around midday, ten Hurricanes flew a patrol over their Base and El Adem. They faired little better and landed without having made contact with the enemy.

The third patrol of the day comprised of six aircraft from No.80 Squadron in company with eight Hurricanes from No.274 Squadron. Together they searched for a large concentration of enemy fighters, which had been reported over the forward area. Although no hostile machines were seen, it was reported that shortly after the allied aircraft had landed, fifteen Italian Macchi fighters dived out of the clouds and carried out ground-strafing attacks.

Sergeant Bill Marsh, piloting Hurricane Z5313, accompanied by Pilot Officer Graves, undertook a local patrol at 15.45 hours, but landed without incident. Unlike the Squadron diary, the former's journal recorded a different story!

During the course of the evening a party ensued to celebrate the return of Flying Officer Thompson, who had been shot down a couple of weeks previously. It was also a way of saying farewell to Wing Commander Linnard, who was to take up a new posting at RAF Headquarters, Middle East Command. His place, as Officer Commanding, No.274 Squadron, was to be occupied by Squadron Leader Dean.

Tuesday, 17th March 1942

*Readiness 07.30. Scrambled at 10.00 hours.
Stooged around over Gazala, near Tobruk with
Browne, Eagle and Samuels. At 11.00 hours
intercepted an Me 110, and made 3
attacks before it reached cloud. No hits
observed. Eagle, my No. 1, attacked first.
He followed it through cloud, disabled both
engines, but could not wait to see it prang.
Claimed damage.*

Although twelve Hurricanes had been at readiness from 08.00 hours, only six aircraft were scrambled when an order came through two hours later. Their orders were to patrol the forward area, where a hostile aircraft had been reported.

Sergeant Eagle, (Z5382) was first to observe the enemy aircraft and identified it as a ME 110. He immediately dived into the attack and opened up with a long burst of fire. Strikes were observed around the rear cockpit area, and are thought to have killed the rear gunner. As Sergeant Eagle peeled aware, other Hurricanes from the Squadron followed up the attack, including Sergeant Marsh, who fired a three second burst of machine gun fire before the enemy took evasive action. The Me 110 dived down into the cloud cover for protection, but Sergeant Eagle saw it and again gave chase. Lining-up the enemy aircraft in his sights he opened fire a second time, and last saw the swastika marked aircraft diving away to the west of Gazala, with it's port engine on fire.

Not having seen it crash, Sergeant Eagle could only claim it as a probable.

Thursday, 19th March 1942

*Boys doing free-lance sweeps in fours formation,
over Gazala, Tmimi, etc. Diced with Me 109s, but
no result. At 16.00 hours a Kittyhawk force-
landed having been shot-up by 109. A top cover
sweep was washed out.*

No.274 Squadron detailed twelve Hurricanes to take-off in three formations, each comprising of four aircraft, at different intervals, during the course of the morning. Their respective tasks were to be offensive sweeps of the forward area.

The third formation, which took-off at 10.25, had completed their task and were returning to base, when they sighed two Messerschmitt Me 109s over the Gambut area.

The four Hurricanes turned towards the enemy who, although outnumbered, accepted the challenge of the Royal Air Force.

The rattle of machine gun fire reverberated through the air, but the outcome was inconclusive. No claims were made by either side.

The same however could not be said for an American built Curtiss Kittyhawk which, having been in a different fight with Me 109s, sought refuge at Gambut Main airfield. The aircraft sustained slight damage, and was probably claimed as such by the German pilot who attacked it.

During the course of the afternoon, No.274 were to have flown an escort patrol to Boston bombers, who were returning from their mission. However, this was canceled at the last moment.

Friday, 20th March 1942

Released then placed at readiness. Slight sandstorm. No. 172 Squadron Beaus arrived, with them is George Tuckwell. Last met him at Gib.*

Bristol Beaufighter aircraft, of No. 272 Squadron (*which Bill Marsh recorded in his journal as No.172) arrived. They were a long-range fighter squadron and undertook such duties as convoy patrols, intruder missions and long-range ground attack operations.

One of their pilots was George Tuckwell, who Bill had not seen since his departure from Gibraltar. Needless to say they spent some time catching-up with each other's news.

A Curtiss Kittyhawk, wearing RAF markings..

A Bristol Beaufighter, coded TJ-C, creates a sandstorm as it takes-off in the North African desert.

Saturday, 21st March 1942

Evening, close escort to Bostons near Martuba.
Bostons made four runs over the target area at
1,500 feet. Sgt. Mullis hit by ack-ack and spun
in. Four Hurricanes force-landed on the way
home – short of petrol. My motor cut out when
taxiing in after landing at dusk.
A very horrible show!!!

Twelve Hurricanes were scrambled at 11.05 hours, to carry out a patrol to the south of Bir Hacheim, in order to search for a reported outflanking German column, heading eastwards.

The Squadron broke into two sections with one flying top cover, whilst the other section went down below the cloud level. Although the lower section were flying at only a couple of hundred feet above ground level, no reports were made of any movements.

During the late afternoon, at 17.00 hours, No.274 Squadron flew as close escort to three Boston bombers who were detailed to bomb a target west of Martuba. The cloud which remained very low not only forced the bombers down to approximately 1,500 feet, but also prevented them from observing the result of their labors.

Flight Sergeant Earl Mullis, RCAF, flying Hurricane Z5313, was hit by ack-ack fire on the return journey. His aircraft spun-in from 2,500' and was seen to burst into flames. His name is recorded on the Alamein Memorial.

Chapter 6: The Western Desert

Sunday, 22nd March 1942

*Day off. Ray Woodcraft here. Went to see
him during the afternoon.*

When Bill was informed that a Bristol Beaufighter, crewed by Yves Tedesco and Ray Woodcraft had landed, Bill went off in search of his friends.

To his disappointment, by the time he got to the visiting aircraft, Ray and Yves had departed and could not be located.

However, inclement weather the next day intervened and curtailed many activities, which meant the three friends met and spent some time together.

They also spent Tuesday, 24th March, together and finished with a binge in the evening, downing quite a few beers in the process.

Wednesday, 25th March 1942

*Ray and Yves in panic fly-off. Saw them
take-off in Beaufighter Z, for Idku.*

Sgt Roy Macfarlane, "General" Mullis and Bill at Gambut, photographed a few days before Mullis was killed in action.

Yves Tedesco, Bill Marsh and Ray Woodcraft at Gambut.

Ray Woodcraft and Yves Tedesco had arrived during the build-up of a sandstorm, which persisted for some days. Having been re-called urgently to their base at Idku (Landing Ground No. 229), they had no option but to take-off in the same type of conditions. Unfortunately, on landing back at their base, the aircraft crash-landed, causing damage to the belly, engine nacelles and propellers.

Friday, 27th March 1942

Hurricane, Z4944. Gambut – Sidi Haneish
Barwick shot down, strafed, but returned o.k.

No.274 detailed twelve Hurricanes to be at readiness at 07.00 hours, to act as a striking force, in conjunction with No. 450 Squadron.

Yves Tedesco (standing) and Ray Woodcraft, after their crash landing at Idku.

At 11.30 hours, as a large formation of enemy aircraft was reported approaching Tobruk and El Adem, the two allied squadrons received orders to patrol over the forward area. The axis formation however changed course and headed for Gazala before returning to the west.

It was not too long before the Hurricane pilots sighted their adversaries in the form of three Messerchmitts Me 109s and three Macchi M.202s flying above them.

As battle was joined, Pilot Officer Conrad was able to bring his guns to bear on a Macchi. He fired a number of short bursts and saw pieces falling off the Italian fighter.

During the skirmish, two pilots, one of whom was Sergeant Barwick, became separated from the main group, and were immediately attacked by Me 109s and M.202s. With enemy machine gun and cannon fire bursting around his aircraft, Sergeant Barwick turned the Hurricane into an evasive maneuver and stole the advantage from his attackers. He opened fire with two long bursts at a M.202, which was last seen going down leaving a trail of thick black smoke. The Macchi was reported, by the South Africans, who had captured the pilot, to have crashed five miles south of El Adem.

Sergeant Barwick found, to his dismay, that some of the machine gun and cannon fire directed at him by the enemy had found it's target and he was forced to land his damaged aircraft at Bir Saleima.

Friday, 3rd April 1942

1 Macchi 202 damage: Engaged by 6+, one of which turned on to Sgt. Persse, my No. 1. Pukka dog-fight for ten minutes, 202 looping and

Parbury (jumping off truck), F/Lt Keefer, Sgt Lerche (on truck), and P/O Browne (in shirtsleeves), greet Sgt Barwick (center) on his belated return to the Squadron.

> *rolling, got in snap shots at bottom of loops.*
> *Broke off combat when a second 202 appeared -*
> *my ammo finished too.*
> *Sgt. "Tiny" Howell shot down.*

Ten aircraft took-off at 10.50 hours, having been on standby for only twenty minutes. Two of them returned early due to engine trouble, but the remaining eight carried out a sweep over the Gazala area as detailed.

During the patrol they sighted and intercepted a mixed flight of Messerschmitt 109s and Macchi 202s, the outcome of which resulted in Pilot Officer Hunter and Sergeant Garwood each claiming a probable, whilst Sergeant Bill Marsh (piloting Hurricane IIB, serial BD820, "D") claimed a Macchi 202 damaged.

The latter exhausted all but fifty rounds of his ammunition, which he would have expended, had he not been forced to break off combat when attacked by a second Macchi fighter.

No. 243 Wing reported that Sergeant Howell was shot down during the melee and, although wounded, was safe.

Sunday, 5th April 1942

> *Flew No. 2 to Dodds on sweep – Gazala,*
> *14,000' top cover. Flew in BD827, a ropy*
> *kite. Two Kittyhawks went in as we landed.*

Four Hurricanes from No.274 were scrambled, when it was reported that two Me 109s were approaching the former's base. The defending fighters roared off across the desert sand and climbed to an altitude. They identified the hostile aircraft and gave chase, but the enemy aircraft turned and headed towards the coast. Unfortunately, due to a hazy sky, the intruders were lost to view, leaving the Hurricanes to return to base.

At 14.00 hours, eleven aircraft from the Squadron took-off for a sweep over the Gazala area, accompanied by Hurricanes from No.33 Squadron.

Still a relatively new boy to operations, Bill Marsh flew as a wingman to Sergeant Hamish Dodds, who was beginning to make a name for himself when it came to a scrap, but not during this patrol.

The sweep however was uneventful, and all the aircraft, except for that flown by Sergeant Barwick, returned to base. Barwick's Hurricane force-landed, west of Tobruk, due to a glycol burst. The pilot, who had just made his second force-landing in ten days, was reported as safe.

Four Hurricanes scramble into the air.

Monday, 6th April 1942

Eagle got a 109F. Bruckshaw got a cannon shell in the cockpit.

A crescendo of noise filled the morning air, as twelve Rolls Royce Merlin engines started up, signaling the start of another mission. The task detailed involved a sweep over the Gazala area.

At 08.55 hours, the pilots turned their aircraft into the wind, powered-up their engines, and raced for the sky. Their eagerness for a fight was to be rewarded when they sighted an enemy patrol, comprising of both Me 109s and Macchi 202s.

The inevitable dogfight developed, with the Hurricane pilots racing into the attack. Sergeant Eagle opened fire at a Me 109 which was seen to bank over and fall away to earth, definitely out of this fight and all future ones. Sergeant Dodds not content with having shot down a Macchi 202, which was credited as a probable, then turned his guns on a Me 109. This went the same way, but was only credited as a damaged.

Although all the Hurricanes returned safely to base, one was found to have incurred slight damage. Unbeknown to the pilot, Sergeant Bruckshaw's aircraft had received a cannon shell in the cockpit, which could have inflicted injury upon him or serious damage to his aircraft!

On the 7th April 1942, No.274 Squadron returned to Sidi Haneish for the start of a month's well earned rest, and a period of leave.

Bill Marsh, along with Sergeants Harrington, Macfarlane, Bruckshaw and Lerche, and Flight Sergeant Neil, went to Alexandria, where they visited the cinema and a few bars.

On Wednesday 15th April, Bill went to Landing Ground No. 229 at Idku, where he teamed up with Ray Woodcraft, Yves Tedesco and George Tuckwell. An invitation from the latter to go for a flight in his Beaufighter was eagerly accepted by Bill.

The aircraft, coded "O", flew at low-level across the desert and, during the forty-five minute flight, Bill, who was more often than not armed with a camera, took approximately ten photographs.

Sgt Michael Bruckshaw, of Bolton, Lancashire.

The traumas of war were put behind him when Bill, accompanied by Ray and Yves, decided to spend the rest of their leave on a sight-seeing trip.

Having returned to Alexandria, where they could get transport, Bill and his two friends then made their way to El Quantara, where they caught a train to Lydda. Although there was a party of noisy Israeli school children also traveling on the train, Bill, Ray and Yves all managed to catch up on some sleep.

They arrived at their destination at 14.30 hours on the afternoon of Friday 17th April, and found accommodation at the YMCA

The following afternoon, they visited Bethlehem, and then continued on to the Dead sea, where they witnessed the unusual sight of a Sunderland flying boat sharing the Dead Sea with a group of swimmers.

They made their next overnight stop at Tel Aviv, where they took a room at the Imperial Hotel. They were impressed by the facilities and visited the bars and two cabarets. It was whilst they were dining that they saw a brawl arise between an Australian and a member of the South African Air Force. The result of the fight was South Africa one, Australia nil.

The return journey was made by air, from Lydda, in a Lockheed Lodestar, which took-off at 16.00 hours, and arrived at Cairo at 17.45 hours.

Whilst Ray and Yves went to stay with some Belgian friends in Cairo, Bill checked in to the Oasis Hotel for a couple of nights.

During his stay, he met two friends from his training days in Canada, Jimmy Hairs, whom he had last seen in January at the Commonwealth Hotel, and Dick Lawes.

The last time Bill had heard of the latter was prior to Lawes taking-off from the Ark Royal, bound for Malta.

Over the palm trees at 260 knots, at an altitude of 30 feet, in a Beaufighter of No.272 Squadron, piloted by George Tuckwell.

Over the coast . . .

Over the landing ground at Idku. At least two aircraft are visible to the right of the picture.

A Short Sunderland flying boat, photographed minutes before taking-off, shares the Dead Sea with a number of swimmers.

Ray Woodcraft and Yves Tedesco sample the delights of the Dead Sea.

It was through this chance meeting with Dick Lawes, that Bill heard No.605 Squadron had been disbanded.

When Ron Jones, ex.No.605 Squadron pilot, walked in it seemed as though all the guys were in town. Jones imparted the news that he was based at Almaza Transit Camp, where he had been for the last eight weeks awaiting a posting. He also added to Dick Lawes' news by informing Bill that of those on No.605 who had gone to the Far East, most were either dead or POWs of the Japanese!

Their time in Cairo coming to an end, the trio met and caught a train to Alexandria. They then hitched a ride to El Daba, and finally arrived back at base at 18.45 hours, on Saturday 25th April.

Sergeant Marsh and No.274 Squadron returned to war on Monday, 11th May.

Monday, 11th May 1942

Scramble Tobruk – Gazala, 12,000'
Attacked from above by four Me 109s
who appeared out of the sun.

Although the Squadron had twelve aircraft at readiness from 06.00 hours, no operations were detailed and, at 13.00 hours, were permitted to stand six of them down, whilst the other six remained at fifteen minute readiness.

It was at 17.30 hours that a scramble was ordered, and all twelve Hurricanes responded to the order.

During the patrol, four Messerschmitt 109s dived down out of the sun. Pilot Officer Conrad, to whom Sergeant Marsh was flying as wingman, rolled his Hurricane over onto its back and dived. At that same moment, a Me 109, with white wing tips, flew across in front of Bill Marsh's Hurricane, but to Bill's dismay, he could not get near the enemy aircraft.

All the Hurricanes returned to Base and landed at 18.05 hours, with the exception of Flight Lieutenant "Bags" Playford, who force-landed at El-Gubbi due to a glycol leak. His aircraft (NH-T) was repaired and he returned to the unit the following morning. Unfortunately, as Playford landed at base, his undercarriage collapsed and he pranged!

Sunday, 17th May 1942

Scramble El Adem – Tobruk, 12,000'
1 Ju 88 & 2 Me 109s observed. Out of range.

Bill, piloting Hurricane BG700 was scrambled along with Flight Lieutenant Playford and Sergeant Dodds, at 12.30 hours to patrol to El Adem area.

The main building and control tower at Lydda airport.

During the course of the patrol, a Ju 88 and two Me 109s were sighted, but due to the enemy aircraft being out of range, no interception was made.

Monday, 18th May 1942

Close escort bomber, N. Gazala. Recalled.

Eleven aircraft from No.274 Squadron took-off at 07.30 hours, to fly as close escort to a flight of Boston bombers. No.33 Squadron had been detailed to fly top cover, but having taken off they promptly lost their charges. However, due to the loss of the top cover, the operation was canceled by control who ordered all aircraft to return to base. The Bostons immediately jettisoned their bomb loads into the sea, and returned as ordered.

Following another aborted mission on the 20th May, ten aircraft from No.274 took-off during the afternoon and flew to Kilo 8, where they exchanged their MK.IIB Hurricanes for Hurri-bombers.

Monday, 25th May 1942

> *Going on special leave – Presland flew*
> *instead of me They ran into some 109s*
> *and 202s. "Bags" shot in his rear part,*
> *flesh wound. Pranged kite – wheels up.*

Lockheed Lodestar, coded 2147, wearing RAF markings, at Lydda.

A poor quality photograph of Bill Marsh (left), Yves Tedesco (centre) and Ray Woodcraft waiting to board the Lodestar.

The first, and only, mission of the day involved twelve aircraft from No.274 being scrambled, at 17.05 hours, to intercept four plus enemy aircraft, approaching Gazala from the west.

Due to the fact he was going on leave, Bill did not participate in this operation. Instead, Sergeant Presland was authorized to fly in Bill's place.

The Squadron encountered Me 109s and Macchi 202s in the reported area and, giving the fighter pilot's war cry, "Tally Ho", on sighting the enemy, they swung into attack.

Ray Woodcraft relaxes amongst the palms . . .

. . . whilst Yves Tedesco, looks pensive during a meeting with a lady friend.

Only the best views, from hotel windows, for Bill.

During the ensuing combat, Flight Lieutenant "Bags" Playford was shot in the butt, causing a flesh wound. He returned to base, but, for the second time in two weeks, his aircraft landed on its belly.

Flight Sergeant Parbury had to force-land his Hurricane two miles west of the base, due to shortage of fuel.

Claims were put forward for damaged enemy aircraft by Flight Lieutenant Keefer, Pilot Officer Sammy Samuels and Sergeant Jack Neil.

A letter from Ray Woodcraft informed Bill that the writer had been temporarily grounded due to ill-health.

CHAPTER SEVEN

The German Push

The ground war took a major turn when, on the 26th May, General Rommel launched a full scale offensive against British armored forces, with the intention of capturing Tobruk.

The plan was to attack from the south, capturing Bir Hakeim, moving north to Acroma and east to El Duda and Sidi Rezegh, taking Tobruk from the south and south east. However, the attack against Bir Hakeim, by the Italian Mobile Corps, was thwarted by the Free French Forces. Although some enemy armor did achieve its aim and reached the escarpment to the north of Arcoma before being repelled.

The attack to the east was partially successful, some troops reaching Sidi Rezegh and El Duda before being pushed back.

After four days of inconclusive fighting, Rommel's forces made their escape by forcing two passages through the British minefields to the west of El Ualeb.

Tuesday, 26th May 1942

Raid – 109s strafed Gambut 2, then pushed off. Then 4 88s stooged over, bombed No.145 Squadron dispersal. Started off on special leave to Alex.

Rommel's offensive was not confined to the ground forces; the Luftwaffe was also involved. At approximately 07.00 hours, on the morning of the 26th May, four Junkers Ju 88 bombers launched a bombing raid against one of the four landing grounds at Gambut.

The Hurricanes of No.80 Squadron and No.145 Squadron, the latter whom had taken up residence the previous day, stood forlornley and indefensive as bombs fell around them.

A sequence of three photographs, taken by Bill Marsh, during an attack by four Ju 88 Luftwaffe bombers, against the landing grounds at Gambut.

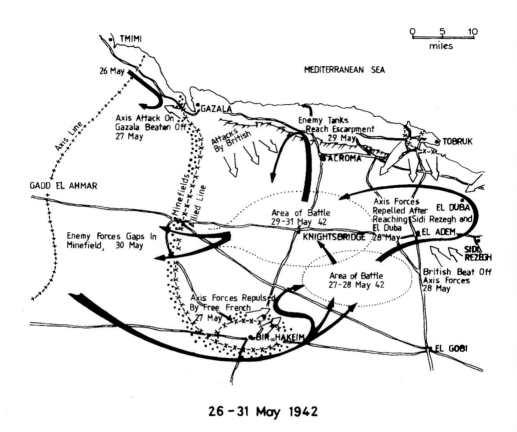

26 - 31 May 1942

Great plumes of smoke and fire rose into the air as the bombs exploded, causing dust, sand and debris to rain down on the unprotected Hurricanes.

Bill witnessed the attack and was able to record the scene, not only in his journal, but also with his camera, before he departed for Alexandria.

Intense fighting, in various areas, kept the ground forces busy during the first two weeks of June, with attacks and counter-attacks.

The pilots of the Desert Air Force were kept equally busy giving aerial support to their colleagues on the ground.

The Squadron lost another pilot on the 31st May, when Pilot Officer Wilfred Ismay, RCAF, was shot down and killed. He was laid to rest in the Tobruk War Cemetery.

Whilst Bill Marsh was enjoying his leave in Alex, the war continued without him.

It was upon his return to the Squadron that he was informed of the loss of his friend, Flight Lieutenant Pat Moriarty, who had been shot down on 2nd June.

Moriarty, accompanied by Flight Sergeant Parbury, had been engaged in a bomber sortie over Cauldron, when they were attacked by Me 109s. Three of the enemy machines

F/Lt Pat Moriarty (facing the camera) plays chess with P/O 'Connie' Conrad, during a period of "readiness" at Gambut.

chased Moriarty and shot him down in the Gazala area, killing him in the process. He was later buried at the Knightsbridge War Cemetery, near Acroma.

Parbury was more fortunate and force-landed near Cuppazza, during a sandstorm. He returned to the unit the following day.

Thursday, 11th June 1942

Top cover to No. 33 Squadron. 20 Ju 88s escorted by Me 109s and M.202's intercepted. P/O. Persse shot down. Returned owing to oil leak, evaded 4 Macchi 202s on my tail.

Eleven Hurricanes took-off at 17.05 hours to carry out a fighter sweep, whilst acting as top cover to No. 33 Squadron.

As No.274 Squadron was patrolling five miles north west of El Adem, they caught sight of twenty Ju 88 bombers escorted by M.202s flying west at 3,000 feet. At the same moment, a group of six Me 109Fs were spotted approaching from the north west at 13,000 feet.

The Squadron took the initiative and attacked the 109s head-on, the bombers having made off at high speed when they realized a fight was about to start. At the same moment, the Macchi 202s climbed up to join in the skirmish.

Pilot Officer Walsh, R.A.A.F. aimed his guns at the leading Me 109 aircraft and opened fire. The bullets struck their target and the German machine burst into flames; it was claimed as destroyed. He then turned in search of another target and found a second 109, which he attacked and claimed as damaged.

Two Me 109s swung into attack Pilot Officer Persse, who had recently been promoted, and Flight Sergeant Neil, the latter responding with a three second burst, but he was unable to observe the results. As to the enemy aircraft turned away, three other Me 109s came in for the attack. Flight Sergeant Neil again responded with another three second burst, but he was unable to observe the results. As the two enemy aircraft turned away, three other Me 109s came in for the attack. Flight Sergeant Neil again responded with another three second burst, on the lead aircraft, from 100 yards. This time he saw it burst into flames and later claimed it as destroyed. Two more avenging 109s came into the fray and attacked Persse and Neil's Hurricanes. The latter fired the remainder of his ammunition at them, but did not observe the results. During the conflict Pilot Officer Charles William Persse was shot down and killed. The Australian, from Queensland, was buried at Knightsbridge War Cemetery.

While all this action was taking place, Bill Marsh's aircraft developed an oil leak, which created a thin coating over his windscreen, obscuring his vision to some degree.

Pondering on what might have been.

His plight was noticed by the enemy and, unbeknown to Bill, four of them lined up astern of his tail. Fortunately this move was noticed by some of Bill's colleagues, who raced to his defense and scared off the four M.202s.

Upon his safe return to base Sergeant Marsh was informed of his close encounter with the Italians; his astonishment later being recorded in his journal.

The outcome of the flight was a credit of two Messerschmitt 109Fs destroyed and a similar machine being damaged, for the loss of Charles Persse.

Friday, 12th June 1942
(First Entry)

Hurri-bomber raid south of El Adem.
Bombed Italian motor transport.
10 bombers, 2 top cover.

Ten Hurri-bombers took-off at 08.00 hours, escorted by two fighters from No. 33 Squadron who were to act as top cover.

Their allotted target was a concentration of Italian motor transport, situated approximately fourteen miles south of El Adem, behind a concentration of German armor!

Bill Marsh, flying BG707, coded Z, watched as the raid developed, and saw bombs rain down on between 50 and 100 axis vehicles, three of which were destroyed in one direct hit.

There was no interference from enemy aircraft, or the German tanks, and the Squadron was back for breakfast at 08.40 hours.

Friday, 12th June 1942
(second entry)

Sweep Acroma – El Adem, 9'000.
WE JUMPED 3 Ju 88's escorted by 10+ Me 109s
at 6,000ft, west of El Adem. "Z" hit by
ground fire after combat. Burst of 303"
in engine and 6" hole in prop blade.
Me 109F PROBABLE.

Eleven Hurricanes took-off at 11.35 hours to carry out a fighter sweep in the region of El Adem. During the course of the patrol they were advised that a flight of ten plus enemy aircraft were approaching from the direction of Gazala. Within a very short space of time three Ju 88s, one Ju 87, accompanied by six Me 109s and two Macchi 202s were spotted bombing allied motor transport at a location some thirty miles west of El Adem. The Squadron immediately swung into the attack, and Pilot Officer Browne opened fire with a five second burst on a Me 109. The enemy aircraft shuddered under the impact, as the shells hit the fuselage. A plume of black smoke emitted from the aircraft as it was seen to go down apparently out of control. Pilot Officer Browne claimed the 109 as a probable.

Another Messerschmitt 109 flew into the sights of Sergeant Hendersons guns, which he instinctively fired. A five second burst sprayed the hostile machine, off which pieces were seen to break loose. Glycol smoke left a trail, marking the 109s path as it went down into a vertical dive. Sergeant Henderson claimed this as a probable, to go with the damaged claim he made on a second Me 109.

Sergeant Thompson also tangled with a Me 109 close on his tail, with the latter obviously lining-up the allied aircraft in its sights.

Bill Marsh, going to his colleague's assistance, pulled up and attacked the Messerschmitt with a perfect deflection beam attack. He closed to a range of 70 yards and opened fire with a fifteen second burst, which sprayed the aircraft from which pieces were seen to fall. The German machine rolled onto its back and fell towards the earth, with a thin stream of glycol pouring from it. Bill followed it down and continued to fire.

F/Lt Hunter has a close shave of a personal nature, whilst P/O. Caen wanders into the tent. The suitcase in the foreground bears the name J. Graves, RAF.

P/O Buckley catches up on some sleep, on a camp bed placed between the guy-ropes of his tent.

At approximately 2,000', the German machine began to slowly pull out of its dive. Breaking the rules of combat flying, Bill continued to follow his opponent west, getting lower and lower.

When the Messerschmitt was about twenty feet above the ground he watched in amazement as the undercarriage came down.

Unfortunately for Bill, in the heat of battle, he had not given thought to his own safety and was brought back to reality when he saw brilliant flashes emanating from the ground. Realizing he was over enemy territory, and was being fired at by their artillery, he made a hasty retreat. A loud explosive crack at the front of his aircraft made him think that he had had it, but the engine kept going and he headed for base as quickly as possible.

Upon landing he checked the nose of the Hurricane and found a six inch hole in one of the propeller blades, and a number of shell fragments in the engine cowling.

As he was unable to see the final outcome of his fight with the Me 109, Bill was only credited with a probably destroyed.

Pilot Officer Hunter claimed a probable after he turned his attention to the Italians and attacked a Macchi 202, at which he fired two bursts. The M.202 turned over onto its back, slowed in flying speed and then fell away, seemingly out of control.

Pilot Officer Buckley also went for the Italian aircraft and attacked a Macchi 202, which was claimed as damaged.

At the end of the skirmish the score was recorded as one RAF aircraft damaged, four Me 109s and one Macchi 202 probably destroyed, with one Me 109 and one M.202 damaged.

Sgt Bill Marsh (left) and P/O. 'Sammy' Samuels (right) pose on the starboard wing of a Hurri-bomber, of No.274 Squadron. Note the 250lbs bomb under the wing.

Although eleven aircraft carried out an offensive patrol over the El Adem area at 14.45 hours, no enemy aircraft were sighted.

Friday, 12th June 1942
(Third Entry)

'SCRAMBLED' – Top cover.
El Adem area, all available fighters.

Another offensive patrol was undertaken by eleven aircraft of No.274 Squadron, at 19.40 hours. It was a big show, and they were accompanied by aircraft from No. 33, 73, 213, 145 and 233 Squadrons. All available fighters took part in the mission, which took place over El Adem.

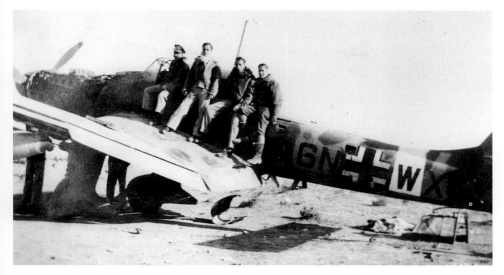

Not necessarily the Ju 87 "Stuka" claimed by P/O Samuels, but a prize worthy of attention.

No.274 Squadron sighted and attacked twelve Ju 87 Stuka dive bombers, escorted by Messerschmitt 109Fs and Macchi 202s, five miles north west of El Adem.

The Squadron dived into the attack and opened fire. Two 109s went down in flames, one to the guns of Sergeant Dodds. The enemy fighters, turning to meet the attack, left the way open to the dive bombers and Pilot Officer Samuels took advantage of this fact. He swung into the attack, opened fire and claimed a Ju 87 destroyed.

Nine American Douglas Boston bombers, escorted by No.274 Squadron, on their way to attack a target at El Duda.

Meanwhile, Hamish Dodds, elated by his victory, tried to increase his score and attacked a second Messerschmitt 109F. Although he saw strikes on the enemy fighter, the twisting turning aircraft did not succumb to his guns and, like Pilot Officer Keefer, Dodds could only claim a damaged.

Flight Sergeant Parbury claimed by Me 109 probable, whilst Sergeant Presland claimed a damaged Macchi M.202.

On the afternoon of 13th June, the British armored forces suffered severe losses having run into concealed axis anti-tank batteries near Bir Behaffer. The British were forced to withdraw eastwards, while the Axis forces kept up the pressure and headed in the same direction.

Towards the end of the same day, Bill Marsh received news that Yves Tedesco had been reported missing following a Malta convoy escort duty.

Three days later, Bill heard that due to his continued ill-health, Ray Woodcraft was likely to be repatriated home

Wednesday, 17th June 1942

Forced to leave Gambut by enemy tanks advancing, 7 miles away when we left.

An early morning patrol, lasting forty-five minutes, over the Gambut area was undertaken on 17th June. Bill recorded Me 109s were spotted in the area, but neither group made any effort to attack.

However, this was not the case during a mission later in the morning, when eleven Hurricanes escorted nine Bostons to attack a target in El Duda. Having carried out their task, the escort returned to their base area, where they were attacked by Me 109s and M.202s.

A United States Army Air Force Kittyhawk.

F/Lt. Darwin (Killed in action 7 August 1942), Sgt Lerche, Sgt Dodds and F/S Harrington, waiting for 'Connie' Conrad to alight from the ambulance following his return to the Squadron.

F/O. 'Connie' Conrad (left), with hands and legs bandaged, reflects on what might have been, as he sits quietly with F/O Hunter.

During the ensuing dog-fight, Sergeant Dodds destroyed two M.202s, whilst Sergeant Lerche damaged another. Pilot Officer Keefer was also credited with a damaged.

Not all the victory laurels went to the Squadron. An Me 109 attacked and shot down Pilot Officer "Connie" Conrad, who was forced to make a wheels-up landing. The German Pilot, however, was not content with his victory and followed Conrad's aircraft down. Opening fire, the German flier strafed the crippled Hurricane before Conrad was able to extricate himself from the cockpit.

As the Me 109 turned to make another run, an unidentified American built Kittyhawk appeared and shot down the aggressor.

Pilot Officer Conrad, although wounded in the left arm and both legs, managed to clamber out of his stricken aircraft and walk a considerable distance before he was rescued by an Army unit. They rendered first aid to the pilot, and returned him to Gambut later the same day.

Flight Lieutenant "Bags" Playford also returned to the Squadron, following his stay in hospital, where he had received treatment for the wound to his rear end!

Two new faces appeared when Sergeant "Pop" Hemmer, an American, from Cincinnati, and Sergeant Hamilton, from Canada, reported for duty with the Squadron.

At 18.00 hours, No.274 Squadron received orders to move to a new base, Landing Ground No. 148, at Sidi Aziz, forty miles to the east.

The convoy arrived there at 23.00 hours that night and, by the time the aircrews landed, the aircraft availability on the Landing Ground had risen to ninety Hurricanes!

Jacky ? (left) and Steen (right) keep Sgt Eagle company whilst the latter waits to start his journey home to England.

Roy Marples, wearing sergeant chevrons on his shirt, appears to be listening for the approach of enemy aircraft.

The following morning the aircraft came to readiness at first light, but instead of receiving a Battle Order, the Squadron received orders to move yet again! This time to El Dwabis. The aircraft, being ready, took-off immediately, whilst the ground staff set off across the desert once more in convoy. The latter arrived at their destination at dusk, tired and weary after their long trek.

There was no operational flying for No.274 the following day, as they sorted themselves out, erected their tents and carried out maintenance work on the ground vehicles. However, later during the day, orders were received instructing them to move yet again!

At 06.00 hours, on the 20th June, an advance party set off for Landing Ground 76, followed four and a half hours later by the Squadron's aircraft.

Having seen the aircraft safely away, the remainder of the ground party were able to leave.

Sergeant Eagle returned from leave, which was granted immediately after he had fainted in the cockpit of his aircraft on the return from a recent Me 109 hunting trip.

However his stay at LG.76 was to be a brief one, as he was informed that he would shortly be leaving the Squadron and ultimately catching a boat home to England.

All the moving, withdrawing from one base to another, was beginning to have an adverse effect on the morale of some of the men, but Flight Lieutenant Roy Marples, DFC (ex No. 616 Squadron, Battle of Britain pilot) kept up their spirits with humorous stories.

At 23.00 hours that night the sound of an aero engine broke the silence. Roy Marples looked up towards the sky, listened intently and then assured his colleagues, with some authority, that the incoming aircraft was friendly. The next moment the sound of machine gun fire erupted, aimed from above, downwards!!

Wally Conrad (still with hand bandaged), F/O. Hunter and F/Lt Keefer rest outside the mess tent. Note the two circular tins of cigarettes on the makeshift table.

Although the British forces had withdrawn to the Egyptian frontier, some of its mobile formations continued to harass the enemy. However, on the 20th June, Rommel's tanks provided yet another surprise by turning their attention towards Tobruk.

The Luftwaffe provided Ju 87 Stuka dive bombers to blast a gap in the south-eastern perimeter defenses, thus allowing Axis tanks and infantry access to Tobruk. The following day (21st) the coastal town was forced to surrender, when it was occupied by Rommel's forces.

Sunday, 21st June 1942

Recco Gambut, Sidi Aziz and Bardia.
Ack-Ack from Bardia and Sidi Aziz.

Six aircraft took-off at 12.23 hours and carried out a reconnaissance of the Fort Cupuzzo area. Although no enemy aircraft were sighted, much ground movement was seen and some fires noted.

A second reconnaissance sweep, carried out by six aircraft later in the day over Bardia to Bir Sherfeyen area, filed a similar report.

Barely had the Squadron settled in to their new location when, at 18.00 hours on the 23rd June, they received orders to move camp again. This time, they were to head east to

Landing Ground 07, at Matruh West. The ground staff arrived at the new location by 12.00 hours the following day.

Wednesday, 24th June 1942

*Recco Halfaya, Misheifa, from LG07.
Some ack-ack 10 miles N.E. Misheifa. Enemy flying
column 20 miles from LG07. Landed, reported, then
panic take-off to reach LG13, our old base.*

A Hawker Hurricane, Mk.II, taking-off from Landing Ground No.76, at Misheifa, Egypt . . .

. . . quickly followed by two other Hurricanes.

At 16.20 hours the Hurricanes were participating in the first of two reconnaissance patrols. However, due to the intensity and movement of the fighting forces on the ground, before the second patrol (which had taken-off at 17.30 hours) had returned, further orders were received instructing the Squadron to move to Sidi Haneish, between Qasaba and Maaten Bagush.

Thursday, 25th June 1942

Battle for Mersa Matruh
Bombing, west of Charing Cross.
Target not identified. Landed with bombs on.

Earlier in the day, three aircraft from No.274 Squadron bombed a German motor transport and tank column with moderate success.

A second force comprising of six Hurri-bombers took-off at 12.00 hours, but by the time they reached the target area the column had dispersed.

As Squadron Leader Dean, who was leading the flight, could not identify a suitable target, he ordered all the pilots to return to base with their bombs.

The intensity of battle was recorded by Bill in his journal when he wrote, "Bostons, Blenheims, Spitfires and Kittyhawks going over all day."

Three Hurricanes set course to attack a German transport column.

Friday, 26th June 1942
(First Entry)

Bombed west of Charing Cross.
Heavy ack-ack over target – Enemy M.T.
Sergeant Thompson missing.

Six Hurri-bombers from No.274 Squadron, again led by Squadron Leader Dean, with Bill Marsh as his wingman, were detailed to bomb an enemy concentration in the battle area.

The formation, flying above the desert sands, soon spotted its target, an enemy column comprising of between 50 and 100 vehicles. The C.O. led the Squadron into the attack, but his bombs failed to release.

Undaunted, Squadron Leader Dean pulled out and turned to starboard, with Bill keeping station with him. A second attempt to release his bombs was more successful, and they whistled down onto some vehicles slightly to the east of the main group. Sergeant Marsh followed his leader's example, and dropped his bombs into the same area.

The rest of the Squadron attacked the main concentration of vehicles, the bursting of their bombs causing plumes of smoke and sand to rise up into the air, blotting out their view of the results.

The enemy responded to the attack with both heavy and light flak which peppered the sky, and provided a dense barrage over the target area. All the aircraft returned safely to base, with the exception of Sergeant Thompson who, it is believed, was shot down by ground fire.

To his utter amazement, when he landed Bill Marsh found a shrapnel hole in the flap of the starboard wing of his Hurricane.

On writing at a later date to his younger brother Gil about the above attack, Bill stated the following. . .

". . .we were over their front line at 9,000', when we ran into the hottest ack-ack I have ever seen. We bombed and came out at 3,000' (one hits 360 [mph] in the dive) and I got caught in lots of their Breda. I got back with a 6" hole in my starboard wing – very lucky too! Touch wood, that's the second time I've collected ack-ack, though I have not been hit by their fighters – I consider that last a very creditable, or lucky, performance for me . ."

Mealtime at LG 105, El Daba with L to R: P/O Andrews, unknown, unknown, S/L Dean, unknown (standing), F/L Marples and "Oppy."

Ron Jones, ex. No.605 Squadron, with a Hawker Hurricane bearing the AK codes of No.213 Squadron, where Jones was posted during the early summer of 1942.

Chapter 7: The German Push

Friday, 26th June 1942
(Second Entry)

Bombed west of Charing Cross.
Lots of ack-ack over target – enemy M.T.
Obscured by bursts, but all in target area.

There was to be no let-up in the fighting, either in the air or on the ground and, once the Hurri-bombers were re-fueled and re-armed, No.274 went back into the fray.

Bill Marsh, as part of the attack force, took-off in Hurri-bomber 112, "H", with a 250lb bomb under each wing.

The target was again located and the attack commenced. As the bombs rained down, the ack-ack fire came up. The scene below the pilots was being blotted out by the black smoke from their exploding bombs rising into the air and merging with the angry black balls of bursting anti-aircraft fire.

Each aircraft ran the gauntlet of the intense ack-ack barrage thrown up by the defending forces, but managed to emerge unscathed. They all returned safely to base.

During the course of the day, a further two attacks were made against enemy motor transport columns, each having similar results as the previous missions.

On two of the sorties, No.238 Squadron flew as top cover to the Hurri-bombers, and saw off two intruding Messerschmitt 109s. A number of enemy vehicles were destroyed and many more were damaged.

The 27th June saw yet another move for No.274 Squadron, when at dawn the unit was ordered east to LG105, at El Daba.

The ground staff arrived at LG105 at midday, and by 13.10 hours the Squadron was operational.

Upon his arrival at El Daba, the first person Bill Marsh met was Ron Jones who, since their last meeting, had been posted to No.213 Squadron.

Normally a beer or two would have been consumed, but there was to be no celebration. Bill was feeling unwell at the time and was depriving himself of all forms of food and drink.

CHAPTER EIGHT

The British Retreat

The enemy, having captured Capuzzo, Sollum, Helafaya and Sidi Barrani took Mersa Matruh on Monday, 29th June.

The Royal Air Force, assisted by the South African Air Force and United States Army Air Force, provided assistance to the British mobile forces, in slowing down the enemy advance, allowing the British retreat to be made in an orderly manner.

Monday, 29th June 1942

Recco. of tank battle area, south of Matruh. Some ack-ack. Went out at 7,000' escorted by Kittyhawks. Circled target (guns shelling main road) dived and bombed at 2,000'. Observation of results impossible, some ack-ack from south. 28th A.L.O. Captain Fields confirms accuracy of bombing – enemy gun posts were silenced for 3 hours, enabling our rear-guard to evacuate Mersa Matruh.

A reconnaissance flight, made up of twelve Hurricanes, patrolled the Fuka-Matruh-Bagush area. Although they saw no enemy aircraft during their patrol, they did observe much ground movement.

They all returned safely to base only to be informed that orders had been received to relocate yet again! This time to Landing Ground 92.

Flight Lieutenant Marples, DFC, received orders to report to No. 127 Squadron, where he was to become a Flight Commander.

Meanwhile two new pilots joined the Squadron, Sergeant "Flash" Gordon and Sergeant Bernard Ott, the latter being a Rhodesian, and a member of the South African Air Force.

No.274 Squadron having moved, spent the next twenty-four hours setting up the camp and getting re-organized as part of No. 244 Wing.

Rommel's advance eastward continued after the capture of Mersa Matruh, and by the 1st July his forces had reached El Alamein. The British decided to stand and make a fight of it, and in the early morning of that same day the two forces engaged, once more in battle.

Repeated attacks were made by the Axis forces, which were repelled by the British Eighth Army, causing the enemy to retire on the evening of the 2nd July. The British positions remained intact.

Sgt "Flash" Gordon, RCAF (left) and P/O. "Hash" Mitchell.

The aftermath of battle.

Wednesday, 1st July 1942

Attempted bombing. 8/10th cloud over target.
Landed with bombs on.

The Squadron detailed eight Hurri-bombers, supported by four fighters, to participate in an attack against an enemy motor transport refueling station.

The aircraft, including Hurri-bomber, BE699, flown by Sergeant Marsh, took-off at 19.07 hours. As they climbed to 7,000', they were informed by ground control that enemy aircraft, flying at 15,000' were reported in the target area. With the cloud base being between only 3,000' and 3,800', and only four fighters acting as top cover, it was considered advisable not to proceed with the attack.

Thursday, 2nd July 1942

Attempted bombing. 10/10th cloud over target.

Bill was detailed to participate in two attempts to bomb enemy motor transport and tanks but due to thick low cloud, both missions were canceled and the pilots ordered to return to base.

On the 3rd July, supported by the Desert Air Force, the British ground forces launched a major counter-attack, which resulted in the destruction of numerous enemy tanks and the capture of hundreds of Axis prisoners.

Friday, 3rd July 1942
(First Entry)

Attempted bombing. Stooged over target
area, could not locate gun posts, returned.

Bill recorded the above, as one of three entries in his log, for bombing operations against enemy gun positions, on this particular day. However, although the two following entries appear in the Squadron's Operational Record Book, there appears to be no comment on an abortive operation.

Friday, 3rd July 1942
(Second Entry)

Bombing Sortie. Bombed enemy gun posts.
El Alamein.

The Squadron detailed six Hurri-bombers, escorted by six Hurricane fighters, to take-off at 08.35 hours, to attack forty enemy gun positions to the west of Bir-Makhkhad. The attacking force gained altitude to 8,000', and followed the coastline to the target area.

The target, gun positions to the north and south side of a main road, were bombed from a height of 5,000', the bombers having dived down from their higher altitude.

The cloud conditions, and drifting black smoke from the heavy ground gun fire, made observing results difficult, but two hits were recorded on assumed gun post positions.

All the aircraft returned safely to base, but one was found to have incurred slight damage, presumably from anti-aircraft fire.

Eight Hurricanes climb into the desert sky in loose formation.

Friday, 3rd July 1942
(Third Entry)

*Bombed enemy gun posts at El Alamein. 3 M.202s
appeared. One climbed up on our port
beam, F/Sgt Garwood attacked. One confirmed.
We bombed OK.*

Six Hurri-bombers, escorted by six Hurricane fighters, took-off from LG92, at 11.45 hours for an attack against enemy gun positions west of Bir-Makhkhad. Bill Marsh, piloting Hurri-bomber, Z9699, climbed with the rest of No.274 Squadron to 7,000', their bombing altitude. Whilst observing the results of their labors, the Hurri-bombers were attacked by three Macchi 202 fighters. Two of the Hurricane escort fighters were ordered to intercept and engage the Italian aircraft. Flight Sergeant Garwood turned his aircraft, BE699, towards one of the 202s which had decided to attack from the beam quarter. Fire spat from Garwood's guns, destroying the Macchi before it could cause any damage to the main Hurricane force.

In the midst of all the Squadron activity, it was decided by higher command that Squadron Leader Dean, the Officer Commanding, had served his time with No.274 and posted him to RAF Headquarters Middle East Command. Squadron Leader Hayter was posted in to take over as the new O.C.

Flight Lieutenant "Bags" Playford was ordered to take over Hayter's previous position as C.O. of the Wing Base.

F/S Garwood, RCAF, carefully picks up Gilbert the snake who, on the original photograph was listed as 'one time bedmate and later a belt'.

Following the success of the operation on the 3rd July, another attack was made against the enemy, by both British and South African forces, on the 10th July. This, like the previous armored assault, was supported by air power.

Twelve aircraft took-off at 06.30 hours, to fly as top-cover to No. 1 Squadron, South African Air Force. Whilst patrolling west of El Alamein, No.274 Squadron was engaged by six plus Me 109 enemy fighters, who made a determined effort and a number of attacks against the Hurricanes.

In the twisting turning melee of fighters one Hurricane was seen going down in a spin. The pilot was not seen to bale out, and neither was a parachute seen to open. Sergeant George Craggs, whose aircraft it was, was later confirmed missing, presumed killed. This was later confirmed.

The second sortie of the day, which took-off at 09.15 hours, enabled the pilots of No.274 Squadron to exact revenge for the loss of their colleague on the previous mission.

They too were flying as top-cover for No. 1 Squadron, S.A.A.F., when they were bounced by twelve Me 109s and Macchi 202s.

The sky turned into an aerial arena as allied and axis fighters twisted and turned in a general melee, each trying to align his sights on an enemy machine.

Cannon and machine gun fire spate from the barrels and leading edges of the fighters' wings as the pilots pressed home their attacks and thumbed their respective gun buttons.

The aerial battle began to diminish as the Axis aircraft began to extricate themselves from the fray, having been damaged or expended all their ammunition.

On return to it's base, No.274 Squadron totaled up its score as one Me 109 probable, two Me 109s damaged, five M.202s damaged and one M.202 probable, the latter claimed by the new O.C. The only casualty to No.274 was Sergeant Hemmer, who was slightly injured.

Friday, 10th July 1942
(First Entry)

Patrol over forward area – No joy.

Bill Marsh must have been cursing his misfortune as he landed back at base, following his first patrol of the day.

His aircraft was one of nine detailed to patrol an area ten miles west of El Alamein, with top cover provided by No.238 Squadron. Although they flew their allotted patrol line for almost an hour, unlike the pilots on the earlier missions, they returned to base with nothing to report. Other than the Axis forces must have been "at home" licking their wounds.

Friday, 10th July 1942
(Second Entry)

Sweep over forward area.
Chased Me 109F but could not catch or engage.

At 19.10 hours, nine aircraft again took-off from LG92 to patrol the same area west of El Alamein, but on this occasion No.80 Squadron were providing the top cover.

As they were patrolling at 10,000', a mixed flight of Me 109s and M.202s was sighted. As the range between the two opposing forces closed, two Macchi M.202s tried their luck and opened fire at the Hurricanes. Sergeant Macfarlane was the recipient of the incoming bullets as they struck and damaged his starboard wing.

In order to stop the Messerschmitts joining in, No.274 went on the defensive. Bill Marsh gave chase after a Me 109 which came into his sights, but found it was too far away to open fire. He eventually gave up the chase and his quarry got away.

Saturday, 11th July 1942

2 Me 109s attacked formation. One climbed away
overhead. Got in two second burst, but could not
catch him again.

A flight of nine aircraft from No.274 Squadron was attacked by two Me 109s, whilst patrolling El Alamein, at 10,000'.

The Messerschmitts made their attack against the bottom cover, on the starboard side of the formation.

The Hurricanes turned-in to meet the attack, whereupon the enemy aircraft broke their formation. One climbed away and was chased by amongst others, Bill Marsh, but the result was the same as the previous day; the quarry got away.

No.80 Squadron scramble.

The second enemy fighter chose a different escape route and dived vertically. Sergeant Macfarlane pulled his Hurricane over in a tight turn and went down after the Me 109. Although he continued to fire at it in the dive, and observed strikes, the enemy aircraft pulled out at 1,000' without any apparent damage. No claim was made against it.

During the course of the late afternoon Bill and Jack Neil, who had both been stood-down, went into Alexandria. They met a number of old friends, including George Tuckwell who, over a drink, related details of his morning's work.

George had been part of a formation of twelve Bristol Beaufighters, from No. 272 Squadron, who intercepted twenty-eight Ju 52 transport aircraft, escorted by Me 110 and Ju 88 fighters. By the end of the ensuing fight, the Beaufighter crews claimed to have shot down twelve enemy machines.

Monday, 13th July 1942

Target 500 enemy M.T. west of El Alamein. Bombers dived from 8,000', then 4+ ME 109s attacked the top cover (4 fighters). Got 12 seconds in short burst at one; he broke away west, diving. 1 ME 109F DAMAGED.

The Squadron detailed eight Hurri-bombers, escorted by four Hurricane fighters to move forward to Landing Ground 151, in preparation for a bombing attack against enemy motor transport. However, being unable to locate LG151, the attacking force landed at Landing Ground 39, where they refueled.

Taking-off again at 13.40 hours, the Squadron flew along the coast climbing to a height of 9,000 feet without incident.

The target, enemy motor transport and infantry concentrations, was located and the bombers carried out their allotted task. Diving to between 6,000' and 4,000' the bombs were well placed in the target area.

Meanwhile, the top cover escort, which included Bill piloting Hurricane, BE699, had encountered four Messerschmitt 109s which dived on them from above. The enemy fighters made several attacks on the Hurricanes, who responded to the challenge. Bill saw a Me 109F just above, and coming towards him. He opened fire in short bursts, whilst climbing in a steep left turn to meet the attack. Also, by turning inside the flight path of the Me 109, Bill was able to slide in behind his attacker's tail. Opening fire, he recorded several strikes against the machine, before the enemy did three rolls, broke off and dived away inverted.

Sergeant Marsh went down after the Me 109, but found he could not keep pace with it. Bill was later credited with a "damaged."

Tuesday, 14th July 1942

*On bombing shows all afternoon.
Bombing enemy infantry and pasting hell
out of German motor transport.
Out at 9,000', dived & bombed at 3,000'.
Some hits; all close.*

The Squadron undertook four separate bombing missions against enemy infantry and motor transport on the 14th July. Bill Marsh flew three of the sorties and on each occasion reported good results, with a number of direct hits.

No.80 Squadron flew as top cover on each of the operations, but they had little to do, as no hostile aircraft were reported.

The retreat continued, as during the course of the day, No.274 Squadron moved to Landing Ground No. 173, located to the south east of LG92.

Wednesday, 15th July 1942

*Top cover on another show in the morning.
To Alex' in the afternoon.*

Having been stood-down for the rest of the day, following an operation during the morning, Bill, Jack Neil, Mick Bruckshaw, and a few other pilots all went into Alexandria where, according to Bill's journal, they all "had some fun."

Their merriment extended into the evening, causing them to stay the night in town and return to base the next morning, when eleven of them arrived in a convoy of taxis!

Thursday, 16th July 1942

*At 10,000', followed bombers down. Accurate
Breda over front line after bombing.*

SGTS HARRINGTON AND PRESLAND MISSING.

As Bill and his colleagues arrived back at LG173, from their night out, the Hurricanes of "B" Flight were arriving back from a mission.

The Squadron detailed eight Hurri-bombers and four Hurricane fighters to attack enemy motor transport. Approaching the target from the north at 7,000', the bombers dived to 3,000' to make good their attack. A number of direct hits were recorded, including one which caused a violent explosion. As they pulled out of their dive, and headed for home, the enemy responded with a barrage of both light and heavy Breda gun fire. "Red" Harrington and Sergeant Presland both flew straight through the box barrage, at an altitude of 200'.

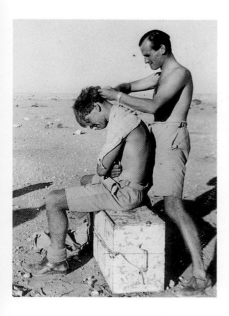

"Mac" Macfarlane gets a trim from "Brucky" Bruckshaw, before going into Alexandria.

Sergeant Presland's aircraft was seen to be hit in the engine cowling, catch fire at the wing root and go straight into the ground.

Sergeant Harrington's Hurricane, streaming glycol, managed to force-land in the desert. The latter was seen to climb out of his cockpit and run off in an easterly direction.

Sergeant Presland was recorded as missing, presumed killed, whereas Sergeant Harrington was more fortunate. He was able to walk back to Allied lines, where he was "picked-up" by the 3rd South African Brigade, and returned to his unit by 16.00 hours that same afternoon.

Friday, 17th July 1942
(First Entry)

Nothing to do in the morning. Went to LG151 in afternoon.

As no Battle Order was posted for the Squadron, the pilots were released from duty and stood-down, leaving Bill and a number of others at a loose-end.

During the course of the afternoon Bill visited Landing Ground No. 151, where he followed the time honored, old English tradition of taking afternoon tea and scones at the mobile canteen.

Friday, 17th July 1942
(Second Entry)

A killer at rest.

*Reported enemy aircraft to port. Me 109s and
M.202s circled and attacked us out of the sun.
We formed a defensive circle; one M.202 dived
vertically, firing at me. Pulled up the nose
and opened fire until he passed through my
sights. 1 M.202 DAMAGED. "F" undamaged.*

Nine aircraft of No.274 were detailed to fly as top cover to No.238 Squadron. They took-off at 18.30 hours, with Flight Lieutenant Keefer, O.C., "A" Flight leading. They climbed to an altitude of 13,000', and zigzagged their way towards El Alamein. It was as they were flying over the town they spotted a flight of some 12+ Me 109s and M.202s, approximately three miles to the north.

Hoping to obtain an advantage, No.274 flew towards the sun and then made a 90' turn, thereby flying a south-westerly course. The axis aircraft, who had a 3,000' height advantage, struck. As the enemy dived down into the attack, Keefer turned his flight into a defensive circle and prepared for the ensuing fight.

The Me 109s came down, through the circle and climbed back up into the sun. Sergeant Bill Marsh, piloting Hurricane, BE487, "F", got in a couple of snap shots. He then spotted a M.202 coming in for a beam attack on him. The M.202 climbed above the Hurricane, flicked over onto its back and came down firing at BE487. Bill pulled his aircraft up, almost into a stall, and thought for one moment the Italian was going to crash into him. The Macchi pilot was still firing, but his aim was wild and instead of pulling round behind the Hurricane, he turned across in front of it. Seeing the M.202 in his gun sights, Bill opened fire and was rewarded with the sight of the cockpit hood of the Italian machine shattering into fragments.

Knowing other enemy aircraft were still around, Bill did not wait to see what happened to the M.202, but went off in search of other prey. He spotted ten or more aircraft stooging around in the distance and identified them as Ju 87 Stuka dive bombers.

As the dog-fight continued and gained in momentum, the Ju 87s flew underneath the aerial ballet and ignored what was going on above. That is until Sergeant Henderson (BE699 "C") saw the group and decided to get himself a Stuka. He pulled his Hurricane over into a turn and dived down, lining-up his sights on the selected target. Fire spat from his guns and the dive-bomber reared up, burst into flames and was last seen falling to earth. Sergeant Henderson was credited with a confirmed kill.

All No.274 Squadron aircraft returned safely to base, where Bill claimed, and was credited, with a damaged against his M.202.

18th – 31st July 1942

Between the 18th and 31st July, Bill was off flying duties. He recorded in his journal, "Have been off flying for a few days – nothing of importance (happening) on the Squadron."

No.274 Squadron continued the fight whilst Bill was off, and his colleagues continued to increase their respective scores. Squadron Leader Hayter, Flight Lieutenant Darwin and Sergeant Lerche each claimed a Me 109 damaged, whilst Flying Officer Hunter claimed a M.202 damaged. Pilot Officer Mitchell and Pilot Officer Bell shared a Me 109 probable, whilst Flight Sergeant Neil was credited with a Me 109 probable in his own right.

Pilot Officer Bell was also credited with a Ju 87 probable, whilst Pilot Officer Browne claimed a similar aircraft damaged.

During this period, a number of pilots with whom Bill had trained, or met and become friends with, became casualties of the intense fighting. Amongst them was Squadron Leader Barclay (No.238 Squadron), whose aircraft is thought to have exploded on impact with the ground.

Two other pilots from No.238, Pilot Officer Morrison and Pilot Officer Jones, were also killed, as was John Leicester, of No. 33 Squadron.

On the 7th August, the pilots of "B" Flight were "jumped" by patrolling Me 109s.

No.274 Squadron had been detailed to attack an enemy encampment, near the coast. "A" Flight were to undertake the bombing side of the mission, whilst "B" Flight flew top cover at 5,000'.

The Hurri-bombers having completed their task, flew out over the sea at zero feet, but their colleagues had to stay and fight, as the Messerschmitts made their intentions clear.

Off flying, with nothing to do and nowhere to go.

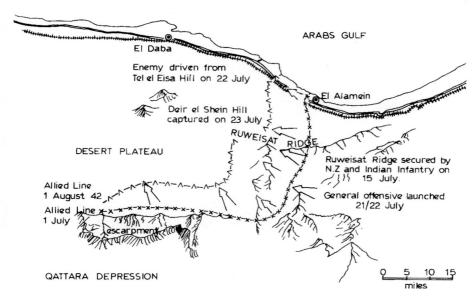

ARABS GULF

El Daba

Enemy driven from
Tel el Eisa Hill on 22 July

El Alamein

Deir el Shein Hill
captured on 23 July

RUWEISAT RIDGE

DESERT PLATEAU

Ruweisat Ridge secured by
N.Z and Indian Infantry on
15 July.

Allied Line
1 August 42

General offensive launched
21/22 July

Allied Line
1 July

escarpment

QATTARA DEPRESSION

0   5   10   15
miles

21 - 27 July 1942

Flight Lieutenant Darwin was shot down and killed, whilst the Hurricane flown by Flight Sergeant "Pop" Hemmer, the American, was seen by Sergeant Lerche to be hit and burst into flames.

"Pop" Hemmer managed to bale out and, as the American floated down on his parachute, Sergeant Lerche protected his colleague by circling around him, until the former landed in the sea.

"Pop" Hemmer's ditching was reported, and the appropriate map co-ordinates given, and a Walrus amphibious aircraft was flown out from Ismailia to pick him up. Although, due to their respective fuel situations, none of the other Squadron members could stay in the vicinity until the Walrus arrived.

Unfortunately the American could not be found and no news was received concerning his fate, other than unconfirmed reports that he had been attacked again, by Me 109s, whilst he was floating in the water.

Around this same time, "Connie" Conrad was promoted to the rank of Flight Lieutenant, and posted to No.145 Squadron.

Result of a night operation in which No.238 Squadron lost three Hurricanes.

When Bill Marsh returned to operations in August, he was transferred to "B" Flight and quickly ushered back on to operations flying Hurri-bomber sorties.

Sunday, 9th August 1942

8+ Me 109s and M.202 attacked from 15,000' - we were at 7,000'. F/Sgt Neil damaged 1 M.202. We funneled down to deck, then eastwards. No one hit.

No.274 Squadron scrambled 12 aircraft for an Interception Patrol over El Alamein. They flew out towards the coast to gain height and then turned-in to about 10 miles east of Burg-El-Arab.

A warning was given that enemy aircraft, flying at 12,000', were approaching from the south west of Burg-El-Arab. The Squadron climbed in order to meet the enemy, whom the top section were first to identify. They called "Tally-Ho" and went into the attack. Flight Sergeant Neil identified a M.202 and opened fire with a good burst. Strikes were seen hitting the enemy aircraft from the stern forward to the mainplane, from where a bright flash emanated. A "damaged" was credited to Flight Sergeant Neil's personal score.

Wednesday, 12th August 1942

F/L Wally "Connie" Conrad on the wing of Spitfire Vb, serial ES386, coded ZX-A, of No.145 Squadron.

F/L Keefer stands on the wing of Spitfire Vb, ES386, whilst F/L Conrad sits in the cockpit explaining the layout.

News of "Pop" Hemmer

Anger, bitterness and sadness filled the Squadron members when they heard the news that everybody feared. It had been confirmed that "Pop" Hemmer's bullet ridden body had been recovered from the sea.

Thursday, 13th August 1942

Came back with a hang-up and engine cut through internal glycol leak when landing: O.K.

The Squadron detailed twelve Hurri-bombers, escorted by twelve fighters from No.11 Squadron, S.A.A.F. to participate in an attack against enemy motor transport. The attacking force approached the target area from the north east, coming in over the sea. As they crossed the coastline they reduced altitude in order to achieve their required bombing height. The bombs rained down from between 3,000' and 4,000', onto approximately 100 vehicles. A Field Hospital, situated fairly close to the target area, narrowly escaped destruction when Sergeant Aron's bombs burst in the vicinity of the tents.

Sergeant Bill Marsh faced a daunting time on landing back at base. Not only did he have the encumbrance of a "hang-up", which could have dislodged from it's mounting as he touched-down, but his engine cut out, due to an internal glycol leak, as he landed. However, luck was with him and he suffered no further setbacks.

The Desert Flyer, Bill Marsh, in the cockpit of a Hurricane, on 10 August 1942.

Packing up the kit again!

Tuesday, 18th August 1942

Keefer posted.

Flight Lieutenant Keefer was posted to RAF Headquarters Middle East Command, in Cairo, whilst Flight Lieutenant May arrived to assume command of "A" Flight.

Wednesday, 19th August 1942

LG173 to LG88

On Wednesday, 19th August, No.274 took-off from Landing Ground 177 and flew ten miles to the north, to Landing Ground 88, which it was to share with No. 7 South African Air Force Wing.

Thursday, 20th August 1942

*Intense and accurate A.A. over target. "P"
hit in starboard wing, 6 inch hole through
trailing edge. Bombed o.k.*

The C.O. leaves the Squadron aircraft and trucks to make their own way to the new landing ground.

The Squadron detailed twelve Hurri-bombers, each carrying two 250lb general purpose bombs, for an attack against an enemy camp and motor transport. Top cover for the operation was provided by twelve Hurricane fighters from No.127 Squadron. Spitfire Mk.Vs, of No.92 Squadron had earlier carried out a preliminary de-lousing sweep.

Bill eventually took-off, with the rest of No.274 Squadron, at 09.00 hours and gained height to 9,000'. He had earlier experienced problems with his engine which, every time he throttled back, would cut out. He made four attempts at starting the engine before he finally got away.

It is not known whether No. 92 Squadron's earlier sweep had made the enemy more cautious or not, but as the main attack force approached the target area from the south east, they noticed the axis vehicles fairly well dispersed and protected by 88mm flak guns.

Undaunted, No.274 dived down to it's bombing height of 4,000' and began its allotted task. The flak responded with intense, and in some cases accurate, bursts as Bill found out. A flak shell exploded against the trailing edge of the starboard wing, fairly close to the wingroot. Recovering his composure, and bringing his slightly damaged Hurricane back onto an even keel, Bill continued his mission and laid his two 250lb bombs with those his colleagues had already dropped. At least six well placed bursts were recorded close to twenty to thirty vehicles.

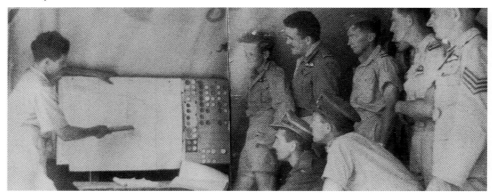

Mission briefing for 274, 238 and 125 Squadrons. L. to R: S/L Hayter, W/O Neil, RCAF, Sgt Gordon, RCAF, P/O Simpson, No.125 Sqdn, Unknown (nose & chin), Unknown, RNZAF, Sgt Meldrum, RAAF. Seated, P/O Wilson, USA, P/O Hill, RAAF.

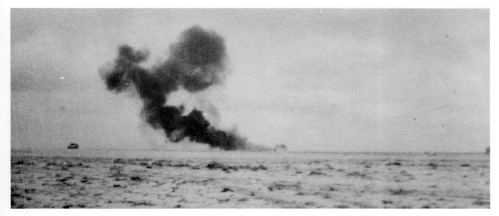

Smoke rises from a tank destroyed in the fighting, on the southern sector of the El Alamein Front, on 31 August.

All the Hurricanes returned safely to base, including that flown by Bill Marsh, who had just been hit by flak for a third time and survived! The circumstances of the incident were identical to those of the 26th June, about which Bill wrote to his younger brother.

Monday, 24th August 1942

Top Cover to 7 S.A.A.F.
Nursery Patrol! to get them used to A.A.; they did.

Twelve aircraft took-off at 07.00 hours, from LG88, to act as top cover to No.7 Squadron, S.A.A.F. The patrol, classified as "Nursery Patrol", was carried out in fine weather, at an altitude of 7,000'. No problems were encountered and all aircraft landed safely an hour and ten minutes later.

On the 25th August, No.274 Squadron were detailed to bomb a column of armored vehicles, but the "Battle Order" did not include the name of Bill Marsh.

The attack was made with the usual determination of No.274, but the Squadron did not have things all its own way. The Hurri-bombers met intense light flak in the target area, and found 4+ Me 109s waiting for them on the way out.

The wreckage of Pilot Officer Wigston's aircraft was found strewn across the desert floor, two miles north of the target area; the pilot being killed in the crash. Sergeant Macfarlane force-landed wheels up, in the desert. He returned to the Squadron later in the day. Sergeant Lerche, whose aircraft had been repeatedly hit by ground fire, eventually landed approximately 15 miles south east of El Alamein. Flying Officer Graves landed at LG28 with his bombs still attached, whilst Flight Sergeant Harrington returned to base with his bombs.

Between the 25th August and the end of the month, No.274 Squadron undertook a number of practice formation flights, in which Sergeant Marsh was involved.

CHAPTER NINE

"Stuka Party"

Wednesday, 2nd September 1942

*The Boys had a Stuka Party. Sgt Carter got
one Ju 87 prob, 2 dam; W/O Neil got 87 dest,
one 87 dam. Col Luftus got one 87 dam and one
109 prob. P/O Henderson and F/O Graves got a
109 dam each. 109s and 202s followed them home*

The Squadron got the new month off to a morale boosting start on the 2nd September, when twelve aircraft were detailed to carry out an interception patrol. The formation, led by Colonel Loftus, took-off at 14.45 hours, accompanied by No.127 Squadron, who acted as top cover.

Unfortunately for Bill, he was not with them when they took-off, as his name was not on the Battle Order. He had been detailed for an earlier show, which did not materialize. He sat in the cockpit of his Hurricane, at readiness, feeling somewhat frustrated, as an armada of 50 Bostons, Baltimores and Mitchells, escorted by Kittyhawks and Spitfires flew-off for a raid.

Bill's mission being "scrubbed", he was stood-down at 13.00 hours. He could only sit, listen and record the details of his colleagues "stuka party", as they called it, upon their return.

Whilst flying at 10,000', approximately fifteen miles south of El Alamein, a flight of ten Ju 87 Stuka dive bombers, were sighted, escorted by seven or more Me 109Fs.

Using their 1,000' altitude advantage, the Hurricanes dived down onto the Stukas, which it transpired were still carrying their bombs. Each selecting a target, the allied pilots waded

An American built Martin Baltimore light bomber, wearing British RAF markings.

into the attack with guns blazing. Within minutes Ju 87s were seen going down, either smoking or with pieces falling off them. Warrant Officer Jack Neil was credited with a Ju 87 destroyed, which was seen to go down in flames, and one probably destroyed. Sergeant Carter was credited with a Ju 87 probably destroyed and one damaged, whilst both Colonel Loftus and Pilot Officer Henderson were each credited with a Ju 87 damaged.

The Messerschmitt escort endeavored to protect its charges, but at least two of them retired from the fray damaged. One being credited to Colonel Loftus and the other to Flying Officer Graves. No.127 Squadron were not left out of the party, and claimed five Stukas.

Realizing they were no match for the allied pilots, the remainder of the enemy aircraft extricated themselves from the fight, dived down to the ground and were last seen heading in a south westerly direction.

All the Hurricanes returned safety to base, where they landed at 15.40 hours.

Four B-25 Mitchell bombers form-up prior to setting course for a mission.

At 17.00 hours, twelve aircraft from No.274 took-off (again without Bill), to fly as top cover to three Hurricane IIDs, of No.6 Squadron, each of which were equipped with a pair of 40mm anti-tank cannons their allotted target being three enemy tanks. No.7 Squadron, South African Air Force, joined the "party" by flying as medium cover.

Their task completed, the attacking force, flying at an altitude of 7,000', turned for home. Flying 3,000' above them were six enemy aircraft, comprising of two Me 109s and four Macchi 202s, who had been waiting their chance. The two 109s dived down in an apparent attack, but pulled up out of their dives without firing a shot. They were quickly followed by the four M.202s who meant business, and a general fight ensued.

The two Me 109s, having shown their mettle, were set upon by Jack Neil and Sergeant Carter, who respectively damaged one and destroyed the other.

Sergeant Bernard Ott, S.A.A.F., was credited with the destruction of a Macchi 202, but both he and Sergeant Carter paid for their victories. In the heat of the battle Nick Carter was shot down and reported as missing, as was Sergeant Ott.

However, they both subsequently returned to base, where Ott reported his aircraft had been destroyed following a collision with an Me 109. Both he and the German pilot had been able to bale out of their respective aircraft, but Ott had the ignominy of landing on his head.

Carter's aircraft had sustained category II damaged to the airframe, and category III damage to the engine, which made it necessary for him to bale out as well.

Thursday, 3rd September 1942

Bounced by "Molders Mob" of 109s, No.145 Sqdn (Spits) did good top cover. P/O Mitchell got a 109 damaged.

The Squadron undertook four separate operations during the course of the 3rd September. The first involved twelve Hurricanes, flying as top cover to No.127 Squadron, on an interception patrol against enemy transport aircraft.

During the patrol, whilst flying at 7,000', a formation of Boston bombers, escorted by Curtiss Kittyhawks, was observed being attacked by two Messerschmitts 109s. Before No.274 had a chance to join the fight they found themselves in one of their own, as six Me 109s came in for the attack. In the twisting, turning melee of machines Pilot Officer Mitchell opened fire at a passing Me 109E, and saw strikes hitting the enemy aircraft. He later claimed it as, and was credited with, a damaged.

Flight Sergeant "Suds" Sutherland had a hole blown in his wing, by a cannon shell, from an attacking Me 109.

The second operation of the day involved ten Hurricanes patrolling over Burg El Arab. Although they were ordered to intercept fifteen enemy fighters, nothing was seen and they returned to base without incident.

Sgt Bernand Ott (Rhodesian Air Force) returns to base, head bandaged and carrying his parachute and flying helmet, after his collision with a Bf 109.

The third operation saw a return to active flying for Sergeant Bill Marsh, when he joined ten other Hurri-bombers for an attack against a column of enemy transports. No.127 Squadron flew top cover and No.7 S.A.A.F. flew medium cover.

Each of the Hurri-bombers carried two 250lb bombs, all of which were dropped on or very close to the estimated 200 stationary vehicles. Unfortunately the results were not observed.

As they were leaving the target area, the Squadron was attacked by two Me 109s, who were met and engaged by Pilot Officer Bell and Sergeant Macfarlane. Again the results of the interception were unobserved.

Bill Marsh also participated in the final operation of the day which involved eight aircraft on another interception patrol. Again they were escorted by both No.127 and No.7 Squadrons. The patrol was fruitless and they again returned to base without incident, apart from Pilot Officer Mitchell who had landed twenty minutes after take-off due to an oil leak.

The Squadron welcomed a new Commanding Officer on the 3rd September, when Major John R. Wells was posted from No.7 Squadron, South African Air Force, to command No.274 Squadron, RAF.

Friday, 4th September 1942

*Good clean fun – No enemy aircraft, but 7 SAAF
lost 4 aircraft to A.A. 3 pilots returned OK.*

Messerschmitt Bf 109F, "Yellow Four" of III/JG 53. German ace Werner Mölders commanded 1./JG 53 in 1939.

Eleven aircraft took-off at 10.15 hours to fly as medium cover to No.6 Squadron's tank-busting Hurricanes, whose targets were detailed as four tanks, three motor transport and one eight-wheeled armored car. No.7 Squadron, S.A.A.F. flew as top cover.

The target was attacked successfully, without the hindrance or intervention of enemy fighters. However, groundfire was heavy and fairly accurate, and was responsible for downing four aircraft from No.7.

Around this period, four pilots, Sergeants Cordrey, McKinnon, Danny Burman and Keith Rostant, the latter from Trinidad, all joined No.274 Squadron. Some were experienced fighters, having been posted in from No.145 Squadron.

P/O Mitchell takes-off, but returns early.

Chapter 9: "Stuka Party"

Monday, 7th September 1942

Wrote a letter to brother Gil.

> *. . .I am still sweating on [getting] my Flight Ser-geant, which when it arrives should be dated 1st May; my Canadian colleagues – all of whom left Canada after me, are all "flights" and Jack Neil got his W.O. through the other day! Red Harrington was at OTU with me and got his F/Sgt through a month back, but I remain the humble Sergeant. . .*

Wednesday, 9th September 1942

To Idku for three weeks rest!

Nineteen aircraft took-off from Landing Ground No.88, at 08.20 hours, and flew north-east to Landing Ground No.229, at Idku, east of Alexandria.

Even though some of the Hurricanes were carrying 250lb bombs, including Bill Marsh's aircraft, they flew in close formation to their destination, where they arrived after a fifty minute flight.

F/S Danny Burman, RNZAF (left), assisted by Sgt Rostant, RAF, (right) prepare to 'string-up' Sgt Don Cordrey, at LG.37.

Thursday, 10th September 1942

Went over to No.272 Squadron.

Things being very quiet, Bill took the opportunity to visit George Tuckwell, at No.272 Squadron. Whilst there, Bill heard all about some of the alterations, and additions, made to George's Beaufighter. These included the facility to carry two 250lb bombs under the belly of the aircraft, a Vickers K gun in the turret and two fixed rearward firing scare guns, situated in the engine nacelles!

Bill was also pleased to hear the news that Yves Tedesco had been promoted to the rank of Pilot Officer, and that the latter had also been awarded the Croix de Guerra (Belgium).

Monday, 14th September 1942

To Alex to celebrate.

Four days later, on Monday 14th September, Bill received good news of his own, when he was informed that he had been promoted to the rank of Flight Sergeant. To add to his joy, the promotion was, as he had hoped, back-dated to the 1st May and came with four months back pay.

The occasion was celebrated by Bill, and a number of colleagues, who went to Alexandria, where they took advantage of some of its hotels, bars and clubs.

Sunday, 20th September 1942

Wrote to mother and sister Lilian

> *. . .I received the [lighter] flints and cigarettes a long time ago – thanks a lot, but don't bother to send anything but the papers [Ormskirk Advertiser], as most things, though dear [expensive], are in good supply. Beer is going even dearer [more expensive]. .*
> *.*

During the two middle weeks of September, the remainder of the Squadron who were still at Landing Ground No.88 undertook a number of interception patrols, shipping patrols and shadow firing patrols.

All missions were without incident until the 21st September, when the recently promoted Flying Officer Mitchell and his No.2, Sergeant Carter, sighted and engaged a Junkers Ju 88 north west of Cairo. With the enemy aircraft 500' below the two Hurricanes, Flying

Bill, at readiness, at Idku, September 1942.

Recently promoted to Flight Sergeant.

Officer Mitchell opened fire and, after several attacks, saw black smoke emitting from the starboard engine.

With a faster machine than his No.1, Sergeant Carter took-up the chase and gave the German bomber several more bursts of fire. The bomber was last seen in a steep dive, its progress earthwards marked by a trail of thick black dense smoke.

The influx of new pilots to the Squadron was continuing, and another three joined No.274, Sergeant McLean was posted in on the 9th September whilst Pilot Officer Brickhill arrived on the 22nd September, as did Flight Lieutenant Green, RAAF, who was to take over as a Flight commander.

Two days later, Flight Sergeant Cooper reported for duty, together with Sergeants Bodger, Connell, Wise and Hedley Lyle. The latter was to become a good friend of Bill Marsh's.

Tuesday, 22nd September 1942

Bombed at 04.00 hours

The Luftwaffe paid the RAF an early morning visit on the 22nd September and dropped three 1,000lb bombs, which fell 300 yards from No.274's sleeping quarters. Unfortunately another Squadron who had a detachment at the landing ground, had three sergeants killed in the attack, whilst the C.O. of that Squadron lost some of his toes.

Wednesday, 23rd September 1942

*Pancaked – Petrol leaking into cockpit. Traced
leak to gravity tank filler cap. Patrolled Amriya – no joy.*

Ten aircraft took-off at 16.45 hours for a formation flying practice, Bill being the pilot of one of the aircraft included. Within minutes of leaving the ground he knew he had a problem, when petrol started to penetrate the confines of the cockpit. His training and experience as a fighter pilot came immediately into play, as he calmly and gently nursed the Hurricane round the circuit and brought it in for a safe landing. The problem, created by a gravity tank filler cap, was soon rectified.

Tuesday, 28th September 1942

*4 Hurricanes at 5,000', acted as top cover
to four M.T.Bs, to prevent 6 Beaufighters
striking. We jumped them, took 10 ft film.*

The war stops for tea, with L to R: Visiting SAAF pilot, F/L Marples, DFC, W/O Jack Neil (standing), F/O Hunter, P/O Bell, unknown.

Two Hurricanes took-off at 11.00 hours for cine-gun practice, with six Bristol Beaufighters and two other Hurricanes. The exercise being to prevent the "enemy" twin-engined Beaufighters from "attacking" motor torpedo boats, who were supposed to be their adversaries. Bill met each "attack" with the pressure of his thumb on his gun button, thus activating the machine-gun cameras which recorded his accuracy and ability to press home his attacks.

Thursday, 30th September 1942

Scramble, 15,000 ft.

Throughout the course of the morning, the Squadron detailed aircraft for shipping patrols. They flew in pairs, and took-off at regular intervals; the first pair being away at 06.40 hours.

All pilots landed safely, and no incidents were reported. During the course of the morning, the Squadron received orders to scramble two fighters for an Interception Patrol. In response Flight Sergeant Bill Marsh, piloting Hurricane BN113, "J", accompanied by one of the "rookie" pilots, Sergeant Danny Burman, flying Hurricane BP949, "Y", raced in formation across the landing ground and were airborne at 09.35 hours. The leader and his wingman turned onto their allotted course and patrolled for forty minutes. In the event nothing was sighted and they were ordered to return to base.

However, the mission was not without its element of danger. Over Abuqir, at 15,000', Bill closed down the rad flaps a little and thereby, and without realizing it, pinched the oxygen tube and cut off his oxygen supply.

Having climbed to 20,000', the pair were vectored over Amiriya, but Bill was experiencing difficulty controlling his aircraft. He was weaving all over the sky, both vertically and horizontally, at one point losing 5,000' of altitude. It looked to his wingman as though Bill was trying, unsuccessfully, to carry out aerobatics. Eventually Bill regained his senses and heard the controller, in his earphones, telling him and Danny Burman to land. However, their troubles were not yet over, for as Danny approached the landing ground, a panel blew off his port wing. He managed to land without further incident, but strained the port wheel in the process.

The first two weeks of October saw the Squadron undertaking a mixture of operations and practice flying. The operations consisted of shipping patrols, interception patrols and standing patrols whilst the practice flying saw them "brushing-up" their formation flying and bombing techniques. The latter using 12lb practice bombs.

Wednesday, 7th October 1942

Squadron anniversary party.

Two Hurricanes take-off for an anti-shipping patrol.

A Squadron anniversary party was held at the Fleet Club attended by, amongst others, Major John Wells, the Officer Commanding the Squadron.

Wells made a speech, during which he made reference to the Air Officer Commanding, who had expressed his displeasure.

The incident, which had invoked the A.O.C.'s wrath, involved the tossing of forty electric light bulbs, by unknown culprits, into the rotating blades of ceiling mounted electric fans.

As a punishment, all members of the Squadron were confined to camp.

On the 9th October, Flight Lieutenant Browne was posted away from No.274 Squadron.

Between the 9th and 11th of the month, the Squadron relocated to Landing Ground No.89, which they shared alongside No.6 Squadron.

Saturday, 10th October 1942

Wrote to mother and sister Lilian

> *. . .although we bind [moan] about things here, there is always flying to work off one's grievances, especially the odd spot of dive bombing, which is great fun if everything goes well.*
>
> *We have the hard times – and will have them again when this desert winter sets in – rain, gales, mud – but when we get into town there is plenty of food and drink – at a price, of course, but one can't argue, we just eat, drink and make merry!*
>
> *Anyway, I got my flight sergeant through with four months back pay, so that was a bit of a windfall. . .*

Monday, 12th October 1942

Went over to 212 Group

W/O Jack Neil in party mood.

151

F/S "Red" Harrington (left), P/O Browne (center) and P/O "Hash" Mitchell, at Idku.

It was whilst he was visiting No.212 Group Operations that Bill met Wing Commander Jerry Edge, his former Commanding Officer on No.605 Squadron, but who was now the Commanding Officer of the Operation Training Unit at Aden.

Together they talked over old times, and discussed the fortunes of their mutual acquaintances, most of whom appeared to be prisoners of war!

Tuesday, 13th October 1942

Balbo and practice strafe.
F/Sgt Beckett + Sgt Lyle collided, both pranged.
Lyle o.k.

Bill Marsh, whilst leading Blue Section, flew some practice Balbos and formation strafes, over the range and Dekheila rocks, during the morning.

Later in the day, during the afternoon, the C.O. lead a flight.

Flight Sergeant Beckett was one of the eleven squadron members airborne for practice flying, when his Hurricane turned-in for an air to ground strafing run and collided with Sergeant Lyle's machine.

Beckett's aircraft was destroyed in the collision and he was killed. Sergeant Lyle's Hurricane sustained Category II damage, and he managed to belly-land his aircraft fairly

Jack Neil, Steen, Becket and Roy Marples considered the implications of another move.

close to the firing range. The Hurricane was seen to skid across the sand before coming to rest; the pilot clambering out and waving to his colleagues to indicate that he was o.k.

The remaining nine aircraft landed safely without further incident.

Wednesday, 14th October 1942

Sergeant Lyle returned to base.

Sergeant Lyle returned to base and related to Bill the details of what had occurred the previous day. It transpired that Sergeant Beckett's aircraft had turned in across the path of Lyle's Hurricane. Unable to take avoiding action, the propeller blades of Lyle's machine chewed into the tailplane of Beckett's aircraft. The latter, totally uncontrollable, fell the short distance to earth, before the pilot could bale out.

Later, during the day, when Bill was leading a section on a shadow firing exercise on the range, he saw the wreckage of both machines.

Sergeant Beckett was buried the following day. His friends, including Bill, Red Harrington, Nick Carter, "Sammy" Samuels, Flight Sergeant Howie, Flight Sergeant Maclean, Flight Sergeant Cooper and one other Squadron member acted as bearers.

Major Wells was also present and represented the officers. After the ceremony, a wake was held, with tea and cakes, arranged by Flying Officer "Spy" Hands, the Intelligence Officer and prepared by the Squadron Mess Catering staff.

Friday, 16th October 1942

Hell of a sandstorm began.

Whilst the Squadrons were lined-up in ranks, ready for the arrival of Marshal of the Royal Air Force, Lord Trenchard, a sandstorm began to engulf the landing ground.

After waiting for an hour in the swirling sand, an order to stand-down was received; Lord Trenchard's visit having been canceled.

The pilots of 274 and 80 Squadrons retired to the mess, where they downed a few beers. Had it not been for the choking dust outside the mess tent, the pilots may well have thought that the dull orange glow that was appearing was due to the effects of the alcohol. It was however due to the khamseen that was about to blow in.

About 18.30 hours that evening, the tent in which Bill slept was blown away, and terrific rain brought down part of the mess tent.

Bill extricated himself from the debris and, finding his tent gone, decided to sleep the night in the C.O.'s staff car!

Saturday, 17th October 1942

The worst Khamseen, followed by lashing gales, ever experienced.

Flying operations were suspended following the damage caused by the Khamseen. The Khamseen, a hot southerly wind that blows across the Sahara, hit Landing Ground 89 during the night. Tents, including the pilots mess, were ripped apart and blown down, as was virtually every other tent on the airfield.

No.274 Squadron Mess Staff, L to R: Brett, Lumb, Ernst Honig (Czech) and Paul.

The pilots put the tents up . . . Howard, Everingham (standing left), Neil (front), Burman (standing right).

. . . and the Khamseen blows them down.

The morning after the Khamseen L to R: Sgt Mckinnon, Sgt MacLaren, F/L Clough-Camm and F/S Sutherland.

Needless to say, the day was spent re-erecting the tents and repairing the damage.

Pilot Officers Henderson and Walsh were posted away from the Squadron the following day, having become time expired.

Tuesday, 20th October 1942

Vectored after Bandits for 50 mins, seen but not contacted, over Burg El Arab after two 109s at 23,000'.

Twelve aircraft took-off at 08.20 hours for an interception patrol over Burg El Arab. They were flying at 17,000', when they sighted two Me 109s flying approximately 6,000' feet above them. The enemy aircraft presumably, being outnumbered, chose to use their height advantage and ignore the allied fighters and flew away. The pilots of No.274 therefore, on landing, reported no incident.

Sergeant Ott was forced to land at LG. 98 with a glycol leak. He returned to the Squadron later in the day.

Three more pilots left the Squadron when Sergeants Ross, Wise and Becks were all posted to No.80 Squadron. Two days later Flying Officer Samuels was posted to No.601 Squadron.

Chapter 9: "Stuka Party"

Friday, 23rd October 1942

*On 23rd October 1942, No.7 South African
Air Force Wing, No.212 Group, of which No.274
Squadron was a component, moved to Landing
Ground No.37, at El Hamman, in Tunisia. At
once we commenced a series of patrols of El
Alamein, and dive bombing sorties.
We gave escort on two occasions to No.6
Squadron (Hurricane Tank Busters), and carried
out several dusk sweeps to forestall Stuka
raids on our troops.*

Although No.274 Squadron spent the day at either readiness or 30 minutes availability, as fighters their services were not called upon.

They therefore took advantage of the situation and prepared for their imminent move, which was made at 18.10 hours. The Squadron's eighteen Hurricanes took-off from LG.89 and headed west to their new base at Landing Ground 37, approximately 30 miles east of El Alamein, where they landed at 18.50 hours.

The basic creature comforts were not in place by the end of the day, causing Bill to record in his journal that he slept on a stretcher provided by Flight Lieutenant Clough Camm, the Medical Officer. However, with what was to take place that night, it was a wonder he got any sleep at all!

CHAPTER TEN

El Alamein

Bright moonlight bathed the desert sands on the night of the 23rd October 1942. It seemed like any other night until 21.40 hours, when the "peace" was shattered by the thunderous roar of an unprecedented artillery barrage, the like of which had not been seen (or heard) during the course of the war to date.

The battle of El Alamein (Operation "Lightfoot") began when Allied artillery, ranged along a six mile front, opened fire on the command of General Bernard Montgomery.

The heavy barrage continued to rain shells down on the German positions, before the Eighth Army moved forward. The intention was to make an all out assault, with infantry, armor and air power against enemy minefields and positions. The air power being employed at first light.

Supported by aerial bombing, the ground troops of the British and Dominion infantry advanced towards the enemy lines, and by dawn on the 24th October, had successfully penetrated a gap in the enemy minefields.

Fighting continued throughout the day on the ground, as it did in the air. The Allied Air Forces undertook non-stop attacks against enemy troops, motor transport columns and supply lines. During the first day of the battle the Allied fighters and bombers flew over 1,000 sorties in support of the Eighth Army.

Saturday, 24th October 1942

*Top cover to No.127 Sqdn. 4 109s and 2 202s
above, attacked. Sgt. Bruckshaw (109 prob) and
self pulled up and fired – I spun, saw no results.*

Allied artillery signals the start of the battle of El Alamein.

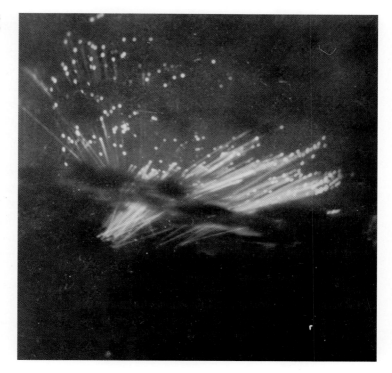

Major Wells, leading "Red" Harringon, led Red Section, whilst Flight Sergeant Marsh led Blue Section, as part of the top cover escort to No.127 Squadron who were in turn led by Colonel Loftus.

As they flew over El Alamein at 8,000', through thin patchy cloud, No.274 Squadron saw a mixed flight of Messerschmitt 109s and Macchi 202s, flying at higher altitude, following a formation of Baltimore bombers returning from a mission. The enemy aircraft left the bombers to fly off unmolested, and waited to see what the Allied fighters were going to do. They soon found out. Accompanied by Sergeant Bruckshaw, Bill climbed almost vertically to effect an attack. Nearing his chosen target, a M.202, he opened fire, with a four second burst, whilst still climbing.

As fire spat from his machine guns, his aircraft slid over and went into a spin. Major Wells witnessed the event and nearly had heart failure.

Mick Bruckshaw got a shot at a Me 109, which was seen to peel over and go down. Although nobody followed the enemy aircraft down, a splash and a column of white smoke was seen in the bay. On return to base Sergeant Bruckshaw was able to claim a probable, whereas Bill could make no claim at all.

Sunday, 25th October 1942

*Involved in a Stuka raid, in the course of
which No.274 Squadron stayed up so long, and the
Stukas came so late, that the landings at LG. 39
were the most sensational I have ever seen.
A hastily laid flare-path, and a shortage of
"gravy" caused two of our less experienced pilots
to prang in no uncertain manner. Sergeant Ott,
from Rhodesia, approached at some 180 m.p.h. and
went through the Greek's dispersal area like a
bomb, losing his undercarriage in the process.
Sergeant Howard Everingham (RAAF) approached in a
steep glide and achieved a perfect 3 pointer
without the disadvantage of a landing run; to wit,
spinner and wheels touched earth at the same time
XIII Corps was ordered by General Montgomery to
press its attacks further, whilst XXX Corps was
orderedto press forward supported by both armor and
artillery barrages.*

No.274 Squadron had ten aircraft airborne at 06.50 hours, in support of No.335 Squadron, to whom they were flying as top cover. Although they patrolled the forward area for ninety minutes, they reported no incidents on returning to base.

A Macchi M.202 single seat Italian fighter.

At 10.30 hours, twelve aircraft from the Squadron were ordered to scramble. They were instructed to fly at 20,000', on a course seven miles south of El Alamein. Again, having been airborne for seventy minutes, no incidents were reported.

Enemy aircraft were reported as being active and No.274, again, scrambled twelve Hurricanes at 17.30 hours. The Allied aircraft climbed to 9,000' and headed for the coast, where they were informed that the enemy "snappers" were west of Alamein.

Arriving at the given map reference, the pilots reported no contact. They were, to their frustration, given a new co-ordinate where the enemy fighters were now thought to be. Although the Hurricanes climbed to 12,000', and were given several more vectors, they were not able to make contact with the enemy.

As they flew home in the fading light, the Allied artillery opened fire, creating a brilliant, although potentially dangerous, firework display.

By the time they reached their Landing Ground, the light had all but gone. There was no flare path, only dozens of red and green Very cartridges to guide the pilots in.

Those to land first got down with the narrowest of safety margins, but Bernard Ott, trying to land in a hurry, touched-down at too high a speed. He rocketed through the Greek's dispersal area, wrenching off his undercarriage.

Sergeant Everington's landing was less spectacular, but equally dangerous. He could not see the ground, dived down, hit the deck and the aircraft stopped abruptly, but its pilot did not.

Sergeant Everington continued forward and cracked his head on the gun's reflector sight, cutting his forehead.

Monday, 26th October 1942

Reported 4+ Snappers in the sun. Went on west
of line and saw bomb bursts, then engaged by 6+
Me 109s, not effectively.

Ten Hurricanes were airborne at 09.30 hours, to act as top cover to No.127 Squadron, with Major Wells again leading the formation. Their allotted task was to patrol over Alamein at 10,000', but two of the pilots were not able to carry out this task. First, Flight Sergeant McLaren pulled out of the formation with glycol trouble, then Flying Officer "Gravy" Graves' aircraft began to stream glycol vapor, and he too went down in a hurry.

Keeping a look out as the Squadron turned onto a southerly heading, Bill saw some flashes in the sun. He identified and reported four Me 109s flying some 5,000' above them, but no action was taken and no engagement made.

The Squadron turned onto a westerly course and climbed to 16,000', where it was reported they would find fighter-bombers twenty miles west of El Alamein.

Arriving in the area, they saw bomb bursts below but could not see any aircraft! Diving

A sudden stop can cause one to lose one's head.

down to 11,000' for a closer look, the Allied pilots suddenly realized there were six Me 109s stooging around above them – the fighter-bombers!

Bill failed to understand how he, and his colleagues, had not seen the enemy aircraft, as they so obviously passed straight through them!

Preparing to engage, they turned to meet the enemy. Bill also prepared himself, and hoped to achieve better results than on his last encounter with 109s, but as the Hurricanes waded into the attack, the Messerschmitts broke into two groups and pulled up and flew away. This was probably just as well, for the Allied pilots were well over enemy lines!

Sergeant Mclaren, who had retired earlier due to engine trouble, managed to land at base, but Flying Officer Graves gave cause for concern when he was reported as missing. To the relief of his colleagues, Graves was listed safe the following day.

Tuesday, 27th October 1942

Some interesting targets were attacked, between
27th and 31st October, including Rommel's presumed
Headquarters, the Headquarters of the 90th L.I.
and the 15th Panzer Division respectively.
Other targets attacked ranged from the Taqua
Plateau, near Quatlara Depression, to the coast
road in the northern sector.
A few enemy aircraft were seen, but surprisingly,

they displayed some reluctance to engage the "dreaded" Hurricanes.

Flying as Hurri-bombers, each with two 250lb bombs under their wings, the Squadron detailed twelve aircraft to attack enemy motor transport, tanks and encampments. On this occasion, No.127 Squadron acted as top cover for No.274.

Approaching the target from a west-south-westerly direction, the Hurri-bombers unleashed the deadly cargoes as they dived down from an altitude of 9,000'. The first loads were dropped on an estimated 200-300 motor transports, and one direct hit was observed on a tank, which erupted into a fireball of brilliant red and orange flame and thick black smoke. Near misses were also reported on many other vehicles.

One by one, the Hurri-bombers dived down onto the targets, as ground fire from Breda machine guns, and heavy ack-ack, arced up into the sky to meet them. Flying through the bursting shells of ground fire the Hurri-bombers succeeded in causing destruction to the enemy vehicles and camp, without loss to themselves.

An attack, by No.274, during the course of the afternoon on a similar target had like results, with columns of thick black smoke rising into the sky by the time they left the target area.

Sergeant Bernard Ott returned to base, fifteen minutes later after taking off for the second attack, due to an oil leak. He landed safely.

Wednesday, 28th October 1942

12 Dug-in heavy art, 10 miles behind the lines.

Tasked with carrying out an armed reconnaissance, the Hurricanes of No.274 Squadron flew as bombers, each armed with two 250lb bombs. No.335 Squadron flew as top cover.

The target consisted of 200 motor transport, which were fairly well dispersed, with light ack-ack in the target area and heavy ack-ack concentrated on the Taga Plateau.

Diving down from their formation height of 9,000', each aircraft released its bombs at an altitude of 4,000'. Ignoring the return ground fire which burst around them, each pilot placed his bombs in the target area, which was left with the familiar columns of black smoke rising into the air.

Having become time expired, Flying Officer D.C. Mitchell was posted away from the Squadron.

Friday, 30th October 1942

2 sorties against dug-in guns and mortars

holding up the Aussies in the northern sector -
bombing excellent, enemy line soon cracked.

Each carrying two 250lb bombs, twelve Hurri-bombers from No 274 were airborne from LG37, at 09.35 hours.

Their allotted task was to bomb dug-in enemy artillery and mortar sites, situated near Risl-Shaggig. The fighter bombers were protected by the Hurricanes of No.80 Squadron, who provided top cover.

The attacking force approached Risl-Shaggig, which they used as a turning point, at an altitude of 8,000'. Turning on to a bearing of 215 degrees, they located the target entrenched by major crossroads. Their bombing run was made from a north-easterly approach, and they released their loads from an altitude of 2,500'.

As the Squadron commenced its dive in for the bombing run, two Macchi 202s appeared from the south-east at 5,000', but they posed no threat to the Hurri-bombers.

The bombs rained down, spewing great fountains of sand and debris into the air, whilst in return the enemy greeted the attackers with volleys of ground fire, which burst around them. Despite the bursting shells, the bombing was recorded as very accurate.

Within forty-five minutes of landing, the groundcrews had refueled and re-armed the Hurricanes in order for them to undertake another sortie. The target was to be the same one they had bombed less than one hour before, thus giving the enemy no time to recover.

Bill participated in both attacks, which were later recorded in his log-book.

The following day the Squadron carried out two bombing raids, the first against motor transport and the second against Rommel's presumed headquarters, situated one mile south east of Ghazal Station.

Flight Lieutenant Green was posted away to join RAF Rear Air Headquarters, Western Desert.

Although recorded in his journal, Flight Sergeant Bill Marsh did not participate in either of these attacks.

Saturday, 1st November 1942

In the northern sector a pocket had been formed,
the Aussies having broken through a few miles from
the coast and almost surrounded by enemy strong
point. This consisted of mostly dug-in guns and
mortars, located between the railway and road.
Three dive-bombing attacks were carried out
before 1.00 o'clock, and at that zero hour (we
heard later) the Aussies were able to walk in and
capture the point.

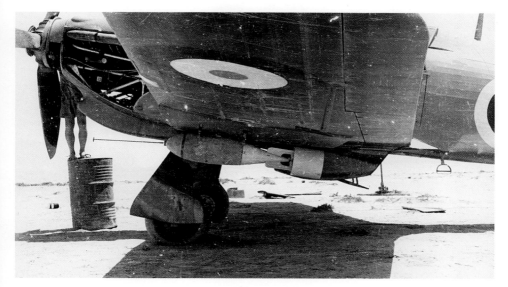

The "hardware department" under the wing of a Hurri-bomber. The 250lbs bombs were fitted with rods to cause them to explode just above ground level.

The first mission of the new month was an attack against the assumed Headquarters of the 90th Light Division.

The Squadron detailed twelve aircraft, each carrying two 250lb bombs, to undertake the attack. They took-off at 09.50 hours and were escorted by Hurricane fighters of No.80 Squadron.

Flying at 10,000', the attackers crossed the coast at Ras Gebeisa and then began a dive to between 2,500' and 2,000'.

The Hurri-bombers powered into the attack and unleashed their bombs, which were seen to fall along a stretch of road and amongst three dugouts.

Although a heavy barrage of ack-ack fire was thrown up from the ground, all aircraft returned safely to base.

Rommel misjudged the intentions of the Eighth Army when the latter attacked the strong German position in the north, instead of going for the center.

The Allied armor followed the infantry through the wedge in the enemy minefield defenses, which resulted, on the 2nd November in a decisive tank battle.

Sunday, 2nd November 1942

Attacks on the crowded north coast road; the
start of the great trek westward.
Flight Sergeant Wesley Stirling Howie (RCAF)

*and Sergeant Robertson (RAF) were shot down while
bombing and strafing. Robbie baled out and just
made our lines; he returned the next day, slightly
hurt, after having spent many hours in an advance
gun post of ours. He was shelled incessantly by
both sides, then bombed by the U.S.A.A.F. Wesley
Howie was captured and made a prisoner of war.
A dusk sweep that evening was jumped by 12+ Me 109s,
a dog-fight ensuing, but no losses were incurred.
I chased a Me 109 westwards, but could not catch or
engage it. I returned to our lines climbed and zig-
zagging all the way home*

The Luftwaffe were much in evidence on the 2nd November, the Squadron encountering the enemy during each of the three missions it undertook on that day.

The first operation commenced at 09.20 hours, when twelve aircraft from No.274 took-off accompanied by Hurricanes from No.335 Squadron, Hellenic (Greek) Air Force.

The allotted task was for No.274 to fly a patrol at between 7,000' and 9,500', with the Greeks 2,000' above them. This they were doing when a report was received of six plus Me 109s flying "in the sun." Mindful of the warning, "Beware of the Hun in the sun", No.274 turned in towards them. Using what advantage they had left, the enemy aircraft dived down for the attack. They made one or two half-hearted attacks, but pulled out when the Hurricanes tried to engage them.

The second operation of the day was a sweep over the battle area by twelve Squadron aircraft, again escorted by No.335 Squadron.

Again the Squadron encountered the Luftwaffe in the form of three Messerschmitts Me 109s, flying 8,000' below the Hurricanes.

On this occasion, the Allied aircraft dived into the attack, and a general melee ensued as the enemy stayed to fight it out. In the heat of battle Warrant Officer Neil and Pilot Officer Brickhill each damaged a Me 109, but not before both Flight Sergeant Wesley Howie and Sergeant Robertson were shot down.

As Bill recorded in his journal, Robbie Robertson returned to the unit to continue the fight, but for Howie the fight was over. He was captured and made a prisoner of war.

Taking off at 16.30 hours for a dusk operation, twelve aircraft from No.274 headed for the battle area again, to carry out another sweep.

They were at 15,000', south-south-west of El Alamein, when they were informed of the presence of six more enemy aircraft twelve miles to the south of Alamein.

As the Squadron were turning onto a new heading four enemy aircraft were spotted to the north east of them. At the same moment another eight were seen coming in from the south east.

The fight started when a single 109 dived in towards the Squadron, but then pulled out and away. Bill turned after it and gave chase, but the enemy was already pulling away. He had no alternative, but to give up any thoughts of catching the 109.

By this time the two elements had met, and the sky to the south of El Alamein had become the scene of a mass of twisting turning machines; an aerial ballet, punctured by the noise of cannon and machine-gun fire.

Surprisingly, at the end of the battle only one claim was made against an enemy machine by Sergeant Bruckshaw, who was awarded a probable.

With so many Messerschmitts around the area, Bill weaved his way back to LG 37, keeping a watchful eye open, particularly on his rear view mirror.

Having divided the Axis armor into two sections, the Allied infantry turned southwards towards the Italian infantry divisions, who were isolated on a desert plateau. Meanwhile, the Allied armor chased the Afrikakorps towards Libya.

Monday, 3rd November 1942

All enemy forces are in full retreat! Our bomb line moves hourly forward. We carried out one sortie on the presumed Headquarters of 90th L.I. and another sortie on the familiar cost road, which was black with traffic. We bombed along the road and got excellent results, starting one big fire!

Escorted by the Greeks from No.335 Squadron, nine Hurri-bombers from No.274 Squadron, took-off at 09.40 hours for an attack against the presumed Headquarters of the 90th Light Division.

The formation, flying at 9,000', headed north from LG 37 and flew out over the coast, before turning onto a heading of 290 degrees enabling them to run straight-in to the target.

Leaving the Greeks to provide top cover, No.274 dived down to release their bombs from between 2,000' - 4,000'. As the bombs whistled down towards the ground, the defending forces threw-up an intense curtain of exploding shells from the ack-ack positions.

The Hurri-bombers flew through the curtain of steel, and fortunately emerged unscathed. Their respective bombs exploded between the dugouts and motor transports, throwing debris, sand and smoke into the air.

Their allotted task completed, as they returned for home the allied airmen sighted twelve plus Me 109s flying north-east, at approximately 9,000'; six more were observed at 5,000'.

A pair of inquisitive Me 109s, who were appearing to break away from their formation, felt the wrath of Flight Lieutenant May's guns, as he turned into them and opened fire. He

A British Army transporter, complete with Matilda tank, joins the advance . . .

selected one of the two Me 109s and gave it a good burst, but did not observe any results. No claim was made against it.

The Hurri-bombers and their escort all returned safely to base, where they touched down at 10.30 hours.

The aircraft, refueled and re-armed, took-off again for a second attack on the retreating forces at 12.20 hours. As before, the escort was provided by No.335 Squadron.

No.274 were briefed to bomb motor transport on the coast road between Ghazal and El Daba, and therefore used the same tactics as the previous attack, by crossing out over the coast and making their bombing dive from in over the sea.

All bombs, except three, were recorded as exploding along the road, scoring at least six direct hits, and a large fire was started following an equally large explosion.

The three bombs which went astray were not wasted, as they too created fires.

The attackers had things much their own way, and were not even bothered by the return of ack-ack fire.

Seven aircraft from the Squadron undertook a third operation at 14.40 hours. Their mission, on this occasion, was to strafe enemy motor transport.

. . . quickly followed by the infantry, who hitch a ride.

Bill Marsh, having been operational on the previous two missions, found his name was not included for this one.

When the "boys" returned they reported a very good attack, with twenty-four trucks set on fire, or damaged, one staff car and one lorry damaged and one large lorry overturned. Two gun positions were silenced, a number of tents were set on fire and many personnel were killed or wounded.

Such was the speed of the Afrikakorps retreat that thousands of its men were captured and made prisoners of war, and large quantities of equipment and materials were left behind.

Tuesday, 4th November 1942

Bombed 10 miles south of Daba; the Headquarters of the 15th Panzer Division

The Squadron participated in two missions on the 4th November, the first being an attack against retreating motor transport, which took place in the late morning.

The second operation was a return visit to the headquarters of the 15th Panzer Division, and the battle order included the name of Bill Marsh.

As with the previous attacks, each Hurri-bomber was armed with two 250lb bombs, and was escorted by Hurricane fighters of No.335 Squadron.

They took-off at 16.15 hours and flew west. As they flew over the British lines, ground control ordered them to return and hold station over, and to the south east, of El Alamein. A short time later, the controller gave clearance for the planned attack to continue.

Having reached the target the Hurri-bombers made their attack from between 3,000'-4,000', and bombs rained down on the enemy vehicles. Three direct hits took out approximately forty motor transports, whilst four other bombs straddled a cluster of vehicles, creating damage to those within the perimeters of the explosions. A near miss was also recorded on a trailer type vehicle.

All aircraft returned safely to base.

Following this attack, Flight Sergeant Bill Marsh wrote in his log, "H.Q. of 15th Panzer Div. Got a bomb on a large enemy motor transport."

Wednesday, 5th November 1942 (First Entry)

Two sorties were flown against traffic past Galal Station. The burst of the bombs obscured the road from sight. Flight Sergeant Danny Burman (RNZAF) came out of his bombing dive north of us, near the coast, and

*saw a Fieseler Storch (German communication aircraft)
and brutally shot it into the sea.
[Later in the day] At 13.00 hours, as we were
listening to the BBC proclamations of victory etc.,
Air Marshal Sir Arthur Tedder called into our Mess;
having arrived by Fieseler Storch! He was in time to
hear the King congratulate General Montgomery and
himself on the outcome of the battle.
The Air Officer Commanding-in-Chief, Sir Arthur was
not amused by Flight Sergeant Burman's action. Before
leaving he advised us that we should not shoot down
Fieseler Storch aircraft as he needed them!!*

Eleven aircraft took-off at 07.15 hours, each armed with the usual bomb load, for another attack against enemy motor transport. No.335 Squadron again acted as top cover.

The enemy vehicles, which were stationary adjacent to the main coast road, were not
dispersed, leaving themselves open to air attack. The Hurricanes came in over the sea, at an
altitude of 8,500'. Each diving down to approximately 2,000' to release the bombs and then
pulling round and back out over the coastline.

Flight Sergeant Danny Burman, who had joined the Squadron two months previously,
pulled out of his bombing dive to see a German Fieseler Storch aircraft flying in front of
him! Not being able to believe his luck, he held the Hurricane steady, lined-up the enemy in
his gun sight and pressed the "tit." Flames spat from the leading edges of his wings, as he
raked the German aircraft with a good burst of machine gun fire. He watched in amazement, as the strut supporting the high wing collapsed. The aircraft flipped over and spiraled
down into the sea, closely followed by a fluttering wing which had completely broken off.
He later claimed, and was credited with, a destroyed (kill).

Danny Burman's jubilation was not however totally shared by everyone, as Bill recorded in his journal. The Air Officer, Commanding-in-Chief, would sooner have had the
German aircraft down intact!

Wednesday, 5th November 1942
(Second Entry)

*This is certainly our greatest day. Lieutenant
Colonel Loftus in No.80 Squadron (flying top cover)
watched us do our stuff!
The bombing was accurate and we started a large
fire. As I was pulling out of a dive, at two
thousand feet, I saw a lone Me 109 heading west at*

Abandoned equipment is put to good use by L to R: Jack Neil, George Meldrum (sitting), Sgt Mckinnon and F/L McKay.

Another abandoned Bf 109 is inspected for souvenirs.

Similar in appearance to a Fieseler Storch, this Henschel Hs 126 multi-role aircraft was found intact in the desert, at El Gobbi.

> *deck level. I turned and dived towards it, but*
> *despite having the extra height, and following it*
> *to Fuka point, I could not get closer than about*
> *600 yards. I fired a short burst in exasperation,*
> *and then turned and climbed up into cloud as a*
> *Breda opened fire from the coastline below.*

The second attack of the day began when twelve aircraft from No.274 took-off at 10.10 hours. The Hurri-bombers, carrying their usual load of two 250lb bombs, were escorted by No.80 Squadron, led by Colonel Loftus.

Tasked with bombing 200 enemy vehicles, the Squadron flew its usual course out to sea, followed the coast road and then turned in for the attack.

Two main fires were started by the exploding bombs, one of which emitted thick black smoke.

Although heavy ack-ack fire was returned from the ground, no casualties were incurred by the Squadron.

Wednesday, 5th November 1942
(Third Entry)

The advance is now leaving us behind. During the afternoon another bombing trip was detailed. They set off and encountered thick cloud over sea. Warrant Officer Jack Neil, with whom I share Hurri-bomber coded X, got a glycol leak whilst climbing through the cloud. The aircraft went into a spin which he was unable to correct, neither could he jettison the bombs the aircraft was still carrying! At an altitude of one thousand feet he decided to bale out, his chute fully opening as he hit the sea. He spent eight hours in (and out) of his dinghy, before being washed ashore, around midnight, at Fuka Bay (near the bombing target). After spending a lousy night with the dead "Ities", he was picked-up at dawn and returned to the Squadron at 16.00 hours.

Thick cumulous cloud, down to 4,000', prevented positive identification of the target allocated for the third raid.

As they were flying in an area north Gahal, at approximately 13.30 hours, six Me 109s swooped down and attacked in line astern.

Realizing what was happening, some of the Hurri-bomber pilots released their two 250lb bombs over the desert. Having jettisoned their deadly cargoes, the Allied aircraft turned-in to meet the enemy. Twisting, turning, diving, climbing aircraft filled this particular part of the sky as the opposing pilots endeavored to gain an advantage over each other.

Bill took advantage when he saw a single Me 109 dive alone, out of the fray. He pulled the Hurricane over into a tight turn and dived down after it, but even though he gained speed during his dive, he found to his disappointment he could not catch it. In a fit of desperation, he pressed his thumb against the gun button at the top of his control column, but did not see the results. Ground fire from the coast below caused him to seek cover in the clouds.

During the course of the main fight, Warrant Officer Jack Neil's Hurricane was seen to spin down through the clouds, out of control, everybody assuming the worst.

Fortunately, Neil was able to bale out, at about 1,000' above the water, and was last seen three miles out to sea! His dinghy was washed ashore some miles along the coast, and he returned to the Squadron the following day.

CHAPTER ELEVEN

The Advance West

Monday, 9th November 1942

Moved to Landing Ground 104, Qotafiyah II, at
El Daba, scene of much destruction both by bombs and strafing.
I made a bivvy under the tailplane of a
crashed Wellington Bomber.
Went on scrounging expeditions, found Italian
uniforms, trench boots and breeches. Got an Italian rifle.
We also found a Me 109G, which was obviously
the victim of many strafing attacks.

On arrival at Landing Ground No.104, the first thing Bill noticed was the varied amount of equipment left behind by the retreating Germans and Italian forces.

The opportunity was too good to miss, and a group of pilots, Bill included, decided to go out on a scrounging expedition.

Their haul, amongst other undocumented items, included German and Italian uniforms, boots, helmets and firearms.

In photographing a battered, abandoned Me 109, Bill commented that "This was the best way to see one." The machine resembled a colander, and had obviously been the victim of much strafing practice.

In preparing for his stay at L.G.104, Bill made himself as comfortable as possible. He set up a bivouac under the tailplane of a crashed Wellington bomber. To shield himself further from the sun, he acquired a panel, still bearing the cross from a German airplane, which he hung vertically as a "screen."

ABOVE: Photo-call during a scrounging expedition. L to R: Macfarlane, Cordrey, unknown, Brickhill, Meldrum, May, Bell, unknown and Maclean (kneeling).

RIGHT: Sgt Mckinnon, RNZAF, parades in "borrowed" German kit.

A Messerschmitt Bf 109 resembling a colander.

It was in the confines of his "bivvy" that he took time out to catch up with the news from home, and read copies of the local newspaper, the Ormskirk Advertiser, which his mother had sent to him a month or two earlier.

Bill's stay at L.G.104 was to be a short one as, two days later, No.274 was to move again.

Apart from motor transport being used, a Bristol Bombay aircraft was also utilized to carry equipment.

The move on this occasion was in a westerly direction to Sidi Haneish South, otherwise known as L.G.13. The Squadron had been based there for a few days in June, before withdrawing to L.G.105.

Wednesday, 11th November 1942

Another move, this time to Landing Ground 13, at
Sidi Haneish South, where the Squadron had resided
on a previous occasion.
Found a number of abandoned Me 109s, one of which
we had just started to work on when No.80 Squadron
claimed it as theirs and took it. Flight Lieutenant
Jerry Wade decided to fly it. On take-off he had the
"prop" in fine pitch, and went across LG13 making
a noise like seven Harvards. Having got airborne, with
the engine at 3,800 revs, he was out of sight when the
aircraft caught fire. The Me 109 pranged in a wheels-
up landing at Quasaba, Flight Lieutenant Wade receiving
a burnt chin in the process.
Sergeant Mick Bruckshaw found a Mercedes Benz staff

car in fair condition, but minus its wheels. From
somewhere he managed to scrounge another set and, after
tinkering around with it, finally got the car going.

With no operational flying on the agenda, and so much abandoned equipment and material left lying around, the pilots decided to go on another scrounging expedition.

Their major find, an Me 109, which they felt worthy of their attention was prized away from them, as noted by Bill in his journal.

However, Mick Bruckshaw, who found the Mercedes staff car, was able to retain his find.

The car was a valuable asset and allowed the pilots some mobility, other than the usual method of traveling around on the back of a Squadron truck. The Mercedes was however proudly adorned with the Squadron code letters of NH, which were displayed on the front passenger door.

Wednesday, 18th November 1942

We move west yet again, this time to Bu Amud
(LG147), some 20 miles from Tobruk. The landing

Bill catches-up on news from home.

177

ground is very wet, with pot holes of soft mud.
Pilot Officer Brickhill (RAAF) landed crosswind onto
this surface and wrote-off another aircraft coded "D."
There is certainly a voodoo on Hurricanes
which carry the "D" code.

Pilot Officer Paul Brickhill was posted to No.92 Squadron during December 1942. It was whilst he was flying on operations with this squadron that he was shot down on 17th March 1942. He baled out of his stricken aircraft and spent the rest of the war as a PoW.

In post-war years, Paul Brickhill achieved fame as the author of a number of books, including "Reach for the Sky" and "The Dam Busters."

Thursday, 19th November 1942

Airborne for nearly two hours on convoy patrol.
Told to "pancake" at Gambut, as Bu Amud was u/s
due to a sandstorm, but then so too was Gambut.
Flying Officer Caen, my No.2 and I eventually
landed at Con. Flight.

F/O George Caen (left) and F/O 'Gravy' Graves in pensive mood on the wing of an abandoned Bf 109. In the background a Bristol Bombay transport aircraft lands behind Hurricane, HL733, coded 'E', of No.274 Squadron.

A Bristol Bombay flies low over LG104, at El Daba.

An intact Bf 109 is worthy of attention by members of No.274 Squadron.

Repainted in RAF markings, the Bf 109 is made airworthy.

The natural enemy of any desert flyer, a sandstorm, blew up whilst Bill and Flying Officer Caen were flying a shipping patrol. There had been no indication of it when they took-off at 09.30 hours, but in a short space of time the weather had deteriorated. Having eventually landed safely at Conversion Flight Landing Ground, they sat out the sandstorm and returned to base at 12.45 hours.

Tuesday, 24th November 1942

*More convoy patrols, followed by a patrol near
Tobruk. I, and my No.2, stooged around at 5,000'
some five miles north of Tobruk. Nothing to report.*

Three shipping patrols, and two area patrols, were flown on 24th November, with Bill participating in two of them.

The first, a convoy patrol, comprised of four aircraft flown by Flying Officer Graves, who led the section, Flight Sergeants Marsh and Burman and Sergeant Barker.

They took-off at 09.45 hours, and flew a ninety minute patrol before returning to base. No incidents were reported.

The second patrol flown that day by Bill was over the Tobruk area. Accompanied by Sergeant Barker as his No.2, Bill patrolled the area for an hour before returning to base. As with the previous patrol, this one was also uneventful.

Friday, 27th November 1942

*We continue to move westward, this time to Martuba I,
former landing grounds of Me 109s and Macchi 202s.
Now it is a series of rocky bumpy landing areas,
but it has GREEN GRASS and SHRUBS!!
I met Bill Doig (No.238 Squadron) and Ron Jones
(No.213 Squadron) and heard much about their long
range strafing attacks against Ageila and Marble
Arch, from landing ground No.125. LG125 is a hidden
and inaccessible drome many miles inland, south
of the coast.*

At 07.30 hours, the nineteen aircraft operated by No.274 Squadron, commenced taking-off from Bu Amud and followed the advance. They formed-up and flew to their new base at Martuba I, some ninety nautical miles to the west, where they all landed safely an hour later.

The result of P/O Paul Brickhill's crosswind landing.

Monday, 30th November 1942

*I took my new No.2, Sergeant Barker, for a
"work-out" at 10,000' over Memelao Bay. I flew
Hurricane coded "O", a very ropy kite, in which
I did all the tricks I knew – dogfights, evasive
action and bombing dives etc. On landing I found
the starboard wheel fairing had split and folded
back, but I must admit she handled o.k.*

Flying Hurricane, BP716, coded "O", an aircraft he did not like, Bill took-off at 08.25
hours, accompanied by Flight Sergeant Danny Burman, for a shipping patrol lasting ninety
minutes. The mission was uneventful and they both returned to base at 09.55 hours.

Another one safely down. Hawker Hurricane, coded NH-D, with a u/s air speed indicator, is escorted
home by Bill Marsh who took the photograph.

"It has green grass and shrubs"

Later in the day, Bill took the same machine into the air, for a "work-out" with Sergeant Barker. The Hurricane appeared to handle well as he chased Sergeant Barker around the sky, giving no hint of the potentially dangerous situation occurring beneath him. As Bill threw the aircraft into tight turns, loops and dives, unbeknown to him the starboard undercarriage fairing had split and was folding back on itself. It could have been the end of his flying career, but he was blissfully unaware of this fact, until he landed.

Although he disliked the aircraft, Bill found within himself a certain admiration for the Hurricane; she had, after all, got him down safely.

Wednesday, 2nd December 1942 - Friday, 4th December 1942

We continued to undertake further convoy patrols. On one of these Flight Sergeant Gordon and Sergeant Aron intercepted a Ju 88. They expended all their ammunition, and saw it make contact with the sea, but it kept flying!

During a convoy patrol later in the day, Flight Sergeant "Flash" Gordon and Sergeant Aron intercepted and attacked a Junkers Ju 88. They made numerous individual attacks against the aircraft, expending all the ammunition, but still it continued to fly! Twice they thought they had a confirmed "kill", when they saw it hit the sea, but it bounced off the waves on each occasion and still kept flying!!

Back at base they could only claim a shared damaged.

Saturday, 5th December 1942

I went on leave to Cairo.

Bill went on leave and flew as a passenger in a Lockheed Hudson aircraft to Heliopolis, Egypt, where he landed after an uneventful trip lasting three hours, twenty minutes.

He made his way into Cairo, where he browsed around and made a number of purchases in the bazaars.

F/O George Caen (standing left) and P/O Ron Jones (213 Sqdn) with a Bf 109 wearing the emblem of JG 53 "Pik As."

Whilst having a drink in the New Zealand Club, Bill met Don Ormesher, a native of Ormskirk, Bill's home town, and a friend whom he knew from way back. The last time Bill had met Don, the latter was wearing civilian clothes, now he was wearing an RAF uniform, and was a Sergeant Air Gunner on Bristol Beauforts. Bill had no idea his friend had joined the Royal Air Force.

After six days of rest, away from the war, Bill returned to Martuba, on the 11th December, in another Lockheed Hudson. The return journey being accomplished ten minutes quicker than the outward journey.

Saturday, 12th December 1942

7 pilots to Benina in a Hudson.

Major Wells, Flying Officer Graves, Pilot Officer Bell, Warrant Officer Neil, Flight Sergeant Harrington and Sergeants Macfarlane and Meldrum flew off to Benina in a Lockheed Hudson. From there they departed (with the exception of Jackie Neil who was without kite), for Malta in long range Hawker Hurricanes.

The flight was led by two Hudsons with Wing Commander R.G. Yaxley, D.S.O., D.F.C., M.C. in command. The Hurricanes were led by Wing Commander Burton.

Beer break at LG173, Amriya. L to R: Red Nicholls, Bill Doig, "Red" Harrington, Jack Galyer, Unknown.

A Grumman amphibian (Air Sea Rescue) aircraft at Martuba.

Grumman Goose, wearing RAF markings.

From Malta the Hurricanes flew to Bone, Algeria, crossing the Tunisian coast at zero feet between Sfax and Gabes, in order to avoid the standing patrols flown by the Me 109s over the Sicilian channel.

No incidents occurred as they crossed onto the battle area, in spite of their having permission to strafe.

Tuesday, 15th December 1942

Hundreds of aircraft at Bone.

The airfield at Bone was surrounded by mountainous terrain, and as airfields went was quite small. During their stop-over there, the pilots from No.274 Squadron saw some clot over-shoot and prang a Spitfire!

Hundreds of aircraft including Spitfire Vs, Beaufighters, Hudsons and several Liberators and Lockheed Lightnings were about, both at Bone and Algiers. There were so many aircraft that dispersal was impossible, and a shortage of fuel bowsers meant that all the aircraft had to be refueled by hand from cans!

Around this time the pilot of an American P-38 Lockheed Lightning misidentified a Consolidated Liberator, and shot it down, killing several of the crew!

Sgt Jack Aron photographed against the tailfin of a Ju 52.

The old voodoo struck again when the pilot of an over-shooting Wellington bomber lost control and collided with an Hawker Hurricane fighter coded "D"!

Leaving the Hurricanes at Bone, the No.274 pilots boarded the Hudsons and flew far to the south, reaching El Adem at 22.30 hours after an eleven hours non-stop, low level flight.

It was later revealed that, whilst circling El Adem, Wing Commander Yaxley had only 60 gallons of fuel left, and orders were to bale out if they failed to locate the airfield.

Friday, 18th December 1942

Afternoon off.

Bill had the afternoon off on the 18th December, and made use of the time by going to Derna. As always, whenever possible, Bill had his camera with him, and took the opportunity of taking some photographs.

He purchased a few curios, including a cigarette case with a Swastika on it, a "souvenir of Libya" and some Italian silk.

Saturday, 19th December 1942

A rookie pilot killed.

A rookie pilot from No.213 Squadron, whilst participating in a formation turnabout at 500', lost control, spun in and was killed.

No.274 Squadron. Back Row: Bruckshaw, Macfarlane, Cooper, McElhanney, Neil. Center: Graves, Bell, Robertson, Caen, Connell, Harrington, Sutherland, Wells (C.O.), Maclean, Matthews, Berryman, Lyle, Caldwell. Kneeling: Meldrum, Carter.

The overshooting Wellington bomber meets the static Hurricane.

Hedley Lyle, pilot and motorcyclist.

Squadron pilots hitching, a ride including "Chick" McElhanney (fifth from left) and "Flash" Gordon (second from right).

Knowing of Bill's interest in photography, "Red" Harrington asked Bill's help regarding some pictures the latter had taken in Malta and Algiers. On inspection, it was obvious to Bill that the film was not much good. He wrote in his journal "only a few will print. Examining the films shows he has under-exposed abysmally!!"

Sunday, 20th December 1942

An order suddenly arrived to the effect that
the Squadron would go to Benina (Benghazi LG)
on loan to No.212 Group until the next battle period.
Our troops are now past Sirte, on the Libyan coast.
I was going to travel with Sergeant Lyle on
his motorcycle, but it packed up at Derna.

I went back to Martuba and just caught the
last remnants of "B" party as they were leaving.
We spent the night east of Barce, a fertile area
dotted with the white farm houses of "Ente Colonnizione
Libia", an Italian settlement, where we found iron beds for all.
The next day we moved on via Tocra and Driana
(Adrianopolis) to Benghazi and then Benina.

The retreating axis forces had cunningly blown up several bridges over Wadis, but as there was always a by-pass cut round the side, their action was pointless.

Friday, 25th December 1942

CHRISTMAS DAY

Quite a party ensued at the "B" Flight Xmas Dinner. In accordance with the time honored custom, the Officer Commanding the Squadron, together with the "B" Flight pilots waited table for the men, before partaking of their own feast.

CHAPTER TWELVE

The Fall of Tripoli

Saturday, 2nd January 1943

Practice Balbo, flew as Red 1.

**We have not received any mail since Xmas,
and read on DROs that all mail between 2nd
and 9th September 1942 has been lost, that
probably includes my Xmas parcel.**

News was received that the Squadron was to be placed under the jurisdiction of the RAF, Air Headquarters, Egypt.

Major Wells released a bombshell at mid-day by announcing that as the Air Officer Commanding, Egypt, was visiting, the pilot's mess would have to be split into Officers and Non-Commissioned Officers' messes, in keeping with the new Air Officer Commanding ruling. This news was not to be well received by the pilots.

During the afternoon a practice Balbo was flown, with the aircraft flying in fours formation. Bill Marsh, piloting Hurricane, BP763, NH-N, acted as Red 1, and led Red Section. Flight Lieutenant May, flying his Hurricane coded "B", took on the role of a Me 109, and "jumped" the formation, from cloud base several times.

Bill managed to get only one deflection shot at him during the exercise. He later commented "It's very instructive, especially when you're not playing for keeps"!

Wing Commander Dudley Honor, DFC (the Station Commanding Officer and C.O. of No.274 Squadron in 1941) made an informal visit to the pilot's mess during the evening.

This resulted in a plot being hatched to maintain the messes in "status quo", with the Wing Commander's assistance and collusion.

Sunday, 3rd January 1943

*Following a night of thunder, the morning
broke wild and stormy, with heavy downpours of
rain which lasted all day.
The C.O., after his entertaining session in
our mess last night, looked rather curdled this morning.*

Four aircraft were detailed to take-off at 11.55 hours, to locate, intercept and shoot down a number of barrage balloons which had broken free from their moorings in Benghazi harbor.

The inclement weather persisted and although a report was given that the balloons were floating northwards, nothing was seen owing to the dense cloud.

Monday, 4th January 1943

*The weather continued wet and windy, and damn
cold too. Last night, by judicious placing of a
petrol tin under the eaves of our tent, I collected*

The morning broke wild and stormy.

enough rain water to do my dobey (washing).

Our advance patrols are active south of Misurata,
Wadi Bir el Kefir, and we are waiting for the next
moon. Meanwhile we are soon moving to Bersis,
near Tocra, where there are certain buildings which
can be used as mess premises! The C.O. sent "A"
party on ahead to consolidate our position there.

Although aerial activity was curtailed by the bad weather, the Eighth Army's Royal Engineers were kept extremely busy, for many days, clearing the roads of mines and booby traps, left by the retreating Afrikakorps, in the Wadi Bir el Kefir area.

On the 5th January the Allied forces secured Buerat-el-Hsun, between Sirte and Misurata.

Tuesday, 5th January 1943
(First Entry)

Today dawned clear and still; at last the bad
weather has left us in peace.
With the change in the weather, a Balbo was
organized for the afternoon with the C.O. leading.
Naturally, with all the rain of the past few days,
the dispersal area was bogged and Major Wells
tipped his new Hurricane on to its nose, holding us all up.
Eventually we took-off downwind towards the hangers,
formatted and flew to Tocra to have a look
at the aerodrome It seems to be a very pleasant
place and right by the sea.

The Squadron took advantage of the clear weather conditions, and detailed twelve aircraft to participate in formation flying practice, led by Major Wells.

The take-off, which commenced at 15.10 hours, was delayed due to a mishap involving Major Wells' Hurricane. As he was taxiing out, the undercarriage of his aircraft sunk into soft sand, and the tailplane rose into the air.

Held by the propeller, which had buried itself in sand, the Hurricane remained in this position as Major Wells clambered out uninjured.

Having found himself a replacement machine, Major Wells took-off, accompanied by the rest of the Squadron, and completed their task without further incident.

"How did he manage that?"

Tuesday, 5th January 1943
(Second Entry)

There is a rumor going around that a Lockheed
Lodestar aircraft, which left here on Sunday for
Alexandria, has crashed near Martuba, in overcast
weather. The passengers include Lady Tedder, wife
of the A.O.C.M.E.

On this date, Bill received his first piece of mail since Christmas. It was an aerogram, from Flight Lieutenant Russell Frowde, D.F.C., dated 4th December 1942. In it he wrote:

. . ."You're getting a real old-timer. It's about time
you came home How many notches have you got any-
way?. . ."

Wednesday, 6th January 1943
(First Entry)

Flight Lieutenants Clough-Camm (M.O.) and Sarell
returned from leave and confirmed the news of the
Lodestar crash. It apparently came down in the

foothills around Heliopolis.
They also brought news that all hotels etc. in
Cairo are now "in bounds" to all ranks, much to
certain peoples dismay. They are concerned about
the accounts of lack of respect, etc.

Wednesday, 6th January 1943
(Second Entry)

At 06.00 hours enemy bombers carried out a sharp
low-level attack against Benghazi. Nick Carter and
I, being readiness section, went early to "ops" and
took-off before dawn. We patrolled Benina, but saw nothing.

Flight Sergeant Carter, accompanied by Sergeant Berryman, took-off at 07.00 hours, to intercept reported enemy bombers.

Five minutes later a second section was ordered into the air, to assist in the same task. Flight Sergeant Marsh was to lead the second section, but as his No.2 could not get airborne, Bill took-off alone.

He soon sighted and joined-up with Carter and Berryman and, although they patrolled the Benina area, they saw nothing. They landed, without incident, forty minutes later with little to report.

F/S Mick Bruckshaw (right) advises Sgt
Macfarlane where to put the excess water!

Hotel Ack-Ack, tariff 1 Bint (female).

Friday, 8th January 1943

*Up at 06.00 hours, and on readiness at 06.30 hours
for an expected German (paratroops) attack on
Benghazi. A bombing raid had been carried out by
three or four Ju 88s at 04.00 hours, but was thought
to be only a nuisance raid. Not the sort of show to
require sixteen Hurricanes to do dangerous night
take-offs. However, as nothing happened it was stand-
down for breakfast as 08.00.
A sudden panic broke at 10.00 hours, when 'Gravy's'
(Flying Officer Graves) section were scrambled and the
rest of the squadron was brought to readiness. The
scare turned out to be fifteen U.S.A.A.F. Liberators
approaching without identity signals.
Having been released for the afternoon, I got in
some practice flying with the new boys.
Sergeant Jack Aron sustained a glycol leak and was
forced to land.*

Four aircraft, led by Flying Officer Graves, were scrambled to intercept a reported
flight of fifteen enemy aircraft.

F/O "Gravy" Graves.

Flying on their given course, the Allied fighters soon sighted a large formation in the distance. Closer examination revealed the "enemy" aircraft were in fact Liberator bombers from the United States Army Air Corps. When this fact was reported to Ground Control, the Hurricanes were ordered to land immediately.

During the course of the afternoon, seven aircraft carried out practice aerobatics. Unfortunately Hurricane, BG750, developed a glycol leak, which resulted in the aircraft making an emergency landing. The pilot, Sergeant Aron, was forced to land, wheels-up at Bersis, ten miles west of Torca. Although he was unhurt, the aircraft sustained some damage.

Saturday, 9th January 1943

More bangs in the night, but earlier than usual.
A Beaufighter from No.89 Squadron got a Heinkel III
east of Benghazi, on a night practice flight, in sight of Benina.
Ten Wellington bombers took-off to bomb the
cross-road at Misurata, one returned early, the rest
came home when the job had been done.

Sunday, 10th January 1943

Up at 06.00 hours again, but due to heavy rain
through the night the drome was u/s.

A Heinkel He 111 which made a crash-landing in the desert.

"Dinger" Bell back from Alex (Alexandria) says
a Liberator was shot down over El Adem at night by
an Intruder 88; instead of going elsewhere the
crew of a second Lib went up and baled out!
Also, No.213 Sqdn, on a second Malta-Algeria
trip, saw their leading Hudson shot down into
the sea by a U.S.A.A.F Lockheed Lightning!
Some of the boys went into Benghasi, including
Mac and Jackie, in the Mercedes, where they were
stopped by the Provost Marshal.

Due, again, to the inclement weather, and the unserviceable nature of the landing ground, all flying duties were canceled.

Some of the pilots decided to go in search of action of another kind, and drove to Benghasi in their Mercedes staff car. It was there that they had an encounter with the Provost Marshal, who stopped them and demanded to know who they were and what they were doing! The outcome of this meeting was that the Provost Marshal threatened to requisition the car!

Monday, 11th January 1943

Received an aerograph (letter) from Gil at
Bomber O.T.U., at Ossington – he says he likes twins
(engines) now.
We are supposed to be moving to Agedabia. F/Lt
Mackay flew there this afternoon and reports 300 yards
of serviceable runway, the rest is under water.
As no convoys are allowed past Benghasi, we

The Mercedes staff car, complete with squadron code on the door, which Sgt Bruckshaw found and nearly lost! Nick Carter is the front seat passenger.

> *cannot move yet, I hope. This blow after finding*
> *excellent quarters at Bersis Tocra.*
> *After readiness, as dusk, taxied "N" (in and out*
> *of a filled bomb crater) to its absurdly distant dispersal.*

Gil Marsh, having completed his course at No.22 Service Flying Training at Thornhill, Rhodesia, returned to England at the end of October 1942. On 17th November he was posted to No.14 (Pilots) Advanced Flying Unit, at Ossington, from where he wrote to Bill.

Having carried out his initial flying training on single engined aircraft like the Harvard, Gil had now progressed to the twin-engined Airspeed Oxford, which he obviously enjoyed flying.

Tuesday, 12th January 1943

> *Had just finished breakfast when the phone rang.*
> *A Wimpey (Wellington Bomber) had wrapped itself*
> *round "N." I went out to see and found the rudder,*
> *elevators and a longeron smashed – a RSV job. Now*
> *I'll lose that prince amongst swine of a Hurricane.*

For the second time in less than a month, a Vickers Wellington twin-engined bomber had collided on the ground with a Hawker Hurricane fighter. Unfortunately, on this occasion, the Hurricane was NH-N, the one Bill Marsh enjoyed flying more than any other. He was beginning to dislike twin-engined aircraft.

Wednesday, 13th January 1943

On a "Balbo" at 10.00 hours – did a practice bombing dive from 9,000' and reformed. F/Lt Mackay leading. F/Lt Appleford, Leader 3. Flying Hurricane "S", which is surprisingly fast, did a shoot-up on the circuit and then landed. Then W/O. Neil came back from a convoy at zero feet and beat-up the dispersal area against the circuit; he got a big strip torn off. I hear we are moving to Agedabia, "A" Flight leave at first light tomorrow.

Twelve Hurricanes from No.274 Squadron, led by Flight Lieutenant Mackay, took-off at 10.10 hours for practice formation flying.

Bill was allocated Hurricane HL733, coded NH-S, which to his pleasant surprise was a decent aircraft to fly. He found it handled well and was surprisingly fast. It made the loss of his beloved "N" that much easier.

After fifty minutes flying, the formation landed, followed twenty-five minutes later by six aircraft which had been out on a shipping patrol.

On approaching the airfield, one of the six Hurricanes broke away.

Acting Sergeant Gilbert Marsh.

W/O Jack Neil "beats-up" the landing ground, watched by two colleagues . . .

. . . carries out one more circuit . . .

. . . and comes in for a landing and a "rocket" from the C.O.

It roared in fast and low over the dispersal area, just a few feet above the tents and then turned-in against the circuit. When Hurricane BE281 had landed and taxied to a halt, the pilot, Warrant Officer Jack Neil, was told to report to the Flight Commander, where he was the recipient of a few harsh words.

Rumors were beginning to circulate about another move forward, but it was to be a week or so before they were proved correct.

Thursday, 14th January 1943

Lots more rain during the night, which continued during the day.
"A" Flight got away with difficulty, and our move is postponed.
Heard that F/O Samuels is missing, and that S/L
Marples D.F.C., got shot into the sea, but got a
Macchi 200 first. He's O.K.

All round it was a miserable day for Bill. The weather was wet, the Squadron personnel were despondent about their move being postponed and there was no flying. On top of all this Bill heard some distressing news.

Information was filtering through that his friend, Flying Officer "Sammy" Samuels, who had been posted to No.601 Squadron the previous October, had been shot down and was listed as missing.

Likewise, Squadron Leader Roy Marples, who had been posted back in June 1942, had also been shot down. It transpired that some Macchi 200s were intercepted by No.145 Squadron, who shot down a number of them.

During the course of the fight, Squadron Leader Marples was shot down into the sea. The good news relating to Roy Marples was that, apart from being rescued by two army officers, who swam out to him, he had taken a Macchi 200 down with him.

Friday, 15th January 1943

Nothing of importance all day, but then, at about 21.00 hours all the flak in creation was over Benghasi. It transpired that two Liberators were stooging over without I.F.F. showing. Two Beaufighters were scrambled from here, then one nearly shot down the other.

Again it was a day of low spirits, with no flying and little all else to do except write letters, journals or look at sand. Unbeknown to the pilots at the time, this was the day that the 8th Army began its push against the Beurat line.

Saturday, 16th January 1943

Major Wells returned from leave today. A Balbo flown this afternoon, but I was not flying - played chess. The Squadron is non-operational now,

Spitfire Vb, ES386, coded ZX-A, of No.145 Squadron.

though when we move Lord only knows. The destination
has been changed to Nofibia, so perhaps we shall be
in the thick of it soon.
Spit Sdns lost 13 aircraft – Jerry is strafing
our landing grounds, leaving a heavy top cover overhead.
Lots of promotions coming through.

Although the Squadron was officially declared non-operational, the boredom of the last few days was relieved for some, when Major Wells led a practice formation flying exercise.

Twelve aircraft took-off at 14.15 hours, but they were back on the ground forty-five minutes later! Bill was not included in the flying exercise, so took himself off to find somebody to play chess with.

Some of the "boys" were cheered-up by the news that they had been promoted. "Chick" McElhanney was promoted to Flying Officer, whilst Mick Bruckshaw, Don Cordrey and Sergeant Barker were all made up to Flight Sergeants.

Sunday, 17th January 1943

The new Air Officer Commanding, Egypt, A.V.M. Saul,
visited us today and had a few words with some of us.
I heard on the 3.00 pm news that the 8th Army
had occupied the Buerat positions (the offensive
started last Friday, but was only mentioned as
patrol activities). General Montgomery's spearhead
is driving north-west to Tripoli, and by-passing
the Misurata front. Also, the Free French driving
north from Chad and Fezzan have linked-up with the
1st Army in Tunis.

Monday, 18th January 1943

Galvanised into action today for visit of A.O.C.
in C. Sir Sholto Douglas, who has taken over Middle
East Command from A.M. Sir Arthur Tedder, who has
been posted home

Bill had previously seen Sir Sholto at RAF Honily, when the latter went there to bid No.605 farewell, on behalf of England, prior to the Squadron going overseas. Bill was in some trepidation as to the augury (omen) of this latest visit, but he need not have worried.

Sir Sholto Douglas did not appear, and the long wait for his arrival was enlightened by one of No.33 Squadron's aircraft going round and round the circuit, unsure as to whether his wheels were locked down. After a total of some ninety minutes stooging around, he landed safely.

The air of despondency was lifted from the Squadron's pilots, as they prepared for the move they had all been waiting for. Their new home was to be at Misurata and the move, which was to be carried out in stages, was to be made over the next three days. The first stop was scheduled to be at Agedabia, followed by further stops at Marble Arch, Tamet and Hamieriet. This allowed the ground staff time to catch up with the pilots, whose flying time for the whole trip was recorded as four and a half hours.

Wednesday, 20th January 1943

Left Benina at 09.30 hours and flew to Agedabia
where we landed. F/Lt Appleford taxied into a hole
at 9 boost and broke his fan (propeller).
I went over to No.213 Squadron and saw Ron Jones.
They have no ground party, so (they) are having to
sleep under their aircraft.
The C.O. was posted to No.2 Wing, S.A.A.F.,
but this was later canceled.

Thursday, 21st January 1943

Got cracking early, did a shoot-up at Agedabia,
and then flew up to Marble Arch.
After refueling there,
the C.O. and I took-off and flew to Tamet
on the coast, just past Sirte. Met our maintenance
party there, and heard about three ground gunners
being killed there yesterday by mines! Spent an
hour sorting out an accumulation of mail, and got
one parcel (Xmas) and two newspapers.
Later took-off to fly to Hamariet, 20 miles south
of Tamet, a very rocky drome
Met our new C.O. – Sqdn Ldr Paul Webb.

Flight Sergeant Marsh and his companions spent the night at Hamariet, where they were entertained by No.2 Wing, South African Air Force. Their host provided a sumptuous dinner, the main course of which consisted of locally shot gazelle.

Marble Arch.

The guests enjoyed their meal, and refrained from giving in to the temptation of shooting a very mischievous monkey, and adding it to the menu, especially as the creature was the Wing's mascot. However, Mick Bruckshaw could not resist playing with the animal the next morning, before he took his leave.

The social occasion also gave the pilots the opportunity to meet their new C.O., who would be taking over from Major Wells in the near future.

Friday, 22nd January 1943

*Messed about a Hamariet for some hours after an
excellent breakfast, then took-off with Major Wells,
Gravy, Neil, Bruckshaw, McElhanney and Eaglen.
We flew up from Hamariet to Misurata, passing many road
blocks, blown by retreating Jerries, and ploughed up
landing grounds. We all got down O.K., except for one
or two burst tyres, since they made a bad job of the
ploughing. No.213 Squadron arrived later in the afternoon,
and we all got installed in villas near the
drome; very pleasant surroundings, with palm trees
and the usual white-walled buildings.
Heard that Sammy was dead. Heard also that Kittyhawks
were strafing Castel Benito landing ground to stop
Jerry ploughing it up.*

Mick Bruckshaw and friend.

Nick Carter and Tommy Matthews at Misurata.

Before leaving Hamariet, Bill, never one to miss an opportunity for a photograph, persuaded his fellow pilots to pose for a picture.

The group included Flight Sergeant Mick Bruckshaw, and Sergeant Roy Macfarlane, who received news that they were both being posted to No.601 Squadron, which flew Spitfires.

Also included in the photograph was Sergeant "Badger" Eaglen who, not to be confused with another Sergeant pilot with a similar name, had joined No.274 Squadron late in 1942.

Other news of a more disturbing nature was confirmed, when it was announced that Flying Officer "Sammy" Samuels was dead. His aircraft, a Spitfire, was last seen turning in to meet an attack from eight Messerschmitts, an action for which he paid the supreme sacrifice.

No.92 Squadron, led by Flight Lieutenant Neville Duke, escorted a flight of Kittyhawks to Zuara, to the west of Tripoli, where the latter bombed and strafed the retreating Axis forces.

Saturday, 23rd January 1943

TRIPOLI fell at 5.00 am this morning. Some of the boys out early looking after a convoy near Homs, which continued until dusk.
At about 3.00 pm Sgt Hedley Lyle, from Scotland, took-off with an air intake cover still in place. He came back, removed it and took-off again for a one

Waiting to leave Hamraiet. L to R: Roy Macfarlane, "Red" Harrington, "Chick" McElhanney, MacLaren, Jack Neil, Mick Bruckshaw, George Meldrum, "Gravy" Graves, Robbie Robertson, Nick Carter, "Badger" Eaglen, George Caldwell.

> *hour twenty minute patrol over Homs. On the way back*
> *he ran out of fuel and pranged.*
> *F/Lt Jerry Wade, now of No.601 Squadron, visited us.*

Tripoli, the last capital of Mussolini's new Roman Empire, was taken by the Eighth Army, at 05.00 hours, on the 23rd January, 1943. The victory came exactly three months to the day since the commencement of the Battle of El Alamein, during which time the Allies had advanced over 1,000 miles.

Flying during the day, for No.274, was limited to shipping patrols. Flying Officer Graves and Flight Sergeant Cooper gave air cover to a convoy for over one and a half hours. The convoy, code-named "Desert", which comprised of ten barges and escorts, was anchored off shore, sixty miles east of Tripoli. Needless to say, with the Germans in retreat, no incidents were reported.

The only action that day was provided by Sergeant Hedley Lyle who, having run oil on super rich mixtures for the whole of his patrol, ran out of fuel. He crash-landed approximately ten miles west of Misurata, with the landing gear still retracted!

Squadron Leader Webb was not impressed by Sergeant Lyle's escapade and, by way of punishment, wrote a sign which he hung over Lyle's bed. It simply read, "PERMANENT DUTY PILOT."

Sunday, 24th January 1943

> *"Bruck" and "Mac" left for No.601 Sqdn this morning.*
> *Another all-day convoy patrol. Jack Neil and I*
> *patrolled between 2.00 – 3.30 pm. Low flying along the road*
> *from Homs to Misurata.*
> *Major Wells is to remain as C.O. – Sqdn/Ldr Webb*
> *is posted to Wing as Squadron Leader Flying.*

Air cover was again provided by No.274 Squadron, for the convoy anchored off the coast. Permission to proceed to Tripoli having been given, the convoy headed west to the harbor, shadowed from above by Flight Sergeant Cooper and Flight Sergeant Mclaren, who took the first two hour watch. As with the previous day, no incidents were reported.

It was the same story throughout the day, as each section of relieved pilots returned to base and made the same report.

Flight Sergeant Marsh and Warrant Officer Neil, who flew as a section between 15.30 hours and 17.25 hours, took advantage of flying home along the coast road, once they had been relieved. As they flew fast and low along the road between Homs and Misurata, they noticed that most of the villas had white flags flying. Furthermore, not only were they still inhabited, but the occupants were waving at them as they flew over!

Warrant Officer Jack Neil.

Having been given notice of their impending posting two days earlier, Mick Bruckshaw and Roy Macfarlane said farewell to No.274 and moved to No.601 Squadron. However, Major Wells' posting had been rescinded; he was to remain as C.O. of the Squadron.

Monday 25th January 1943

Took-off at 08.00 hours to cover the convoy again,
with "Chick" McElhanney.
Returned to base and I had to pump down both the
wheels and flaps in order to land.
"Red" Harrington finished his two hundred hours at
10.39 am and in celebration, shot the place up.
Heard that half the aircraft are to go to Castel Benito tomorrow.

Life for the pilots of No.274 Squadron was becoming routine, as they continued to patrol above the convoy which was still heading for Tripoli Harbor. However, when he took over the task as second section of the morning, Flight Sergeant Marsh found the convoy at anchor, thirty miles west of Homs.

He flew a ninety minute patrol, accompanied by Flying Officer McElhanney, before returning to base and making the now usual report, apart from the fact that his aircraft had developed Hydraulics failure prior to landing.

Tuesday, 26th January 1943

Took-off at 09.00 hours, with my kit in the belly
of the aircraft, and flew the 50 miles to Castel Benito.
Its very nicely laid out, with both Spitfires
and Kittyhawks operating from here.
Took off again in "Y" to cover the convoy off Tripoli;
Got installed in very comfortable billets.

Nine aircraft from No.274 took-off from Misurata, at 09.00 hours, and flew to Castel Benito, where they landed fifty minutes later.

Bill, like most of the other pilots, packed his kit into the belly of his Hurricane for the flight, which went without incident. However, on landing, NH-N punctured the tyre on the port side of the undercarriage.

The airfield was a virtual paradise, with properly laid out buildings, including hangers, billets and palm trees.

The hangers, although showing signs of damage, housed a number of "treasures" in the shape of abandoned German and Italian aircraft.

The business of finding a suitable billet, and settling in, had to wait, as another convoy was in need of air cover.

Riding at anchor in the roadsteads outside Tripoli Harbor was "Anger", the code-name given to a convoy comprising of six merchant ships.

Due to his own aircraft being unserviceable, Bill , flying again with Flying Officer McElhanney, took-off in Hawker Hurricane, BE490, NH-Y, at 13.50 hours for his seventy minute sortie. As was becoming expected, all pilots reported no incidents.

With flying finished for the day, the pilots were permitted to stand down.

Naturally they went off in search of a suitable billet, which was not too difficult to find.

The permanent accommodation blocks, abandoned by the Italians were, in Bill's view, built to high standards, and were also very comfortable.

Their estimation of their new surroundings rose even higher, when a search of the place revealed the wine storage area! Bill later recorded in his journal, "stayed up drinking Chianti till 10.00 pm!!"

Wednesday, 27th January 1943

More convoying – but only one for me today, at

A Fiat G.50 Italian fighter in the hangar at Castel Benito.

A German Henschel Hs 129, the first aircraft of its type to be captured during the desert war.

A moment of reflection at the end of the day, for Nick Carter, at Castel Benito.

11.00 hours. Lots of cloud and rain squalls.
Spent the afternoon searching stores abandoned
by the Ities.

Major Wells and the remaining pilots who had stayed at Misurata flew to Castel Benito to rejoin the rest of the Squadron.

Having flown earlier in the day, Bill was released from further duty at lunch time. He spent the afternoon searching the stores left by the Italians.

The number of aircraft, and the amount of material left behind caused him to write in his journal. . .

"...colossal waste, millions of quids worth of stuff; this was their base with workshops like ours at Abourkir and Heliopolis. I found an "Itie" oxygen mask, some files, a screwdriver and a chisel...These Ities did themselves well. [I also] got a mirror, arm-chair and a table..."

Saturday 30th January 1943

A quiet morning, fine but cold, so lit a bonfire.
Flew with George Caldwell, as No.2, on convoys.

Bill woke up to a fine, but chilly, morning, which was not to his liking. Utilizing the up-turned fin casing from the tail of a bomb, he endeavored to light a fire to keep himself warm. His goal was achieved, but at the cost of having to endure a thick blanket of smoke floating around his room.

Having survived his self-imposed ordeal, Bill found he was to lead a two man section on a shipping patrol, with Sergeant George Caldwell flying as his No.2.

They took-off at 11.45 hours, and headed for Tripoli Harbor, where they were to relieve Flight Lieutenant Sarll and Sergeant Bickford-Smith, who had been patrolling over convoy "Anger" for the last hour and twenty minutes.

The entrance to Bill's accommodation.

213

Hurricane, BN173, coded "R", piloted by George Caldwell.

A Savoia-Marchetti S.M.79 Italian bomber.

Although he was flying on a mission, Bill had taken his camera with him and, from the confines of his cramped cockpit, he took photographs of Tripoli, the harbor and George Caldwell's Hurricane formatting on his own.

Fortunately the Luftwaffe were, seemingly, still not paying any attention to the convoy.

On Bill's return to base, he heard that three former members of No.274 had been decorated for their work with the Squadron. Flight Lieutenant Conrad and Flying Officer Keefer, RCAF, were both awarded the Distinguished Flying Cross, whilst Sergeant Dodds, RAF, had received the Distinguished Flying Medal.

The action by Allied ground forces, against the rearguard of the retreating Axis forces had continued unabated, and by 31st January 1943, the Eighth Army had taken Zuara. Zuara, which had recently been attacked by Kittyhawks and Spitfires, was the last town in Libya on the Tripolitanian coast, before the border with Tunisia.

CHAPTER THIRTEEN

Application for a Commission

Monday, 1st February 1943

Up at 07.00 am, and took-off on patrol,
with Bickford-Smith. . .did a snappy formation landing.

Flight Sergeant Bill Marsh, flying Hurricane, BP662, coded "X", took-off at 07.50 hours for the first patrol of the day. His wingman was Sergeant Guy Bickford-Smith, who was piloting Hurricane, BN270, coded "R."

Together they headed out over the coast to carry out their allotted task, a shipping patrol incorporating Tripoli Harbor.

No incidents were reported and they returned to base where, instead of landing individually as usual, they put on a bit of a show and made a perfect formation landing, at 09.40 hours. Leaving Bill feeling rather pleased with his efforts.

As he was not detailed for another patrol until 15.30 hours, Bill spent the day preparing for the proposed move to Mellaha, which the Squadron was using as a satellite Landing Ground.

Impressed by what he saw at Mellaha, Bill noted in his journal that the mess and sleeping quarters were a "veritable castle", approached by a half mile long drive lined with palm trees.

It was obvious Bill fully intended to make himself comfortable whilst there. He acquired a ground floor room, facing south, and moved in the furniture he found at Castel Benito.

The entrance gate to Mellaha airfield, littered with the wreckage of two Luftwaffe and one Italian aircraft.

Entrance leading to 274 Squadron Officers Mess.

The avenue of palm trees, outside the Officers Mess, looking back towards the main entrance gate.

The Officers' Mess.

The tennis courts at Mellaha.

Tuesday, 2nd February 1943

We were called upon for harbor and convoy duty during the afternoon, with Bickford-Smith.

When he landed from his afternoon shipping patrol with Sergeant Bickford-Smith, Bill was less than pleased with the ground controller.

The pair had taken-off at 15.30 hours for the usual standing convoy patrol, which lasted for approximately ninety minutes duration.

Having patrolled their allotted area for the requisite time without incident, they searched the sky for the incoming pair of Hurricanes from the Squadron who would relieve them. Their searching however was in vain, due to the fact that the relief section had been canceled, but the ground controller omitted to inform Bill and his wingman that their patrol was to be the last one for the day!! Consequently, Flight Sergeant Marsh and Sergeant Bickford-Smith remained on patrol for two hours, ten minutes without being recalled.

Wednesday, 3rd February 1943
(First Entry)

Up about 09.00 am and had just finished breakfast when F/Lt Sarll asked me to take his place on readiness in "Z."

Wishing to stand-down from his allotted patrol duty, Flight Lieutenant Sarll asked Bill to take over as readiness pilot on Hurricane coded "Z." The latter agreed to the officer's request, gathered his flying kit and prepared himself for the forthcoming flight. He was scrambled, along with Sergeant Tommy Matthews as his No.2, at 09.50 hours.

Matthews was piloting Hurricane, HL795, coded "O", which was a fairly fast machine, but Bill was not impressed with "Z." He later wrote in his journal. . .

> . . ." "Z" is a bit slow for an HV [HV484] kite.
> Tommy Matthews had to ask me to go faster at 14,000',
> over Tripoli Harbor. . ."

Wednesday, 3rd February 1943
(Second Entry)

> About 4 pm heard that Sgt Eaglen had pranged. . .
> "H" written-off, "Badger" may be badly hurt.

Sergeant "Badger" Eaglen, flying as wingman to Sergeant Meldrum had taken-off with the latter, for a patrol over Tripoli Harbor at 14.15 hours. Their mission proved uneventful and they returned to base, where Meldrum landed safely at 16.05 hours. It was as Sergeant Eaglen brought Hurricane, BE397, coded "H", into land that tragedy struck. As the aircraft came in over flats, it overshot, hit a bump, burst a tyre and cartwheeled over onto its back, damaging the aircraft and seriously injuring the pilot. In the turmoil that followed, an entry was made in the Squadron's Operational Record Book to the effect that "Badger" Eaglen had in fact crashed in Hurricane, BP710, coded "H."

Thursday, 4th February 1943
(First Entry)

> Nick Carter went into Tripoli, trying to find
> his father who is in the 7th Armored Division.

Sergeant Nick Carter, being off-duty, went into Tripoli in the hope of finding his father, who was serving with the 7th Armored Division, and had been involved in the recent ground fighting.

Unbeknown to Sergeant Carter, the Allies were holding a parade in honor of a visit by Winston Churchill, the Prime Minister, and movement around the town was far from easy.

The parade involved hundreds of tanks and military vehicles, together with a massive march past, and was carried out in the presence of the Prime Minister, General Alexander and General Montgomery.

Hawker Hurricane, BE397, coded "H", following "Badger" Eaglen's accident.

Bearing in mind the role played in the recent battle by the Allied Air Forces, it dismayed Nick Carter to see that the RAF was not represented at the parade by any high ranking officer other than Winston Churchill himself, who wore the uniform of an Air Commodore.

Thursday, 4th February 1943
(Second Entry)

On readiness at 2.30 pm. Take-off and
patrol in "N", but it was u/s due to oil leak, had to take "T."

When an oil leak on Hurricane, BP763, coded "N", prevented Bill from taking-off for his allotted patrol, he quickly swapped his defective aircraft for Hurricane, BE281, coded "T."

This action did not please his friend Warrant Officer Jack Neil, whose aircraft Bill had taken. Bill later confided in his journal that he did not like "T", and referred to it as "a ropey kite", but at least he brought it home safely.

The groundcrew, having fixed the problem on "N" whilst Bill was on patrol, left Jack Neil with the problem of having to take "N" into the air for his own patrol. The mission was carried out without incident, but the landing was a different matter.

As Jack Neil touched-down on the bumpy landing ground, a tyre burst, writing-off the undercarriage and causing the pilot to twist his shoulder.

Under the reference he had written earlier about Hurricane "T", Bill added the comment ". . .Aerodrome getting a bad reputation."

A Pipe Band leads the Victory Parade . . . followed by the Regiments who fought in the Campaign.

Friday, 5th February 1943

Sgt Eaglen is dead. . .
. . .S/L Clause landed and wrote-off his undercarriage.

It was with great sadness that Bill received the news that his friend, "Badger" Eaglen, had died from a broken neck, following the accident a couple of days previously. Sergeant Edward William Eaglen, aged twenty-three, was laid to rest in Tripoli Cemetery.

The airfield jinx however struck again during the course of the morning, when Squadron Leader Clause, Officer Commanding No.601, attempted to land his Spitfire at Mellaha, and wrote-off his undercarriage!!

No.601 Squadron were supposed to have a detachment based at Mellaha, but following the C.O.'s prang, the rest of the Flight was diverted to Castel Benito.

Saturday, 6th February 1943

Afternoon tested [Hurricane] "T."

Bill's name was not listed on the Squadron "Battle Order" for operations on 6th February, so he had a free day. He took the opportunity to inspect and collate a number of photographs he had recently had developed.

During the course of the afternoon, he flight-tested Hurricane BE281, coded "T", which was suspected of having a main fuel blockage.

Whilst he was flying over the Landing Ground, Bill saw the C.O., Major Wells, and Sergeant George Caldwell, on the circuit preparing to land. Momentarily a thought passed through Bill's mind and he gave way to temptation. He pulled back on the "stick" and his Hurricane responded by peeling over and diving down upon the two unsuspecting aircraft. Fortunately for the two airmen ahead of him, Bill's attack was only a mock one, for neither pilot saw him.

Now in the mood to practice his skills further, Bill put the Hurricane into a climb, from which he rolled off the top at 7,000' and carried out a mock bombing dive over the salt flats.

Satisfied with his efforts, and that the aircraft was airworthy, he returned to base.

On this date, Bill wrote to his mother and sister Lilian, setting out his hopes for his immediate future.

> *. . .Just got an airgraph (letter) from Ray Wood-craft, who is well and says there may be a Pilot Officer Marsh soon – I hope this is true. Speaking for myself, my present ambition is Warrant Officer, most senior of senior N.C.O.'s and a rank which neatly combines the advantages of officer and N.C.O.*

Sunday, 7th February 1943

> *Wet and windy! Control ordered a section above cloud besides the one below. Mellaha u/s for landing.*

Low cloud, high winds and torrential rain greeted the pilots as they woke from their slumbers, and was to impede their operations throughout the day. All aircraft detailed for missions were able to take-off, but the conditions were deemed too hazardous to allow them to land back at base. They were therefore diverted to Castel Benito.

Bill, detailed to deliver a message, took-off from Mellaha and flew to Castel Benito, where he found total chaos.

At 11.40 hours he took-off (in his own words) very casually with Flight Sergeant Cooper, RCAF, with orders to patrol above the cloud. Bill "fought" with the controls of his Hurricane, HL733, coded "K", and put his trust in his instruments, as the aircraft was buffeted by the elements.

He broke cloud cover at 17,000', after a tough battle, and was amazed to find that Flight Sergeant Cooper had not followed him. Satisfied that Cooper was not going to materialize, Bill carried out the patrol alone. It was not until he landed two hours later that Bill found out that Flight Sergeant Cooper had baled out in cloud, due to his engine constantly cutting out.

The patrols continued throughout the day, as did the rain, and Bill was airborne again at 16.10 hours. On this occasion he was accompanied by Sergeant Bickford-Smith; their mission to patrol Tripoli Harbor.

Shortly after taking-off, whilst flying at an altitude of 10,000', Bickford-Smith developed engine problems and advised Bill that he was returning to base. For the second time that day, Flight Sergeant Marsh was left to carry out the patrol alone.

Visibility was poor and Bill could see very little, but he did try to locate George Meldrum and Tommy Matthews, who had been advised of a "bandit" in their area.

Meldrum and Matthews were flying together as Red Section, when the ground controller informed them by radio that a Ju 88 bomber was in the vicinity.

After being told to alter course at least twice, and gain altitude, the Hurricane pilots sighted their quarry flying at 11,000'.

The fighter pilots made ready to attack, but the bomber pilot knew they were there and dived down to seek sanctuary in the clouds, 2,000' feet below his aircraft.

Sergeant Meldrum gave chase and opened-up with a three second burst of machine gun fire from three hundred yards. Strikes were registered along the fuselage and tailplane of the aircraft, from where pieces were seen to fly off.

Jack Neil, "Chick McElhanney, Unknown, Tommy Matthews, Unknown.

Before further damage could be inflicted, the bomber entered the safe cover offered by the thick cloud, but it was sighted again a short while later, approximately one mile ahead of the attackers, flying very fast at low altitude. It is thought to have jettisoned its bomb load whilst flying in the cloud.

Monday, 8th February 1943

Heard that Major Wells is awarded the DFC

A message was received to the effect that a well deserved Distinguished Flying Cross was gazetted to Major John Wells, South African Air Force, Officer Commanding No.274 Squadron, on the 5th February 1943. The citation stated it was awarded for his courage, determination and devotion to duty.

Major Wells had been on continuous operational duty since November 1940, and led many missions in the air. During a twelve day period in 1942, he led ten bombing missions, which achieved excellent results, despite having to face barrages of intense anti-aircraft fire.

Needless to say that a party was held in the mess that night, at which copious amounts of alcohol were drank.

Tuesday, 9th February 1943

A.O.C., Egypt visiting this morning. . .
. . .says we move back to Castel Benito.

Having been at readiness for a shipping patrol, Bill took-off at 10.30 hours, just after the arrival at the base of the Air Officer Commanding, Egypt.

Flying Hurricane, BN763, and accompanied by Sergeant Matthews piloting Hurricane, BE281, he patrolled over Tripoli Harbor for one hour and twenty minutes without incident, before returning to base.

Whilst they were away, the A.O.C. imparted some information which was not well received by the pilots. He informed them that they were to move back to Castel Benito. The thought of leaving their "palatial" surrounding horrified them, especially when they also heard that all the billets had been taken, and they would have to live and sleep in tents!

Bill, receiving the news upon his return, almost wished he had stayed in the air!

Wednesday, 10th February 1943

General mess meeting, lots of fun.

Following the previous days news, a mess meeting was held during the course of the evening, and a few changes were implemented. Flying Officer "Spy" Hands, the Squadron's Intelligence Officer, to his amazement, lost the secretaryship of the Mess Committee to Flight Lieutenant Clough-Camm, the Medical Officer, who was elected almost unopposed.

Also, Flight Lieutenant Bob Sarll, "Gravy" Graves, Jackie Neil and Nick Carter were elected to form the Mess Committee.

It is not known whether they had any influence, but shortly after their election, news was received that the move back to Castel Benito had been rescinded.

Friday, 12th February 1943

"K" going round circuit with port oleo-leg broken. . .friend Hedley Lyle again!

Whilst down at "flights", Bill watched two Hurricanes on the circuit, one of which had a problem. The two aircraft, HL703, "J" and HL733, "K" flown by Flying Officer Caen and Sergeant Lyle respectively, were returning from a shipping patrol and the latter had to face the problem of landing with a broken port undercarriage strut.

Bill, realizing that "K" was being piloted by his friend, Hedley Lyle, stood and watched, after all there was nothing else he could do.

Lyle, who only three weeks before had had the ignominious sign "PERMANENT DUTY PILOT" hung over his bed by the C.O., retracted the undercarriage and made a wheels-up landing off the runway area, endeavoring to save the aircraft from further damage.

At lunch time that day, Bill heard that his other friend, Jack Neil, had received a commission, and had been promoted to the rank of Pilot Officer. As if a reason was needed, it gave the pilots an excuse to spend the evening drinking!

The next evening much merriment was derived without the aid of alcohol, but from all things a 16mm cine film show, which had been put on by a visiting Canadian Welfare Group.

Bill recorded in his journal. . .

> . . .After an hour's wait it [the film] started. . .occasionally it would slip into reverse. A transatlantic flight became a series of backward flights and take-offs and some hero baling into his aircraft, collecting a stream of flour (his parachute) from mid-air as he did so.

On 15th February 1943, the British Eighth Army captured the town of Ben Gardane, Tunisia approximately twenty-five miles from the country's border with Libya.

F/S "Red" Harrington (third from left) possibly asks Major Wells (right) about the possibility of having a party, whilst "Chick" McElhanney (center) looks pensive.

Having occupied the town, together with its airfield, the Allies were able to begin their advance towards Medenine and the Mareth Line.

Tuesday, 16th February 1943

This morning my room mate Guy Bickford-Smith,
using the 15cwt (truck) to facilitate his duties as duty pilot,
drove [the] near side front wheel over

F/O "Spy" Hands, astride his Arab steed, restrained by F/L Austen Clough-Camm. F/S Syd Barker (right) watches from a safe distance.

*the three feet high parapet wall of our fountain
and got stuck there; in the dark.
Twisted the track rod. D.G. got a week [as] duty pilot!!*

Thursday, 18th February 1943

A.O.C. in C. visited today.

Air Chief Marshal Sir Sholto Douglas (later Marshal of the Royal Air Force The Lord Douglas of Kirtleside, GCM, MC, DFC, DL), having been recently appointed to the position of Air Officer Commanding in Chief, RAF Middle East, visited some of the Squadrons which came under his overall command.

No.274 Squadron were honored with a visit during the morning of 18th February, prior to which much panic ensued getting things ready.

Operations were not curtailed due to the visit, and most of the pilots flew shipping or interception patrols. Bill took-off at 13.00 hours, piloting Hurricane, BN109, coded "P", for a combined air test (of his guns) and patrol. He climbed to 12,000' and headed west of Tripoli Harbor. On the return leg of his patrol, he air tested his guns, by firing off all the ammunition and later recording two stoppages.

He had just landed back from his mission when the Squadron's Bristol Blenheim hack aircraft touched down. An officer, looking very smart in his best blues (No.1 uniform) with pilot's "wings", emerged from the machine.

Bill looked at the distinguished figure and recognized the face, but momentarily could not place the officer, then suddenly realized that it was Flying Officer "Gravy" Graves!! Bill was so used to seeing his colleague dressed in a dust covered battle dress blouse etc., that he did not recognize him.

Graves had not returned to the unit empty-handed, for on the Blenheim were a number of crates of beer, which needless to say gave an excuse for a drinking session of immense proportions that evening.

Although little was said about the visit of the A.O.C. in C, word had obviously got around about the arrival of the beer, for during the course of the drinking session, the Squadron members were visited by a Group Captain, two Wing Commanders and a Squadron Leader.

"It's a fountain, not a motor pool!"

Saturday, 20th February 1943

Easy day, supposed to be flying to Berka
(Benghasi) in our Blenheim, with George Caen
and the Adjutant, but the Blenheim
is u/s, so had no flying for [the] first time this month.
Applied for an interview with the C.O.

Two days after his application Bill was granted an interview with the C.O., where the former put forward his application for a commission. The C.O. discussed the topic with Flight Sergeant Marsh and concluded the meeting by confirming that he would recommend the N.C.O. for a commission.

That evening Bill Marsh, the officer elect, was instructed to attend a lecture given by the Adjutant regarding the Air Force procedures for would-be officers, King's Regulations and other "useful" items of information.

The next day, 23rd February, Bill visited the Orderly Room, where he was given a number of forms to fill in, sixteen sheets of paper in all, regarding his application.

With true British bureaucracy, the RAF demanded that the application for a commission be made in quadruplicate.

Feeling somewhat fed up with all the paperwork, and indignant about a remark made by Flight Sergeant Carter, the entry in Bill's journal for that day read. . .

. . .Spent all afternoon filling the damn things in. .
.Nick Carter [found] that I left school the year before
he started!!

Wednesday, 24th February 1943

Filled in another stack of forms.
Nick Carter's father turned-up.

The quest for a commission seemed to be a never ending task to Bill, as he was instructed to fill in another batch of forms, which necessitated two more visits to the Orderly Room. One can only imagine the thoughts going through his mind.

Flight Sergeant Carter, who three weeks earlier had visited Tripoli in the hope of finding his father, was delighted when the latter arrived at the base to see his son.

Carter Senior, who had been into battle with the 7th Armored Division, was sporting two new stripes on each sleeve of his army battledress blouse, having been promoted to the rank of Corporal.

The Squadron said farewell to Flight Lieutenant Bob Sarll who, through sickness, was

A few 'home' comforts? The wall behind the pilots bar.

being posted to a ground appointment at Air Headquarters, Air Defenses, Eastern Mediterranean.

The next day almost proved somewhat expensive for the Squadron, as Bill recorded in his journal.

Thursday, 25th February 1943

Sergeant George Caldwell [from] Warrington, doing some very nice slow rolls on the circuit, touched down with a drift on and broke the starboard oleo [undercarriage leg], and skidded to rest safely.

The Hurricane, HV974, coded "Y", which Bill thought of as a "nice kite" sustained Category 1 damage.

In making an entry relating to his friend Guy Bickford-Smith, who due to his double-barreled surname was known as "Shotgun", Bill continued. . .

. . ."Shotgun" Smith, flying Hurricane, BP319, at dawn, was very shaken by an internal glycol leak which caused him to make a "dead stick" landing. [He] fortunately had enough height to make base.

Later in the morning Bill flew on a convoy patrol, which had a sequel to the above story. In conclusion of the day's events, he wrote. . .

> . . .*Took-off in [Hurricane] "N" at 11.30 hours, and flew top cover with "Shotgun", over convoy preparing to move off east, after only four days for turnabout. [We] patrolled at 14,000', but "Shotgun" had to pancake (land) early, he had only three gallons of fuel left. I still had a full reserve tank!*

Friday, 26th February 1943

> *Morning off; afternoon at readiness – no harbor patrol.*
> *Scrambled to 25,000' west of Tripoli.*
> *I could have been off the deck in 1 1/2 minutes, did in fact get off in 2, but Barker had finger trouble and took 2.75 [minutes], then lost me on circuit.*
> *We 50 miles north of Tripoli, at 27,000', alone and saw nothing.*

On his return from his "solo" patrol, Bill was informed there had been a mid-air collision whilst he was away.

It transpired that Flight Sergeant Sutherland, RCAF, and Sergeant George Caldwell had taken-off, as a three aircraft formation, with Flying Officer Graves, for a practice flying and shadow firing exercise. Bill recorded the circumstances of the crash as they were told to him.

> . . .*[They] had taken-off just before I was scrambled, to do practice attacks on an A.S.R. Wimpey (Wellington Bomber). It seems that "Suds" (Flt Sgt Sutherland) attacked first, pulled up into the sun, then George Caldwell followed, and didn't see "Suds" until the last second and so could not avoid him. Caldwell's machine "T" had its tail chewed off by "Suds'" propeller and since they were only at 1,800', though Caldwell was probably knocked out, "T" spun right in and exploded. "Suds" in "S" was dazed, having been thrown against the reflector gun sight and cut his chin, but managed to keep control and force-landed, wheels up but into wind amongst some rough sandhills.*

The Hurricane force-landed approximately 150 yards from the shore line, touching the ground one wingtip first. The machine pivoted round, the force of the gyration throwing the pilot out of the cockpit.

The Squadron, alerted to the emergency, swung into action, as the entry in Bill's journal continues. . .

> *. . .Search and first aid parties set off by air, land and sea. "Chick" flew over and reported "Suds" lying on the wing waving. The Doc on his jeep was able to reach the crash site and soon after the air sea rescue launch picked them up and returned to Tripoli.*
>
> *I was duty pilot, so [I was] kept in touch fairly well.*

Flight Lieutenant Austen Clough-Camm, the Medical Officer, obviously known to everybody as "Doc", returned from Tripoli at lunch time the following day. He brought with him the news that Flight Sergeant Sutherland had cracked vertebrae in the lower back and would be in plaster for some months, but would make a full recovery in due time

Sunday, 28th February 1943

Heard that some 417 RCAF Spits due to arrive.

Having spent the previous evening printing three rolls of film, Bill was in a photographic frame of mind when he heard that some Royal Canadian Air Force Spitfires were due to land at 14.00 hours.

Armed with his camera he set off for the landing strip to await their arrival, in the hope of adding more photographs to his collection.

At 14.30 hours, the Spitfires made an appearance, but not even Bill was ready for what was to follow.

The first aircraft came in on a final approach, attempted to land, but decided to overshoot and go round again. The second Spitfire undershot off a climbing approach, struck a barrel and lost its starboard wheel. The aircraft pancaked, and came to a stop fairly quickly without injury to the pilot. The rest of the Squadron came into land without further incident.

During the previous week, on 27th February, some two cannon, MkIIC Hurricanes were ferried to Mellaha from Misurata for use by No.274 Squadron.

The first opportunity that Flight Sergeant Marsh got to fly one, and test its fire power came on the first day of the new month.

Monday, 1st March 1943

*Up at 05.30 for dawn readiness. Supposed
to be no patrol, but Control ordered me
off at 06.35 – told me to pancake at 08.00.
After breakfast did a cannon test on "T",
got nothing first flip, starboard gun fired all
ammo second time
After lunch with F/O Graves, Nick, self
and Barker on practice formation and cannon
tests. Only starboard gun fired again!!*

The practice formation and cannon tests only lasted an hour, and Bill and the others were back on the ground by 15.25.

Following a quick debriefing, the pilots discarded their flying kit and prepared to visit Flight Sergeant Sutherland. Although a whole group of them went, including Bill, only two people at a time were allowed around "Suds'" bed.

On his return to Mellaha, Bill took the opportunity of catching up with some correspondence, and wrote a number of letters before attending a "lecture" by the C.O.

Later Bill wrote in his journal. . .

*. . .Pep talk by the C.O. on airmanship and the
necessity for NOT pranging. In February, 19 machines
pranged or needed engine changes.*

Needless to say, some pilots were more guilty of this crime than others!!

Further cannon firing test flights were made over the next couple of days, but the outcome left Bill in some doubt as to the suitability of these weapons. Sometimes they fired, sometimes they didn't and sometimes only one gun would fire!!

Wednesday, 3rd March 1943

This day, 12 months gone, did my first op. with the Squadron!

The highlight of the day, on Bill's first anniversary with No.274 Squadron, was the unexpected arrival of an American P-38 Lightning, which according to Bill's journal caused quite a panic. . .

*. . .Big Flap. A Lockheed Lightning on the circuit,
so all rushed down to see. Landed o.k. A Yank looking*

The first overshot, the second crashed and the third . . . ?

*for Castel Benito! He took off – after I got three snaps,
and did a shoot-up. It climbs like a 109, first Allied
plane I've seen which can.*

Thursday, 4th March 1943

*Started watering around my new province,
the home farm. Mainly a matter of working
the irrigation systems properly.*

Although it was some four years since Bill had had anything to do with seeds, vegetables or plants, the "veteran" desert flyer was not adverse to trying his hand again at growing things.

The skills he had learned from his father, combined with the experience he gained both at Lathom Vale Nurseries and Clucas Seeds, had not been lost. He knew the answer to a successful garden or allotment, in desert soil, was a matter of good irrigation.

He chose an area of open ground, close to his billet on Mellaha airfield, surrounded by palm trees, where the seedlings and plants could benefit from both sun and shade. When time allowed, in his off-duty periods, he set out the irrigation channels and prepared the ground of the plot he was to call "Home Farm."

During the afternoon, Bill was detailed for flying practice with Flight Sergeant Syd Barker, of whose flying skills he was not totally impressed. Bill entered his thoughts in his journal later that same day, when he wrote. . .

*. . .Chasing and being chased by the docile Syd
Barker, who makes some fair attempts when warmed
up. [He] did one upward roll o.k., but then tried another one and spun.*

Lockheed Lightning, serial 2366, with long range tanks.

Whilst many are happy to view from a distance . . .

An Entertainment National Service Association concert party arrived on the base at 18.00 hours, with a view to providing a show that night.

An improvised stage was set up and, after tea, the show entitled "Hello Happiness" commenced. Bill thought the show very good, and thoroughly enjoyed the sight of Flight Lieutenant Appleford being rebuked by a young lady by the name of Bonnie Downes.

The officer had apparently been talking all through the young lady's act and she, obviously, took exception to this. Finally, Bonnie Downes looked straight at Flight Lieutenant Appleford and informed him that there was a dead mouse under his nose. This was a deadly insult to the Squadron's mightiest mustachio!!

After the show a very rowdy party developed, which culminated in somebody firing a revolver at the ornamental fountain, in which Bickford-Smith had recently parked a truck!

Two promotions were announced on Saturday, 6th March, when Flight Sergeant "Red" Harrington was commissioned to the rank of Pilot Officer and Flight Sergeant Cooper, RCAF, was made up to Warrant Officer.

Consoling himself that his name was not on the promotions list, Flight Sergeant Marsh divided his time over the next three days between flying convoy patrols and gardening.

However, on the morning of the 7th March, the weather took over and lent Bill a hand. It relieved him of the duty of irrigation by raining. He was however able to get back into his garden that evening.

Monday, 8th March 1943

*Nice quiet morning. Jackie Neil
[now] Pilot Officer, back from
Cairo – blue uniform looks o.k.
but is a bit shoddy (rough).
Readiness in the afternoon, then*

. . . Paling (right) and P/O McElhanney get a close-up view of the cockpit.

flew on harbor patrol with Syd.
Vectored after bogey (hostile
aircraft) at 15,000', but after
trying to locate Syd, who was three
miles away! it turned out to be friendly.

The feeling of disappointment regarding the fact there was still no news of his own commission caused Bill to record a detrimental comment about the appearance of his close friend, Jackie Neil, who had recently received his second promotion with the space of a year!

It was also becoming clear that Bill was losing his patience with Flight Sergeant Syd Barker who was not in close visible contact with his leader when the interception order was received.

Unfortunately Bill had cause to write adverse comment in his journal, again about Barker, the following day.

Tuesday, 9th March 1943

Out at 06.20 on convoy patrol, as top
cover to "Gravy" (F/O Graves). Located
convoy of Ras el Hallat, and went up to
8,000'. Some cloud above 6,000', but not
10/10ths until 9,000'.
Syd calls up (on radio) that his gyro-horizon
is u/s and he cannot follow me
[I] sent the clot (idiot) down to a lower
level, then he said he was joining "Gravy",
but even then he kept a good mile behind!
I have had enough of him.

Wednesday, 10th March 1943

Spent morning cutting cauliflower, got
four dozen. Also cut my finger.

The Squadron benefited from Bill's labors, who proved beyond doubt that he had lost none of his gardening skills, when they were able to add "home" grown fresh vegetables to the menu.

Bill at "Home Farm" his vegetable garden at Mellaha.

F/S "Red" Harrington (left) and F/S Cooper, wearing a RCAF sweatshirt, photographed in the rays of a low desert sun.

Thursday, 11th March 1943

On readiness at 07.15 in my new Mk.IIC
[Hurricane aircraft], coded HW783, – a
four cannon job. Just been ferried from Takoradi.
Did readiness until 10.30, then at 11.15
on convoy patrol [code-named] "Curley",
twelve ships file miles from Tripoli, and
"Nation", a rather large one just leaving
harbor for the east.
During my patrol they (the two convoys)
crossed – very impressive.
Fired my cannons into the sea afterwards -
only one stoppage!
[The] Squadron is almost wholly converted to Mk.IICs now.

Bill's spirits, lifted by the arrival of his new aircraft, was now feeling in a better mood. On return from his patrol, having put his new aircraft through its paces, he spent the afternoon tending to his garden.

He even joined in the party that evening to celebrate both the promotion of Flight Sergeant Connell and Rommel's abortive push on the Matreth Line.

On 6th March, the Axis forces had made a determined attack against the British in Southern Tunisia. However, the assault was unsuccessful and the attacking forces were made to retreat.

In all the Germans lost fifty tanks, captured by the British, over a three day period.

The Kasserine Pass, from which the British had once been forced to retreat, was now also retaken due to a successful combined operation by American and British infantry.

Friday, 12th March 1943

Fine morning, so four Arabs from the cook-house
working in the garden. Their efficiency and skill surprised
me, especially in the weeding and irrigating.
On readiness 12.45 until 15.30, but nothing happened.
Back to my land work again at 16.00, and found
my Arabs still working. The weeds had been
carefully stacked on piece of sacking.
Towards 5.00 pm I was approached on the subject
of "Forage, baksheeth" which I found meant they
wished to cart the weeds home for their cattle,
which explained their assiduous weeding! O.K. with me

The labors of their day being ended, the Arabs took their reward home for their cattle, whilst Bill continued to work for another hour and a half. He watered the plant beds and generally prepared them for transplanting the following day.

Saturday, 13th March 1943

Readiness at 06.15 in "N", with Don Cordrey
as my No.2.
Nothing happened. Back at 08.30
breakfast, then into garden to supervise
irrigation and planting of cauliflower.
Back on readiness at 11.00 until 1.00 pm.
Lot of panic about a dinghy in the sea. . .
. . .last night saw verry lights, reported 15
miles east, 5 miles off-shore, but air sea
rescue Bisley (aircraft) failed to locate
[it] after a three hour search.

Bill's new Mk.IIc Hurricane, coded NH-N.

Early morning readiness.

After lunch, co-operating with RAF High
Speed Launch, and assisted by two sections
of 4 Hurricanes, dinghy was found, contents
4 Germans. Usual stuff (brandy, cigarettes
and blankets) was dropped to them, but
they were picked up before dusk. [The] Boys
say the dinghy had everything except an outboard motor.

Bill was spending as much time as possible in his garden. When not there, he could be found searching for and acquiring, all types of discarded machinery, which he could adapt for use in the garden. To date, he had managed to acquire a water pump, made a plough and found a tractor!

The original plot size had grown immensely and was more then just a means of finding relaxation and peace in a world of turmoil. For some it was becoming a form of punishment.

Monday, 15th March 1943

In the garden at 08.45, detailed plot of land
to be dug by Ashton, who has 7 days hard labor,
supervised by [the] Orderley Corporal.

Wednesday 17th March 1943

[During the] afternoon went to see about
my tractor, got it filled with M.T. fuel and
started it up; suffered from misfiring and loss of power,
but found out how to drive it. It has caterpillar tracks
and is steered tank-wise.
Later showed the Commanding Officer around garden.
He says that [the] cost of extra messing
which we get free from the garden would be
2/6 (50 cents) per man per day.
Yet I get very little co-operation, only Mabbs as voluntary assistant.

As Bill got more engrossed in his garden, it seemed as if the desert flyer was fast becoming the desert gardener. The entry for 18th March almost forgetting the war.

Thursday, 18th March 1943

Up early again and in the garden after breakfast -

Learning to drive the tractor.

spent all morning at it. Some Arabs, feeding cattle in a
pasture near the garden, asked for old cabbage leaves -
eventually [I] organized them into a cleaning-up and
weeding squad! At 11.00 o'clock I was approached
by a deputation of Ities (Italian PoWs),
one of whom had lived [for] 15 years in the States
and spoke fair Yank!
Seems they can get hold of a diesel motor
and water pump combined – if we can get permission.
F/O. Hands got some seeds for me at a flower shop in Tripoli.
On readiness at 12.45, flew at 2 o'clock,
bounced McElhanney!
After tea took the tractor to "B" Flight -
an hour journey, almost. Went better backwards!!
They will have a look over it for me
A Spit (Spitfire) landed without flaps, [it]
rolled on and on and came to rest against
another Spit in a hanger. [The] pilot forgot
to use his flaps!

The fact that the war was still being fought was brought home, literally, to Bill and his colleagues during the evening of the following day.

At 18.40 hours, just as some of Bill's "home" grown vegetables were being served with the evening meal, the Luftwaffe arrived. Bill recorded in his journal. . .

> . . .*the noise of several aircraft flying low past the mess gave rise to some speculation, especially as the rain clouds were down to 500'.*
>
> *Within a minute the sound of bombs exploding caused us to evacuate the mess. We then saw the most daring low level attack we have yet seen, carried out by ten aircraft, of which we saw one Heinkel IIIK, two Ju 88s (one of which strafed the beach on the way out) and a Dornier 217.*
>
> *The first three of the formation of six [aircraft] which made the initial attack were shot down, but at least two ships, a tanker and an ammo boat [in the harbor] were hit. Fire burning all night.*

> *Saturday, 20th March 1943*

> *[After] a quick lunch, took-off to relieve Red Section. Sent to north-west of harbor, then 10 miles west at 12,000'. There "intercepted" a Spitfire and, soon after, a Beaufighter. Pancaked (landed) to learn that "Gravy" and Bickford-Smith had a Ju 88 come in over the harbor.*

Flight Lieutenant Graves and Sergeant Bickford-Smith took-off at 12.35, with orders to carry out a patrol over Tripoli harbor. They were not long into their mission when the ground controller informed them there was a hostile aircraft in their vicinity and ordered them to climb to an altitude of 20,000'.

Searching the skies as they gained height, Flight Lieutenant Graves reported the intruder, a Ju 88, flying at 24,000'. The two RAF fighters gave chase, with Graves leading. The enemy aircraft altered course, towards a cloudbank, but Graves was determined it would not get away. He opened fire with several bursts of cannon fire from a distance of 600 yards, followed closely by Bickford-Smith. Thick black smoke began to emit from the port engine. The Ju 88 peeled over and dived down, it was last seen entering the relevant safety of the clouds.

Not having seen the final outcome of their endeavors, the German aircraft was claimed only as a damaged.

Sunday, 21st March 1943

*On readiness 07.20 and did a harbor
patrol at 08.40 – Doc brought breakfast down
[to dispersal] in a jeep.
Two convoys, the first a gunboat supposed to be
going to shell Sfax tonight; the second I
covered on the harbor patrol as
it headed west from Tripoli.
Landed and went on readiness again in "Y",
took-off at 11.50 to cover the second convoy.
Found them 7 miles off Zuara. Kept R.T. (radio)
silence, expect to "o.k." to pancake (land) order from base.
Afternoon in garden, getting seed beds ready
and planting more tomatoes.
At 5.00 pm, an Air Sea rescue Walrus came in here.
F/Lt Wade and F/O Collingridge visited us at night.*

Flight Lieutenant Bob Sarll who, a month previously had been posted to a ground appointment due to sickness, returned to the Squadron on 22nd March, looking fit and well.

Tuesday, 23rd March 1943

MY BIRTHDAY

*Nothing out of the ordinary. Quiet morning,
most of which I spent in the garden. At midday,
[I was] standing outside "ops" tent waiting for Syd Barker
to return from a convoy. He had called-up that his engine
was u/s and that he was landing.
Tommy Matthews took off and replaced him.
Barker came into the circuit wheels down, then
lifted them, did a rate 1/2 turn out to sea,
and started back east. He soon came back and did
one of his usual Blind Approach Landings.
He came into "ops" saying, "I am a clot" (idiot)
and proved it by explaining that, having taken-off
with some flap down, he had lifted the flaps instead of
his wheels (undercarriage), so naturally could
not keep up a reasonable boost. He assumed his*

engine was duff (u/s) and called up for a relief.
[Barker] discovered his boob (mistake) when trying to lower
the wheels to land.

Unfortunately for Syd Barker, the Officer Commanding had been watching the whole incident and, when the former had finished his explanation, the O.C. took him to one side and had a few choice words with the offending pilot.

Bill's birthday did not go unnoticed. No.274 Squadron boasted an excelled Czechoslovakian chef by the name of Jack Herzcovitz, who spent the day making and icing a surprise birthday cake for Bill, and presented it to the latter later in the day.

Wednesday, 24th March 1943

Out in the garden at 08.00. At 09.30
got organized for a trip into Tripoli.

As on Thursday, 18th March, the war for Bill seemed to take second place to the garden.

Accompanied by Flight Lieutenant Graves, a corporal from the Royal Engineers and an Italian engineer who knew where to find a diesel pumping set, Bill set off on an expedition to the Royal Engineer's Depot, situated three miles from the base.

The R.E. Depot had a number of English made diesel pumps, in which Bill was interested. However, he found to his dismay that he would have to officially apply for permission from Colonel Topham, C.R.E., Tripolitania, in order to acquire one!

Jack Herzcovitz with Bill's birthday cake.

Bill did not really want to do this and decided to let the matter rest for the time being.

On the return journey, Bill asked the driver to stop in Tripoli, where he and "Gravy" Graves visited the Cao. Angelo Finocchiario Seed Store in the Piazza Italia.

After a lot of haggling and bargaining, Bill purchased 50 grams each of carrot seeds, beet, lettuce and radish, together with over 200 cucumber seeds. If nothing else, Bill and his squadron colleagues would eat well, in time

The nearest that Flight Sergeant Marsh got to the war that day was on his return to base, when he spent one hour, twenty minutes on standby, strapped into the cockpit of Hurricane "N."

The standby duty was followed by a lecture on the German Dornier 217, given by Flying Officer "Spy" Hands. Not that he found it boring, but Bill found it difficult to stay awake during the talk.

Thursday, 25th March 1943

Red Harrington and Lyle intercepted a Ju 88.

Flying at 25,000', Pilot Officer Harrington and Sergeant Hedley Lyle intercepted a German Ju 88 directly over Tripoli. As they started their attack the enemy aircraft turned across in front of them, at a range of 500 yards, and went into a dive.

At that moment, the ground defenses took action and, due to the accurate ack-ack fire, the two Hurricane pilots were forced to relinquish the chase.

Although he was scrambled at 10.40 hours, with orders to patrol the harbor area, Bill was instructed to land five minutes after taking off.

Having been released Bill naturally made straight for the garden, where he tried to repair the pumping plant which had gone u/s. Having "struggled" with it for some time, he decided to leave it to the more experienced hands of the Royal Engineers. Instead he got on with some ploughing, aided by his voluntary assistant Mabbs and watched by the Officer Commanding!

The evening was spent in belated birthday celebration for Bill, due to the arrival on the Squadron of copious amounts of Sherry and Cognac!

Saturday, 27th March 1943

. . .invaded by caterpillars. . .

The entry in Bill's journal referred not to an attack by the Axis Forces, but to an invasion by the enemy of all gardeners – caterpillars, which were attacking his tomato plants. Needless to say he was not pleased, and expressed concern that they would threaten the west side of the garden.

Tripoli Harbor, with camouflaged shipping.

However, Bill found that not every enemy is a natural foe. Making use of his knowledge of the French language, Bill was able to converse with an Italian, who was trying to repair the defective pump. They chatted for some time and Bill was amazed, after they had parted, at the many expression of goodwill between them; and reflected that only a short while ago they were enemies.

After much fierce fighting, and overthrowing the German rear-guard action, the British Eighth Army captured Mareth and Matmata on 28th March, thus allowing the latter to take the whole of the Mareth Line.

Monday, 29th March 1943

Up at 04.30, took-off at first light with
Syd Barker . . . a shufti (reconnaissance)
88 over harbor . . . Doc's birthday. . .

Flight Sergeant Marsh rose at 04.30 hours and prepared himself for the first shipping patrol of the day, which he was to undertake with Sergeant Barker as his wingman. Having taken-off at 05.30 hours, it was not long into the patrol before Syd Barker advised his leader that he was returning to base with an electrical failure. Apart from losing his wingman yet again, Bill had nothing to report when he landed one hour and twenty minutes later.

After breakfast, the desert flyer put on his gardening hat and spent an hour ploughing with his tractor, prior to attending another lecture by the I.O., "Spy" Hands. The particular talk being on the Savoia-Marchetti SM79, 81 82 and 84 Italian aircraft. It was also the last official duty undertaken by Flying Officer Hands, who had been posted to No.210 Group, with a promotion to Flight Lieutenant.

The new Intelligence Officer, Pilot Officer Chawnor, was to report for duty with No.274 Squadron later in the day.

At 12.15 hours, a German Ju 88 reconnaissance aircraft was reported over Tripoli Harbor at 24,000'.

Flight Lieutenant Sarll and Flight Sergeant Berryman, who had recently returned from leave, were on patrol in the vicinity, and spotted the intruder five miles away. They radioed "tally-ho", the recognition call-sign given by the British fighter pilots to signify they 'have sighted the enemy, and proceeded to give chase.

However, as happened a few days previously, the ground defenses opened-up with a ring of ack-ack fire, before the Hurricanes could close the distance.

They withdrew and watched the enemy aircraft dive down through the ring of ground fire, to an altitude of approximately 12,000', before pulling out over the sea and making good its escape.

Flight Lieutenant Clough-Camm, the Medical Officer, celebrated his birthday by taking tea and cakes at teatime, with Bill and one or two of the other pilots. However, at the birthday dinner that evening, Bill was rather skeptical that the meal served was in fact chicken as stated!

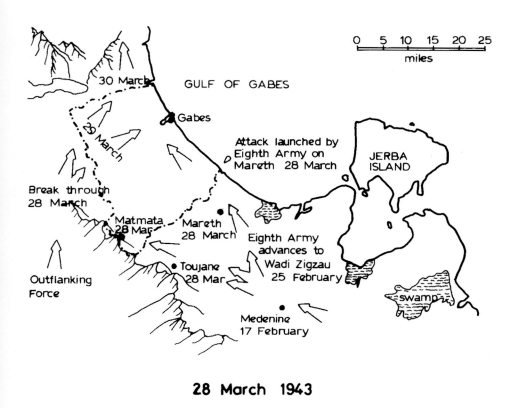

28 March 1943

On 30th March 1943, the R.A.F. used "tank-busting" aircraft to bomb and strafe enemy tanks and artillery positions, in some of the heaviest aerial support since the North African campaign commenced. The attack, which lasted nearly three hours without a break, caused the collapse of the German resistance at El Hamma, to the west of Gabes.

Over the last few days the Allies had taken over 10,000 prisoners.

Tuesday, 30th March 1943

Took-off in "T" for harbor patrol
with Syd Barker, as always

With Syd Barker flying as his wingman, Bill took-off during the afternoon for a harbor patrol, at 12,000'.

Little was happening and, as there were no reports of enemy aircraft in the area, Bill took the opportunity to engage in mock dog-fights with Barker.

Both aircraft were carrying cine-gun cameras, and the leader used his on his wingman, shooting off some thirty seconds of film.

Most of the time, Bill experienced a problem in getting on Barker's tail, the latter smartly turning into the sun each time his leader tried the maneuver. However, in taking the evasive action he did, Barker kept losing sight of Bill Marsh's aircraft. This in turn allowed the more experienced pilot to bounce his wingman on each occasion.

Wednesday, 31st March 1943

P/O George Meldrum back from leave.
He saw "Suds."

The newly promoted George Meldrum returned from leave in Cairo with the news that he had been to visit Flight Sergeant "Suds" Sutherlands, who was still in Aberswoir Hospital after his recent mid-air collision.

Meldrum reported that Sutherland was very happy and on the mend, adding that "Suds" could shuffle about on his legs, but had a wheelchair in which to dash about! It was hoped that full use of both legs and feet would be gained in due time

In the meantime, No.274 Squadron would have to continue the war without "Suds."

CHAPTER FOURTEEN

Victory in the Desert

Thursday, 1st April 1943

Up at 08.30 and had breakfast before
going into the garden.

Being no fool, Bill Marsh did not raise from his bed until 08.30 hours on April Fool's Day; the rest probably doing him good.

After breakfast, as he was not flying, Bill went down to the garden to check out the caterpillar invasion. There, to his amazement and annoyance he found an invasion of another sort, a group of Arabs plundering the bottom end of the garden.

Gesticulating and shouting, he chased them out and then went to inspect the damage. Unfortunately, some of those he chased out were hired help, and showed their contempt by not turning up for work later in the day, thus leaving Bill to do everything himself.

Something else that upset Bill during the day was the news of the impending arrival of an Aircraft Repair Unit at Mellaha.

Being a non-combatant unit, the ARU would most certainly take over most of the buildings on the base, including the hangers, office buildings and billets. The latter meaning that No.274 personnel would be forced back into living in tents!

Bill hoped that the incoming unit would not be able to take the Pilot's Mess, as that was off the camp, but he could see the Sergeant's Mess being commandeered. The final line on the subject in his journal read . . .

. . .I foresee trouble. . .

The only thing that amused Bill on April Fool's Day was the arrival on the base of a Spitfire Mk.IX. The pilot, who had taken-off from England three days earlier, had spent some time in Algiers before arriving at Mellaha. Having landed at the latter, the pilot admitted later that he cautiously looked around for swastikas before taxiing in. He was apparently on his way to Malta, but could not find it! The point of Bill's amusement was that both the pilot and the aircraft were from an R.A.F. Photo-Reconnaissance Unit!!

Bill wrote in his journal. . .

> *. . .he took-off [this] afternoon for*
> *Castel Benito – hope he finds it. . .*

The following day, a situation arose which made Flight Sergeant Marsh very annoyed.

Friday, 2nd April 1943

Up at 04.30, down to "ops" 05.15 for readiness.

In contrast to the previous day, Bill got up at 04.30 hours and reported for duty in the "ops" room at 05.15.

He had only been there fifteen minutes when the first intimation of a convoy patrol came through, but Flight Lieutenant Sarll decided he would fly the mission. Bill gave way to the Officer, but within minutes it became evident that there was a second convoy.

Gathering his flying kit, Bill made his way out to his aircraft, closely followed by his wing-man Sergeant Barker. The pair took-off at 05.55 hours and, after an uneventful patrol, landed back at Mellaha just over an hour later.

On arriving at the mess for his breakfast, Bill found a very bad atmosphere prevailing, caused apparently by his unparalleled error. He was told to report back to "ops" where the Flight Controller ordered him to stay on readiness for an hour or more in case a section of aircraft had to be scrambled.

Having completed his "detention" period, Bill attended a lecture on the Focke-Wulf Fw 200 German aircraft. It was here he found out he was being accused, by the Flight Controller (behind his back) of being late off earlier that morning. By now Bill was feeling very annoyed and returned to the "ops" room to tackle the F.C. where he was amazed to hear his opponent say "Forget it, old chap."

A friendly face calmed Bill down, when Flight Sergeant Bernard Ott, the SAAF pilot who landed on his head after parachuting out of his crippled Hurricane, arrived on a visit.

Ott was serving with No.3 Repair and Salvage Unit where, he told Bill, he was stagnating following a crash-landing in a Spitfire when the Air Officer Commanding was present!

Chapter 14: Victory in the Desert

Sunday, 4th April 1943

. . .general mess meeting. . .

The C.O. gave a short speech at a general mess meeting, announcing the separating of the Pilots Mess into Officers and NCOs.

An election was held to decide on a committee for adjustment and finance and property, the result of which found Flying Officer Graves, Pilot Officer Meldrum, Warrant Officer Cooper and Flight Sergeant Marsh elected as representatives.

Bill and W.O. Cooper immediately called a meeting of the NCO pilots which concluded with the agreement that they (the NCO pilots) would live in the sick quarter buildings, eat in the Sergeants Mess and have their own separate bar as a form of Pilot's Club. This also found favor, when put to him, with the Commanding Officer.

Monday, 5th April 1943

Moving Day. . .to orderly room with Graves, Meldrum and Cooper to settle on [position of] partitions.

The decisions made the previous day at the meeting regarding the splitting of the mess were put into practice when the elected committee representatives agreed a layout plan for the accommodation.

Leaving others to undertake the practical work, Bill made his way to "Ops" Control, where he reported for duty. Being on readiness, he climbed into his Hurricane, strapped himself in and waited for the order to scramble. His task, when the order came through, was to carry out the usual harbor patrol.

The mission, which lasted one and a half hours, was much the same as always, without incident and with nothing to report on landing.

Having completed his operational task, Bill attended a lecture on the Messerschmitt 110 and Me 210., maybe to "refresh" his memory as to what a Messerschmitt looked like; not having seen one for a while.

With the help of Flight Lieutenant "Doc" Clough-Camm, Bill spent the later afternoon getting settled into his new quarters, and generally organizing his creature comforts. He reflected on the thought that if he were an officer, most of his creature comforts would, to some degree, be taken care of. It did not help when Bill heard that Nick Carter had been promoted to the rank of Warrant Officer. The former wrote in his journal. . .

. . .Nick Carter's Warrant Officer came through! Boy, am I sweating on mine. . ."

Tuesday, 6th April 1943

Afternoon to Officer's Mess to collect our half of mess property.

The dividing up of the mess property continued during the afternoon, following the conclusion of two operational missions on which Bill was detailed to participate.

Another Mess Adjustment Meeting was held, with all the fine details being discussed, including the examination of the mess Balance Sheets. Instead of being the separation of officers and NCOs, the situation was more like the end of a marriage!

However, the pilots did not let the situation depress them, when Bill got back to the billets he found a rowdy drinking session going on. When Sergeant Tommy Matthews passed out, the party continued on around him!

Thursday, 8th April 1943

[In] evening developed my Super XX film, which came out excellently.

Having completed his turn at readiness and flown the obligatory harbor patrol during the day, Bill relaxed by spending part of the evening developing some films. He was extremely pleased with the results, which included a time exposure photograph of the British ack-ack firing into the night sky over Tripoli.

Friday, 9th April 1943

C.O. called Barker and myself into Orderly Room, tore me off a strip.

The day got off to a bad start for Flight Sergeant Marsh, and did not get much better as it progressed. Having risen from his slumber at 08.30, Bill had breakfast and then attended a lecture on the Focke-Wulf Fw 190. Immediately following the talk, Bill and Sergeant Barker were instructed to report to the C.O. They were ushered into the Orderly Room where Major Wells proceeded to reprimand them both.

The nature of their crime turned out to be that on Wednesday, 7th April, whilst scrambling for a harbor patrol they had taken-off down wind. As if this was not bad enough, the crime was augmented by the fact that the Wing Commander Flying was watching the whole episode.

Being the leader of the section, Flight Sergeant Marsh was held responsible and punished by given extra nights as Duty Pilot.

Much to his annoyance, Bill's name was removed from the duty roster for a convoy patrol at 10.00 hours; his place being taken by the C.O.! Instead, the errant pilot found he was detailed for readiness duty over the lunch period, an action he felt was deliberately planned as an extra part of his punishment; being strapped into his aircraft and going no-where.

It was 13.30 hours before he finally took-off, upwind, with Tommy Matthews as his No.2., to carry out the usual unexciting harbor patrol. However, when he returned to base, Bill found he had been detailed for another hours duty at readiness!

During the day, Flight Lieutenant Sarll returned from a patrol without his wingman, Don Cordrey, which immediately gave cause for concern.

It transpired that the loss of Flight Sergeant Cordrey was not due to enemy action, but a crash-landing caused by engine failure. The pilot was reported as being o.k., but the air-craft was a write-off.

Saturday, 10th April 1943

Gales blowing from north west and lots of low cloud. Very bumpy too.

Having got up at 05.00 hours, Bill reported for duty and was sent straight out on a convoy patrol.

The weather was atrocious, with gales blowing and low cloud racing across the turbu-lent sea, on which the sixteen ships of the convoy and their six Royal Navy escort ships were being tossed about.

It was not only the ships that found a problem making headway, Hurricane NH-N was also being tossed about in the air making its pilot feel quite ill.

On his return to base at 07.30, Bill made his way to the mess but found he could not look at food, let alone eat it. He returned to his billet and went to bed, where "Doc" Clough-Camm visited him a short while later. The M.O. advised Bill to stay in bed all day, and most certainly until he felt better.

During the afternoon, the sick pilot received some news that certainly went some way to making him feel slightly better. He was informed that he was to report to the Wing Commander on Tuesday, 13th April for an interview concerning his application for a com-mission.

The other news that cheered him up was that Hedley Lyle was to relieve Bill of being Duty Pilot that night and the next two nights! Apparently, whilst taxiing his Hurricane from a standing position, Sergeant Lyle had swung his aircraft round and struck an accumulator trolley with the tailplane of his machine; hence three nights as Duty Pilot!

Sunday, 11th April 1943

Still not very well, but up and about.
[I] didn't fly all day, but kept busy with various small matters.

Monday, 12th April 1943

Did a harbor patrol early, then after
breakfast [attended] a lecture.
Got scrambled at 11.55

Having flown a non-eventful patrol earlier in the morning, Bill and his wingman, Flight Sergeant Barker, were given a scramble order at 11.55 hours. Due to the latter experiencing some form of "finger" trouble in the cockpit, Bill took-off alone.

Hurricane HW659, coded NH-H, climbed out of Mellaha and headed north, gaining height to 24,000'. It then turned onto a compass heading of 170 degrees and continued to climb. After reaching an altitude of 28,000', at a distance of approximately seven miles from the base, Bill was informed that a bandit aircraft was ten miles east of his present position.

Using his radio call sign of "Blue One", Bill repeated the information back to the ground controller, in order to confirm the information. As he did so, he glanced ahead and saw the bursting black balls of exploding ack-ack fire over Tripoli, with a Ju 88 flying straight through the middle of it!

Pushing the "stick" gently forward, Flight Sergeant Marsh put the Hurricane into a slight dive towards the enemy machine, but as he did so the Ju 88 turned and headed towards him. It continued in a head-on attitude, passing very quickly beneath him and going down in a steep diving turn.

The chase was on, and "Blue One" fired a three second burst, from 400 yards, in a quarter astern attack. Black smoke issued from one of the engines. Bill fired another three second burst, but saw no strikes on this occasion, neither was there any return fire.

Although he had full power on, the Hurricane was losing ground to the bandit aircraft as it slowly began to increase the distance between them. The Hurricane was flying at 260 mph, with 13lbs of boost and 3,000 revs on the clock, but still Bill could not catch his quarry!

As the Ju 88 headed north at sea level, flying so low that it created a wake on the surface of the sea, items of equipment were jettisoned from it. The Hurricane pilot noticed splashes and yellow "packages" floating in the water and drew encouragement from this.

From a range of 800 yards distance, he lined-up the German aircraft in his sights in a last desperate attempt to bring down the intruder. Bill took careful aim and opened fire – and one solitary round of ammunition issued from the port outer gun!!

It was as he gave up the chase, and turned his aircraft on a heading for home, that Bill realized that he had been flying his Hurricane on maximum boost for half an hour, instead of the prescribed ten minutes!! It was a wonder the Merlin engine had not blown up.

The British Eighth Army continued to gain ground, having captured the port of Sfax on 10th April, they advanced further north and entered Sousse on 12th April. The latter was taken without any opposition, but the enemy had destroyed all the dock installations in what was Tunisia's third largest port.

Tuesday, 13th April 1943

Interview for commission with G/C Grandi.

Still chasing his hopes for a commission, Bill headed into Tripoli during the course of the morning for another interview, which he felt went quite well.

He also visited the No.24 Medical Receiving Station, where various medical tests were carried out to check his health. The eye sight test which had to be performed by a specialist was scheduled for another occasion. Another agonizing delay!

Thursday, 15th April 1943

Off again to 24 MRS at 10 a.m. to see eye specialist.

The final medical test which Bill had been waiting for came on the morning of the 15th April, at 10.00 hours, two long days after his medical. It was followed by a second interview with the Wing Commander, and meeting with the Officer Commanding, No.24 Medical Receiving Station, when all the final documents were signed.

Friday, 16th April 1943

[During the] afternoon two new Sgts arrived.

Sergeant A.K. Ford and Sergeant C.R. Furtney, two new "rookie" pilots arrived on the Squadron during the course of the afternoon. There was some consternation as to where they were going to be billeted, as the Aircraft Repair Unit had decided to take over the Sergeant Mess! This action forced the sergeant pilots from No.274 Squadron to move into No.417 Squadron's vacant Mess, causing them all to find new billets!

Their new accommodation left a lot to be desired, but Bill, a man for getting things done, organized a scrounging party. He seconded Sergeants Ford and Furtney to accompany him in search of surplus materials, particularly doors, which could be used to improve their new home

The odd one or two things were purchased in Tripoli, but it was amazing what one could find if one looked hard enough, or used a little imagination.

Within a very short space of time, the sergeant pilots had all their creature comforts, including the most important of all, a new Pilot's Bar.

Assisted by two guests, Pilot Officers Neil and Meldrum, an inaugural drinking session started at 17.30 hours and lasted until 23.00 hours.

The fact that Flight Lieutenant Sarll had received a positing (on 18th April) to Air Headquarters Middle East, had no bearing on the reason for the inaugural binge lasting so long.

Tuesday, 20th April 1943

In D.R.O.s a big hand from the A.O.C.

Air Vice Marshall Coningham, via the Daily Routine Orders, congratulated everybody on achieving 1070 hours flying time during March without an avoidance accident. He thought it was a good show and asked them to keep it up.

Friday, 23rd April 1943

Quiet morning, did a convoy patrol at noon in [Hurricane] "Z." Jackie Neil tried to jump us, but got the worst of it.

It may well have been a quiet morning, but things began to liven up during the afternoon, and go into panic state by the evening.

The pilot who had been banished from the Squadron by the Wing Commander for "bending" an airframe, Flight Sergeant Bernard Ott, returned during the course of the afternoon from No.3 Repair and Salvage Unit. He was flown into Mellaha, from Zuara, by Flight Lieutenant Mackay.

Shortly after their arrival, Flight Sergeant Jack Aron returned from leave. Three good excuses, if any were needed, for a drinking session.

However, at 18.30 hours, the proverbial "rocket" went up when the drink got too much for one man.

Leading Aircraftman "Paddy" Holme, an airframe fitter, from "B" Flight groundcrew (mechanics), whilst drunk climbed into the cockpit of Hurricane HL711, coded NH-R and started it up.

He then opened the throttle wide and attempted to take-off, but on seeing some of the rapidly approaching palm trees, must have lost his nerve and heavily applied the brakes. The Hurricane semi-somersaulted onto its nose and the undercarriage collapsed, snapping

The result of Paddy's attempt to fly Hurricane, HR711, coded "R."

the two cannon barrels off the leading edges of the wings. The aircraft came to rest approximately twenty yards from the palm trees, with the cowling covered in oil from its wrecked engine. The aircraft was a write-off!

An oil covered and slightly injured LAC Holme climbed out of the machine and, after some coaxing, was placed into the ambulance by members of the rescue services.

It was whilst he was being examined by the Medical Officer, at Station Sick Quarters (S.S.Q.) that Holme effected an escape. He leapt through a wire-netted window in the examination room, and was away towards the trees which had not long before caused him fear. A search was organized, but he defied capture.

Having recorded the episode in his journal, Bill some time later wrote an addendum which read. . .

> *. . .3 months later, still no further news of Paddy;*
> *He must have sobered up and got clear, perhaps back*
> *to Ireland!*

However, the entry for the following day did impart a little more news implying that "Paddy" Holme had indeed sobered up.

Saturday, 24th April 1943

*Hear that Paddy is on ten charges, but
that in the night he slipped into his
billet and collected his small kit.
He [still] hasn't been seen yet.*

The congratulatory message from AVM Coningham, a couple of weeks previously, regarding avoidable accidents, was rapidly dimming from people's memories, as a second Hurricane was to be written-off within a few days.

Tuesday, 27th April 1943

*Woke up at 08.00, and from the noises
and chatter outside deduced there had
been a prang (landing accident).*

Flight Lieutenant Thompson, D.F.C. of No.601 Squadron, was in the process of taking-off in his Spitfire, when the aircraft struck the windsock.

In the resulting crash, a wing was torn off and the machine disintegrated as it impacted with the dried salt pan ground. The engine broke away and came to rest approximately fifty yards from the main wreckage, whilst the fuselage burst open as it turned over, throwing out the pilot who was still strapped into the seat.

Flight Lieutenant Thompson sustained a displaced knee cap, and cuts to his face; he also suffered a temporary loss of memory.

The latter meant that he did not know where he was or what he was doing. His rescuers therefore informed him that he was in Tripoli during a war. Thompson obviously asked against whom and, on being told the Germans, replied "Good Show"!

The month of May started with a bang, or quite a few in fact, as recorded in Bill's journal.

Saturday, 1st May 1943

All afternoon terrific bangs from explosion.

The cause of the explosions was not an enemy attack, although the shells going off were those of a very recent former opponent.

Some eight miles from Mellaha, at a former Italian ammunition dump, artillery shells were being systematically destroyed. Great mushrooms of black smoke towered into the

The remains of F/L Thompson's Hurricane.

air, reminiscent of battles that took place in the not too distant past, on these same desert sands.

However, the opinion that the destruction of the dump had got out of hand was strengthened, when the noise continued well into the night.

One particularly large explosion caused Jack Aron to take evasive action, and in doing so dislodged Bill's mirror from its stand. The mirror, 48"x18" in size, crashed to the ground and smashed. Seven years bad luck for someone??

Clearing the Axis Forces bombs and mines.

Evidence of a number of changes was in the air, both generally and particularly within No.274 Squadron.

To begin with, the weather had changed and was now becoming unbearably oppressive and sticky, thus affecting the pilots and their flying conditions.

Secondly, equipment, conditions and personnel changes were being implemented.

Sunday, 2nd May 1943

On readiness at 05.00 till 08.00.
Still this oppressive sticky heat.
Hear that "Red" Harrington may solo in a Spit. today.

Being strapped into the cockpit of a fighter, waiting for the order to scramble was, paradoxically, almost as draining for the pilots as the physical effort required when dog-fighting. Especially when the desert sun was rising and getting warmer by the minute, making everything that its rays fell upon hot to the touch.

Flight Sergeant Marsh was by now an experienced desert flyer, he knew the cockpit layout of the Hurricane blindfold. The position of every instrument, dial, knob and lever was immediately to hand. When the order to scramble came, he would be able to instantly bring the machine to life and have it racing across the airfield within minutes, but the order never came; not that morning anyway.

On hearing that Pilot Officer Harrington was probably going to fly solo in a Supermarine Spitfire, Bill realized he had some more learning to do.

The possibility that he too might fly Spitfires meant that Bill would have to learn a new cockpit layout, together with the characteristics of the aircraft. With this thought in mind, he began to "gen-up" on the subject.

"It's a Spitfire,! Let's have a closer look."

Two Hurricanes and two Spitfires were held at readiness, in that same desert sun, through-out the day, until 18.05 hours. Yet, even at the end of the day, the heat could still be too much to bear.

Major Wells celebrated his birthday by inviting his pilots, of all ranks, to the Officer's Mess for dinner and drinks. It was a pleasant occasion, but Bill found the heat too much, and finished the evening with "Doc" Clough-Camm, in the latter's room, drinking WA-TER!!!

Monday, 3rd May 1943

Lots of activity, convoys coming and going.
Still hot, with a sand haze which reduces visibility.

Unlike the previous day when on readiness, the order came for Bill to scramble to fly a harbor patrol over Tripoli.

Flying his beloved Hurricane, NH-N, he climbed into the desert sky only to find his visibility immediately restricted by a sand haze. The haze got worse, reducing visibility to about half a mile, so when he was ordered to fly escort to convoy "Nostril", which was steaming east out of Tripoli, Bill had to ensure that he kept the two destroyer escort ships in view all the time

During the course of the evening further changes were put in hand, when a meeting was held to discuss the closure of No.274 Squadron Sergeants Mess. Bill found the pro-ceedings to be a rather boring business, especially when Jack Aron got up and made an aimless speech!

Tuesday, 4th May 1943

Up at 04.20 hours, took-off at 06.30 on
harbor patrol; still very hazy, ground
and sea [are] invisible from 4,000'

The British First Army, assisted by fighter and bomber aerial support, launched the final offensive for Tunis, at dawn, on 6th May.

Having broken through the German lines at Massicault a few hours later, the British armored columns advanced onto the Tunisian plain. An Advanced element of the First Army entering Tunis during the afternoon of the 7th May.

The American and French forces, who had begun an offensive against Bizerta at the same time as the British, took their objective at 16.00 hours on 7th May, having captured the port facilities at Ferryville first.

Pilot and aircraft, ready for the final assault.

Saturday, 8th May 1943

Up at 05.30, to take-off on convoy patrol at 06.30.
Great news on the radio – Tunis and
Bizerta occupied yesterday afternoon,
only isolated pockets of resistance on Cape Bon left!
Afternoon did another convoy patrol.
Landed at Zuara, refueled, met P/O
George Martin who was in Rhodesia
[training] with Gil.

Flying Officer "Spy" Hands having been informed earlier of his impending posting and promotion, left No.274 Squadron for H.Q. No.210 Group on 11th May. During the evening, prior to his departure, he ventured down to the Pilots Pub to say his final farewells but, naturally, his leaving gave rise to a massive drinking session.

Tuesday, 11th May 1943

Night Flying, so had day off. . .
. . .Took-off at 17.00 hours, up to
Zuara. Then got our beds fixed up.
Standing patrol over Cape Bon and
heavy bombing of Sicily and southern Italy.

Night Flying Training started from Zuara, in accordance with instructions received from Air Headquarters Eastern Defense. Four pilots, including Flight Sergeant Marsh, flew a total of seven and a half hours night flying, before returning to Mellaha at 09.10 hours the following morning.

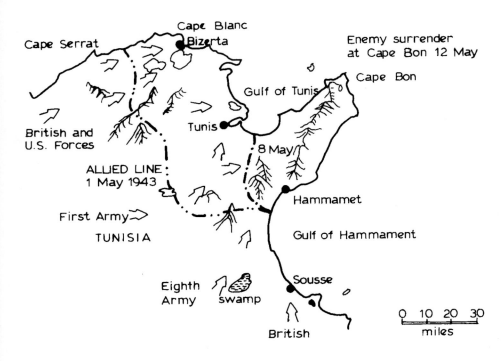

8 – 12 May 1943

The thrusts made by both the British and American forces, in their campaign to take Tunis, pushed some of the Axis forces up onto the peninsula known as Cape Bon. Although they put up some resistance, the enemy forces surrendered on the 12th May.

Thursday, 13th May 1943

Nothing much doing here – [the] war is
definitely over in North Africa. Lots
of prisoners of war working on the camp
under armed escort – 30 or 40 to
one bored RAF Regiment type armed with
a sling rifle!

Bill may well have thought the war in the desert was over, but there was still a lot to be done.

The Squadron detailed two Hurricanes to carry out a shipping patrol, on a rotational basis, between 15.00 hours and 18.15 hours.

During the evening the desert flyer himself, with Flight Sergeant Cordrey as his wingman, flew a convoy patrol lasting an hour and a quarter. At 18.00 hours, the end of their allotted time, they were relieved by a Bristol Beaufighter, twin-engined fighter/bomber.

Taking the opportunity of a little practice before going home, Bill climbed his Hurricane above the "Beau", peeled over and dived on it. He then pulled out, did a loop and rolled off out of a second dive, this time followed by Cordrey.

Friday, 14th May 1943

R.A.F. C.O's PLEASE COPY

Bill read an article in a newspaper which he cut out and pasted into his journal, with a heading implying that every RAF Commanding Officer should take note of. It was headed "Thunderbolts Out-Pace Spitfires."

The content of the article implied that when the American P.47 Thunderbolt fighters began to arrive in England, they were issued to American controlled airdromes as the American pilots knew how to handle them.

The article went on to say how this large American fighter dwarfed the Spitfire both in size and speed. It also stared that Colonel Hubert Zemke issued a decree that the Thunderbolt was not to be flown until he gave permission, the penalty being a substantial fine (in British currency) towards the mess funds.

The pilots under his command soon worked out that the American equivalent was about fifty cents, whereupon a rush was made towards the hangers and soon the air was full of Thunderbolts.

Chapter 14: Victory in the Desert

Saturday, 15th May 1943

*Flt/Lt. Mackay, D.F.M. & Bar arrived here
with two [Bristol] Blenheims. 3 Bostons
flew over at 6 p.m., at 7 p.m. [they] came
in and landed here – looking for Benito
of course – Yanks! And navigation instructors!!*

The three Douglas Boston A.20 bombers which Bill referred to in his journal were from the 97th Bomber Squadron, U.S.A.A.F. They were trying to locate Castel Benito airfield, but in the gathering dusk were forced to put down at Mellaha.

Another aircraft which made an appearance at Mellaha during the day, but not in its recognized form, was a Heinkel He 115 German floatplane. The RAF Maintenance Section at Mellaha had taken a capture example of this machine and, after much work, converted it into a yacht! According to the Squadron diary, when it was launched, it sailed in grand style!

Sunday, 16th May 1943

After lunch 3 Yank Aircobras landed here!

Mellaha airfield was almost becoming a staging post for American Army Air Force aircraft. The day after entertaining the Boston crews, three Bell Aircobras, of No.154 Squadron, U.S.A.A.F., landed at 12.45 hours; in time for lunch.

Monday, 17th May 1943

*Did a convoy patrol, on which Bickford-Smith
and I saw a destroyer peel off and drop seven depth charges.*

An American Bell P-39 Airacobra, serial 24784.

The harbor at Tripoli was a hive of activity with convoys of ships sailing in and out of the port.

As the convoy code-named "Cussed" steamed into the harbor from the north, convoy "Nelson" was heading out in a north-westerly direction.

It was to provide air cover to the latter convoy that Flight Sergeant Marsh and Sergeant Bickford-Smith were ordered to take-off from Mellaha.

As he circled the convoy, Bill noticed one of the escort destroyers peel off and drop seven depth charges, each creating a large white plume of water as it exploded beneath the surface of the sea.

Gradually a dark stain appeared, and a patch of oil developed which grew larger as both aircraft and ship circled the area.

On returning to base an hour or so later, Flight Sergeant Marsh made a full report of all he had seen.

Later, at dusk, he flew a second patrol over the same convoy, accompanied on this occasion by Flight Sergeant Cordrey.

On his way out to the convoy he flew over the destroyer, which was still standing guard over an ever increasing oil slick.

Bill located the five ships which made up the convoy "Nelson" fifty miles on from the scene of the earlier action, and stayed with them until darkness precluded him from continuing his duty in a proper manner.

He flew back to base by dead reckoning navigation and led Cordrey in over the coast, making landfall at the airfield.

Bill heard later from operations that a German submarine had been sunk fifteen miles north west of Tripoli Harbor.

Wednesday, 19th May 1943

Jackie Neil, in a Spit, scrambled after a Ju 88, tally ho'd (saw) it 5 miles away.

Pilot Officer Jackie Neil was scrambled into the air, for an interception patrol, at 10.00 hours, in search of an enemy reconnaissance aircraft.

Piloting Spitfire BR580, coded "G", P/O Neil climbed to an altitude of 20,000' where the "bandit" aircraft was reported to be. Contact was made with the enemy aircraft, which Neil identified as a Ju 88, approximately fifteen miles north east of Tripoli.

Engaging the enemy aircraft he attacked with a three second burst of cannon and machine gun fire, followed immediately by a second burst of equal duration.

As smoke and flames began to issue from one engine of the enemy aircraft, P/O Neil's port cannon jammed, but the damage had already been inflicted.

Pressing home his attack with machine gun fire, Jackie Neil registered fragments fall-

Hurricane at rest.

ing from the tailplane of the twin-engined German aircraft. However, before he could inflict the "coup de grace", the Ju 88 managed to seek sanctuary in the clouds.

As he had not witnessed its ultimate end, Pilot Officer Neil was only allowed to claim the machine as damaged, even though the RAF Air Sea Rescue spent some time searching for it!

Spitfire at rest

The German Forces, having surrendered in mass, gave the Allied Forces victory in the desert.

The occasion was marked with a big parade held in the Tunisian capital, on 20th May. Generals Eisenhower, Giraud, Alexander and Anderson took the salute, as units from all the Allied Forces marched, drove or rode through the town, passing in front of them.

Saturday, 22nd May 1943

*. . .did another convoy patrol, convoy
just off shore and heading east. . .
3 Officer pilots, a Warrant Officer and
2 Sergeants arrived to join the Squadron.*

Piloting Hurricane, NH-P, Flight Sergeant Marsh flew the second of two convoy patrols during the late afternoon. The convoy he was ordered to "protect" was code-named "Hemmingway", and it had the distinction of being the first convoy to sail through the Mediterranean, from Gibraltar to the Suez Canal, since Italy had joined the war in 1940.

During the course of the day, six new pilots reported for duty with No.274 Squadron. Flying Officer H. H. Moon was the most senior in rank and was, according to Bill's journal, an ex-Battle of Britain pilot, although no evidence can be found to support this claim. The other two officers were P/O N. Hunton and P/O D. Stroud.

The two Sergeants, T. Mooney and C. R. Purce, were from Headquarters, No.210 group, as were the officers. The one exception to this was Warrant Officer J. Westcott, who was from No.73 Operational Training Unit.

Sunday, 23rd May 1943

*At 4 p.m. a runner came in with a brief
curt note to the effect that I was posted
to No.22 Personnel Transit Center, with a
Clearance Certificate to sign.*

Bill later found out that he was not the only one on the move, Jackie Neil and "Red" Harrington were also being posted.

That evening a massive party erupted at the Pilots Pub, with well-known squadron faces, present and past, showing up. Amongst those attending the premature "farewell" party were "Dinger" Bell, "Chick" McElhanney, George Meldrum and F/Lt Mackay. The new Intelligence Officer, Pilot Officer Evans attended, as did Bill's friend Pilot Officer Don Gordon, who called in whilst on leave.

Another face from the past walked in to the Pilots' Pub at 9.00 p.m. that evening. It was

Mick Bruckshaw, who had been to No.92 Squadron and was now on his way to No.73 Operational Training Squadron.

Mick had been flying Spitfire Mk.IXs, and spent most of the evening extolling the virtues of this aircraft.

The party broke up at 23.00 hours, but by this time Jackie Neil was well under the influence and did not want it to stop. The other pilots experienced some difficulty getting Neil home.

Monday, 24th May 1943

*Getting organized this morning – reveling
in [the] new prospect before me.
Afternoon went into town with Doc and "Gravy"
- met all the boys there. Had tea at the
Officers Club – disguised self rather feebly
(as an officer?) but it worked o.k.
We are to go by air on the 27th.*

Tuesday, 25th May 1943

*Got cracking with stores and clearance chits
etc. Photographs taken by C.O., George Meldrum and self.*

Morning after the night before! Jack Neil wears his officers cap back-to-front, whilst his colleagues wear 'hang-dog' expressions.

271

No.274 Squadron at Mellaha.

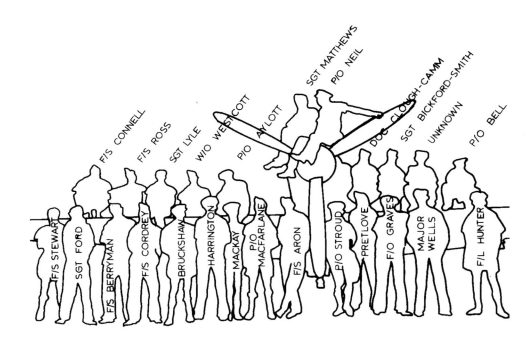

F/S CONNELL
F/S ROSS
SGT LYLE
W/O WESTCOTT
P/O AYLOTT
SGT MATTHEWS
P/O NEIL
DOC CLOUGH-CAMM
SGT BICKFORD-SMITH
UNKNOWN
P/O BELL

F/S STEWART
SGT FORD
F/S BERRYMAN
F/S CORDREY
BRUCKSHAW
HARRINGTON
MACKAY
P/O MACFARLANE
F/S ARON
P/O STROUD
PRETLOVE
F/O GRAVES
MAJOR WELLS
F/L HUNTER

Photo key

As the photographs were being taken, a group began to form outside the Officer's Mess, ostensibly for a dinghy drill, but it did not take long for another drinking session to develop.

This one, like the session the previous evening, broke up at about 23.00 hours. Bill seemed concerned about his state, having confided in his journal that he . . .

. . .went to bed moderately and alarmingly sober!!!. . .

Although Flight Sergeant Bill Marsh was ready to move, things did not go according to plan, as his journal records for the 27th May.

Thursday, 27th May 1943

Up at 03.30 a.m. and packed my bed roll; then
to breakfast at 04.15, and [then] on our way to Benito.
Got there at 05.30 and waited until
06.30 a.m. Then told that as our bookings were
not "priority", POWs had been sent in our place
and the message canceling our departure had been
sent to No.214 Group last night.
Jackie [Neil] and Red [Harrington] played
hell about this, as did a Squadron Leader in the
same fix. Got nowhere, so returned to Mellaha.
[The] good point is that I can now draw a reasonable
amount of pay.

There was not a lot for Bill and the others to do, as they were no longer on active service.

In the hope of finding something to keep them occupied, Bill and some of the others, including Doc Clough-Camm, went into Tripoli during the course of the afternoon. However, even there there was little to keep them amused, and the boredom factor followed Bill into the evening.

Due to the generator failing, there was no power, which obviously curtailed their activities and led to a rather dull evening.

Saturday, 29th May 1943

Up at 04.15 a.m. and to breakfast at 04.45 at
Officers' Mess. Jackie and Red [were] waiting
so got cracking soon after eating.

The trio said their final farewell to No.274 Squadron and headed back to Castel Benito, where they arrived at 06.30 a.m.

Much to their chagrin they could not get a fight until 08.30 hours, and even when they did, they thought they would be going back to Mellaha!

Their allotted aircraft, a Douglas C-47, developed engine trouble in the starboard motor which refused to start. The mechanics worked feverishly on the defective engine and soon got it going.

The twin-engined transport aircraft, known as the Dakota to the RAF, finally taxied out and took-off. Apart from the crew, it was carrying eight passengers and the fuselage of a Spitfire.

There was not much room inside the C-47 and Bill found it difficult to get comfortable, but he soon found a remedy to his problem. He climbed into the cockpit of the Spitfire, got comfortable, and slept for the rest of the journey!

He was woken from his slumbers when the C-47 landed at Benina, where it was to stop for half an hour whilst tea was taken!

Feeling somewhat refreshed, the passengers and crew climbed back aboard the transport aircraft which then continued its journey to Aboukir, where it landed at 16.00 hours.

There Bill, Jackie and "Red" disembarked to continue their journey to Alexandria by train. The Spitfire fuselage was also unloaded prior to the C-47 talking-off for Cairo; its final destination.

Amiriya was the destination of the three ex-No.274 Squadron pilots, but before they went there, they spent a day and night in Alexandria, prior to heading south to Cairo.

Bill walked around the town trying to get used to the idea of being non-operational. In the evening he visited a cinema, where he was able to watch somebody else's war, as he viewed newsreel film of British Beaufighter aircraft strafing enemy convoys in the Pacific.

The next morning, 31st May, Bill met up with Jackie and "Red", as pre-arranged and together they headed south.

In Cairo, Bill stayed at the Manchester House Hotel where he met his old friend Bill Doig, who was now a Pilot Officer.

Jackie and "Red" chose to stay at the National Hotel which, in Bill's view, was much better than were he was staying. That evening they all got together and, surprisingly, downed a few drinks. They talked about experiences past, and what the future may hold.

Tomorrow was not only a new day, it was also a new month and a new beginning.

CHAPTER FIFTEEN

No.71 Operational Training Unit

Tuesday, 1st June 1943

Up at 08.00 a.m., met "Red" and Jackie
and arranged to meet them at 12.00.

Whilst Bill went into town, "Red" and Jackie visited the RAF Headquarters Middle East Command, to try and ascertain where the three friends were to be posted.

"Red" and Jackie arrived back at the National Hotel an hour and a half later than the pre-arranged time of mid-day, making Bill wonder what had happened to them.

It transpired that whilst at RAF HQME, Harrington and Neil had been ushered into an interview with the Officer Commanding Training. They both came out of the interview with a posting to No.71 Operational Training Unit and a pass for fourteen days leave.

The bad news for Bill was that he had to report personally to H.Q., to receive his posting, which he did that afternoon.

Following his interview, Bill hitched a ride in a staff car to No.202 Group, at Heliopolis, where he had a second interview with Flying Officer Goldman. The latter, who had once been Cyphers Officer with No.274 Squadron, informed Flight Sergeant Marsh that he was being posted to No.71 OTU, as Ismailia, as an instructor. First, however, he was to be given two weeks leave.

Sunday, 6th June 1943

Jackie came round to say that "Suds"
and Robbie would be in town this afternoon.
So round to Canada House to meet them.

"Suds" Sutherland was making a good recovery following his crash back in February, and could get around fairly well on a pair of crutches. This fact enabled "Red", Jackie and Bill to take Robbie and "Suds" out for the afternoon, but the crutches created a bit of a furor at one establishment so they all beat a hasty retreat back to Hurricane House, where Robbie and "Suds" were staying.

Having recently drawn a large amount of pay, Bill decided to entertain his friends to dinner that evening at Hurricane House.

Between the rounds of beer and courses of dinner, somebody imparted the news that "Dinger" Bell, "Chick" McElhanney, George Meldrum and F/Sgt McLaren were all being posted from No.274; leaving Flying Officer "Gravy" Graves as the only old hand on the Squadron.

Tuesday, 8th June 1943

Doc arrived in town, went out to dinner with him.

The recent victory in North Africa, coupled with the fact that life was somewhat easier for the Allied Forces, meant that a number of service personnel who would normally be required at the front were now able to take leave.

One person who took advantage of the situation was Flight Lieutenant Austen Clough-Camm, the Medical Officer on No.274 Squadron. He arrived in town and met up with Bill, with whom he later dined and took in a show, but before he did so Doc went to visit "Suds" Sutherland.

During the course of the evening, Doc imparted all the latest news, including who was going to be in town over the next few days. The more they talked the longer the list of names got, and Bill felt a party coming on. By the end of the evening he and Doc had formulated a plan for a party to be held two days hence.

Thursday, 10th June 1943

A party at the National Hotel with
ex-members of No.274 Squadron.

The guest list for the party held a number of names which should have made it go with a swing, but for some reason it fizzled out at 20.00 hours, with most of the guests opting to go for a more sedate dinner at St James Restaurant.

Amongst those in attendance were F/O Heath Hunter, RCAF, F/O Nugent Walsh, RAAF, F/O Ken Wilson from Rhodesia who was hoping to return there soon, F/L Mackay, DFM and Bar, RAF, F/L Appleford, RAF, P/O Jackie Neil, RCAF, P/O "Red" Harrington, RAF,

Austen Clough-Camm (left) and "Suds" Sutherland enjoy at beer, at Hurricane House.

Bill Marsh, "Suds" Sutherland, Austen Clough-Camm and Robbie Robertson, on the balcony at Hurricane House.

P/O Mick Bruckshaw, RAF, P/O MacFarlane, RAF, P/O Don Gordon and of course Bill and Doc.

Wing Commander Linnard, the ex-C.O. sent apologies for the fact that he was unable to attend.

Saturday, 12th June 1943

Out with Doc again.

Knowing that he had to return to his unit at 05.00 hours the next morning, Doc decided to spend the last few hours of his leave with Bill. Together they visited "Suds" and Robbie Robertson again and dined with them that evening at Hurricane House.

A camera appeared and a number of photographs were taken. The last pictures ever that depicted this small group of friends together.

Doc was going back to Tripoli, "Suds" was going to Palestine for convalescence, Robbie was hoping to go home to England and Bill was going to No.71 OTU.

Monday, 14th June 1943

Up at 08.00 and saw the large victory
parade through Cairo, led by Sherman tanks.
Took many films.

The Victory Parade in Cairo, included an armoured car bearing a Mickey Mouse emblem and the legend, 'TOYTA NIKA' . . .

. . . two Sherman tanks bearing the fern leaf emblem of New Zealand . . .

. . . and a heavy gun tractor aptly named "CANTANKEROUS."

Tuesday, 15th June 1943

My leave expires tonight, but since Jackie has till 16th (by some clerical discrepancy) [I] am moving into Canada House tomorrow.

Bill spent a day in Jackie Neil's company at Canada House before going with the latter, on 17th June, to No.203 Group Headquarters at Heliopolis, to collect their posting details, travel warrants and to draw rations.

Loaded down with his bedroll and parachute bag, Bill returned to Cairo by metro train to spend the last evening of his leave at the cinema.

The film he saw, entitled "In Which We Serve" was rated by Bill as one of the most thrilling pictures he had seen, and by far the best war film ever.

The details on Pilot Officer "Red" Harrington's leave documents showed the same information as Bill's leave pass, but unlike the latter, "Red" Harrington reported for duty at No.71 O.T.U. on 16th June.

Friday, 18th June 1943

Out to the station at 10.00 a.m. with Jackie.

Their leave over, Bill and Jackie made their way to the railway station, where they boarded a train for the start of their journey to Ismailia, approximately sixty miles to the north east of Cairo, and approximately ten miles north of the Great Bitter Lake.

They managed to find an empty First Class compartment, which they hoped they would have to themselves, but before the train had moved out of the station, their berth was "invaded" by a Lieutenant Colonel and three Captains!

The two pilots arrived at Ismailia station at 14.00 hours and hired a taxi to take them on the final leg of their journey, out to the airfield.

Jack Neil and Bill Marsh were given a warm reception upon their arrival at No.71 O.T.U., as the latter recorded in his journal.

Friday, 18th June 1943
(Second Entry)

Got fixed up with billets, very comfortable mess.
Met Warrant Officer Harry Crompton (ex-No.213 Squadron)
and Warrant Officer Freddy Etchells.
Had quite a party this evening.

Following a brief interview with the Chief Flying Instructor the following morning, Bill found he had the rest of the day to himself.

His initiation into the mysteries of the O.T.U. would come later, but for the time being he was allowed to settle in to new his life gradually.

After his interview with the C.F.I., Bill was invited by Harry Crompton and Freddy Etchells to join them down at the RAF Sailing Club, for an afternoon on the water.

Bill accepted and enjoyed himself even though, at one point, he nearly capsized the boat!

Accepting another invitation, he spent the evening at the Greek Club where, after experiencing some difficulty gaining admission, the instructor met some of his future pupils.

He became aware of the cosmopolitan nature of the students at Ismailia, and confided in his journal . . .

. . .There are also Turks, Egyptians, Yugoslavs
and a [number] of South African Air Force. [The]
RAF are almost non-existent on this course. . .

Sunday, 20th June 1943

Had a quiet day to let yesterdays sunburn heal!
Went down to the Sailing Club, but sat in the shade reading.
Harry and Freddy got me out yachting for a while,
and we had a lot of fun towing each other on a
surf-board behind the boat.
Evening meant to be quiet, but got
inveigled into a party with Paddy, a
4th Air Formation Signals Staff Sergeant.
Changed my billet to one on the second
floor of a stone building – much cooler.

Although Flight Sergeant Bill Marsh officially returned to duty the next day, for him, things were still fairly quiet.

Monday, 21st June 1943

Reported for duty at 05.30 a.m.!
Met F/Lt E. "Nipper" Joyce, DFM, RNZAF, famous as a
F/Sgt and W.O. for his successes at night with 73 Squadron.
Sat around waiting, with a break for food,
till 12.00, when [I] got away for lunch.
Afternoon read quietly, evening wrote 3 letters home

The Flight Lieutenant to whom Bill Marsh reported for duty was Ernest Leslie Joyce, who was born in Hamilton, New Zealand, on 17th February 1920.

Joyce joined the RNZAF in March 1940 and, on completion of his training, was posted to No.73 Squadron in the Middle East early in 1942.

By the end of July that same year, he had claimed five victories and was awarded the D.F.M. the following month. He was promoted to the rank of Warrant Officer, and became renown as a night fighter pilot adding a further three victories to his score.

At the end of 1942, Joyce received a commission and a posting to No.243 Wing Training Flight, where he stayed until July 1943, when he returned to No.73 Squadron as its C.O.

During November 1943, Joyce was posted to England, promoted to the rank of Squadron Leader and given command of No.122 Squadron, flying North American Mustang Mk.III aircraft.

Squadron Leader E.L. Joyce, DFM, was shot down and killed later in the war, on 18th June 1944, having been "bounced" by Me 109s, whilst strafing a train near Evreux, France.

Tuesday, 22nd June 1943

Up at 05.30 hours, fortunately awakened by Harry Crompton!
At 08.30 we stopped flying, moved and
taxied aircraft into serried ranks, then
went to prepare for visit of Sec. of State.

Sir Archibald Sinclair, Bt, KT., CMG, MP, the British Secretary of State for Air, accompanied by the Air Officer Commanding in Chief Sir Sholto Douglas and Air Vice Marshal W.A. Coryton, made a number of official visits to Squadrons and other units which came under the Middle East Command.

At Ismailia the base was brought to readiness some time before 10.45, the expected time of arrival of the official party.

To the men lined-up in the Egyptian sun, the minutes seemed to drag by. The allotted ETA came and went, and still they stood there. It was to be a further fifteen minutes before the drone of aircraft engines could be heard in the circuit, followed by the appearance of a twin-engined Lockheed Hudson turning on the final approach and landing.

The officers of the station were presented to the visitors, before the latter toured the camp and made a general inspection.

The inspection, Bill reported, went quickly enough, but he felt the speech given by Sir Archibald was a bit dull and boring.

The visitors took their leave at 13.15 hours, after being entertained to lunch at the Officers Mess.

Another familiar face from No.274 Squadron arrived at the Unit on 23rd June 1943, when Flying Officer Bell reported for duty as a flying instructor.

Thursday, 24th June 1943

Overslept by an hour!!!

The lifestyle that Bill had been forced to adopt since his arrival at No.71 OTU, that of sailing, swimming, drinking and making new friends was beginning to catch-up with him. His body had had enough and, on the morning of the 24th June, he overslept.

He rushed around getting ready and, expecting a proverbial rocket, reported for duty one hour late. Bill could not believe his good fortune when he found that not only had Flight Lieutenant Joyce not turned up, but neither had Warrant Officer Crompton.

Although still only a Flight Sergeant in rank, Bill Marsh's first duty at No.71 O.T.U. was to lead a battle formation made up of three students each with a higher rank than his own!

The formation, led by Bill Marsh, comprised of a Yugoslav, Flight Lieutenant Vlandousis, and two Greeks, Flying Officer Cottas and Pilot Officer Demirus.

Friday, 25th June 1943

Up again at 05.20 hours. . .Led two
Egyptian F/Os on practice attacks.
Took Greek F/O Cottas up for dog fighting [practice]. . .
Dinger Bell arrived, posted here.

Whilst Bill was leading two Egyptian Flying Officers on a practice attack formation, during the course of the morning, the weather conditions changed. He was concerned that the low cloud and poor visibility would create problems during the landing procedure, but he need not have worried as everybody got down o.k.

Later in the day, Bill had a problem of a different nature. It was one which almost led to the pupil teaching the instructor how to fly.

Taking off with Flying Officer Cottas for a dog-fighting exercise, it soon became apparent that Bill's aircraft was somewhat slower than the one his pupil was flying. It did not take Flying Officer Cottas long to realize the same thing, and soon he was out-climbing his leader and using tactics similar to an Me 109 to make mock attacks.

The only reply Bill could make to his student's attacks was to turn in and meet each one head-on.

Saturday, 26th June 1943

Air letter from Gil at Waterbeach,
Cambridgeshire, on Stirling conversion
course and recommended for Pathfinder
Force. He has been training 2 years now.

Gil Marsh, now a sergeant, had reported to No.1651 Conversion Unit at Waterbeach, with the nucleus of his crew, on 3rd June.

With a flight engineer and a mid-upper gunner joining them at Waterbeach, Gil's seven men crew reported to "B" Flight and began a conversion course, which would enable them to fly the four engined Stirling bomber.

Monday, 28th June 1943

On Safety Instructor duty from 08.00 until 11.00 hours.

Bill's task, as safety instructor, entailed standing at the end of the runway with a Very pistol, to scare off pupils about to make silly landings.

He watched intently as one pupil flying a Hurricane came in without flaps, but making quite a sensible approach. Bill watched and allowed the Hurricane pilot to land, since the mile long runway was clear. The Hurricane flew past Bill at a speed of 120 m.p.h., about 20' off the deck, with the engine throttled right back. Some 200 yards further on, the pilot opened the throttle to about 2+ boost, as if he were going round again, but no. The aircraft touched down approximately two-thirds of the way down the runway, swerved to starboard and went up onto its nose; the propeller taking the brunt of the damage.

Flight Sergeant Marsh was paraded before Wing Commander Flying, where the former received a reprimand for not making the Yugoslav pilot go round again!!

A tragedy for which Bill could not be held responsible was the death of a pupil, who crashed approximately eight miles from Ismailia.

Sergeant W.E. Davies, a pupil on No.44 Course, was carrying out air to ground firing exercises, when his Hurricane Mk.I Z6177, spun into the ground.

Sergeant Davies was buried at Moascar Cemetery the next day, his funeral being attended by Flight Lieutenant Saunders, the Chief Flying Instructor, Officers and pupils from the Unit.

Tuesday, 29th June 1943

*Down to flights at 08.00 a.m., and flew
to Air Firing range in Harvard flown by
F/Lt. Halliday.
Arrived at 08.30, took over
from Harry Crompton as Range Control Officer.*

Standing out in the desert sun watching the students learning the art of being a fighter pilot did not appeal to Bill, even thought he himself once went through the process.

He felt the Greek students were ground strafing frantically and making some pretty horrible efforts, with huge wide circuits and flat approaches.

Flight Sergeant Marsh did however appreciate the efforts of one student who, in Bill's opinion, "had attack and gunnery weighed-up." The instructor watched as the student made approximately twenty attacks across the range, each of satisfactory standard.

For his efforts in standing out in the open all morning observing the students capabilities, all Bill got was sun burn!

An AT-6 Harvard climbs out of Ismailia, whilst two Hurricanes are prepared for flight.

Wednesday, 30th June 1943

The course goes air-firing so I'm off [duty] or so it appears.
Played tennis after lunch. Wrote a long letter to Doc
and Bickford-Smith, enclosing four snaps (photographs).
Received a letter from Doc and Bickford-Smith;
tells of a flypast with the King, and of Sydney Barker
pranging [Hurricane] "P", four cannon job by landing downwind!

His Majesty King George VI arrived in North Africa on 12th June 1943, at the start of a visit to the battlefront. He took the opportunity to consult with his service commanders, meet the men from his various regiments and air forces and meet American military leaders.

The King arrived at Tripoli by sea, and six aircraft from No.274 Squadron undertook an escort patrol, led by Major John Wells, the C.O.

Although no incidents were recorded, it is not known whether Flight Sergeant Barker, who was Bill's wingman on a number of occasions, pranged his aircraft whilst landing back from the escort duty.

In his letter to Bill, Guy Bickford-Smith wrote. . .

You will be sorry to hear that Sydney unsuccess-
fully tried to do an instrument flying landing down-

wind in "P." He is now Duty Pilot for life!

Later in the day, three Officers and eighty Airman from the Squadron, under the command of Flight Lieutenant J.P. Davies, lined part of the Piazza D'Italia, Tripoli, in honor of the King's visit.

The first week of July saw Flight Sergeant Marsh settling in more to his instructional duties. He was Range Control Officer on a number of occasions, which meant early starts for Bill.

It also saw the arrival of Section Officer C.A. Hand, Women's Auxiliary Air Force. S.O. Hand was the first Administration Officer of the WAAF to be posted to RAF Ismailia. Twenty-nine other ranks were to arrive five days later.

On 2nd June, Flight Lieutenant Saunders, CFI, left Ismailia on posting, and reported to Headquarters RAF, Middle East.

Wednesday, 7th July 1943

Huge armada of ships at Port Said, troops
going aboard at night and coming off in the morning
for the last week. Gen (rumor) is that they sailed last night.
Crete, I suppose.

Bill's supposition was right, as he heard on the radio the following evening.

Thursday, 8th July 1943

Commando Raid on Crete reported on the radio.
Troops landed, attacked bases and airfields, and returned before dawn.
Reports the Ities are destroying the harbor facilities in Sicily!

Friday, 9th July 1943

Last day of this course.
Flew as port sub-section leader to Wing Commander Morris.
[In] evening to the Green Plage, a posh
beach affair on the shores of Lake Tirnsah.

To mark the completion of this particular course, Wing Commander Morris led a flight of five aircraft in vic (vee) formation.

Bill flew, as stated in his journal, on the port side slightly behind his leader, with a fellow instructor by the name of Moulapoulos flying on the starboard side.

Outboard of them, and again slightly behind, flew two students, one on each side.

In this formation, they made four passes over the troops practicing invasion tactics, with tank landing craft etc., before finishing off with a dive-bombing practice over Abusweis.

Having completed their course, the students felt able to "let their hair down" and have a good time They invited their instructors to join them at a Greek club, to partake of home made whiskey, sour white wine and a cold buffet.

At the end of the evening, although he accompanied George Halliday, there seems some doubt in Bill's journal as to whether they actually walked home!!

Saturday, 10th July 1943

SICILY INVADED

No flying. Not feeling well, slept in until 11.00 a.m.
Heard news of Sicily last night. We (Allies) claim to have hit
and wiped out Axis H.Q. and Signals Exchange for the whole island,
in a preliminary air attack.
British and American Airborne Troops mainly
glider transported, were used for the first time by us.

The information received and taken in by Bill Marsh, allowing for the effects of the previous evening, was correct.

Two hours before midnight, on the previous evening, American and British glider borne troops had indeed dropped behind enemy lines on the island of Sicily. They were quickly followed by paratroops, and together they were to make contact with the sea borne landing force who arrived over the next two days.

Having established air superiority, the Allies were able to protect their invading forces with both air and sea power.

Sunday, 11th July 1943

Listened to the news of [the] invasion.
All beaches are holding, and our troops
are advancing on a front of 100 miles.
Line shoot by [a] Yank PRU Lightning
pilot on [the] radio, who saw 40 miles
of ships, with men-o-war darting
in shore, firing furious salvos, then retiring.
He gives his audience a puzzle,
"Someone was catching Hell – guess who."

By Sunday evening, British troops had captured Pachino, numerous bridgeheads had been made at various points and 100 miles of the Sicilian coastline was in Allied hands.

Flying Officer "Chick" McElhanney and Flight Sergeant McLaren, both from No.274 Squadron, reported for duty as flying instructors; how many more would come from No.274?

Tuesday, 13th July 1943

F/O "Chick" McElhanney and F/Sgt McLaren
arrived, posted here. "Chick" in "B" Flt
with Dinger Bell and myself, Mac goes to "C" Flight.
News of the Squadron – 274 Crest presented
by the A.O.C., Major Wells awaits posting.
274 may come down to [Nile] Delta in a
month's time to re-equip with Spits.

No.71 Operational Training Unit was rapidly being the place to send time expired No.274 Squadron pilots.

Flying Officer T.P. "Chick" McElhanney and Flight Sergeant McLaren both received news of their respective postings back in June. They left the Squadron together, on 24th, to report to H.Q. No.203 Group, where they were instructed to proceed to No.71 O.T.U.

Thursday, 15th July 1943

Letter from Gil, now on XV Squadron, Stirlings
at Mildenhall, Suffolk. Also joint letter from Doc
and Bickford-Smith at Mellaha, telling of
a six day leave at a swell hotel 60 miles south
of Tripoli and 3,000ft up in the hills.

Younger brother Gil had completed his training and was now declared combat ready. He, along with his crew, reported for duty to No.XV (Bomber) Squadron, based at RAF Mildenhall, Suffolk, on 1st July 1943.

The Squadron flew the Stirling bomber, the first of the four-engined heavy bombers to be used by the Royal Air Force during the Second World War.

Two days after reporting for duty Gil Marsh flew his first war operation, as second pilot, with a battle experienced crew to gain first hand knowledge of night bombing operations.

By the time Bill received Gil's letter, Gil had captained his own aircraft on two missions, one a mining operation in the Frisian Islands and the other an attack against Aachen, Germany.

Friday, 16th July 1943

*Today, a joint statement to Italy by
Roosevelt and Churchill; the message
is an appeal to [the] Italian people
to overthrow their fascist leaders who
got them into this mess.*

On the day that the British Eighth Army fought desperately for control of Lentini, and the Americans and Canadians together secured the capture of half a dozen towns, the two Allied leaders, Roosevelt and Churchill issued a message to the Italian people.

It was after all now only a matter of time before the Allies invaded Italy.

Saturday, 17th July 1943

*Italian newspapers forced to publish
the Roosevelt-Churchill appeal, owing
to [a] large leaflet raid by us on Italy.*

According to the comment in Bill's journal, the Fascist's reply was to the effect that the Allies would be made to pay the full price in blood and weapons. It also stated that if an Italian listened to the Allied propaganda with a sympathetic ear, that person would be deemed to be a traitor and a coward.

Sunday, 18th July 1943

*Further advances in Sicily – closing in on Catania.
Several people predicted capture of Sicily within a fortnight,
[General] Montgomery says 2, 4 or 6 weeks.
Our bomber offensive switched to toe of Italy -
Messina blitzed heavily.
Italy being attacked from England,
North Africa and Middle East!*

Although the Allies were gaining much ground, their advance was held at Catania by the stiff resistance put up by the German forces. The latter came under the directive of General Hube and the staff of No.XIV Panzer Corps who, on 17th July, had taken command of all the German fighting forces on the island.

Their advance north blocked, the British Eighth Army had to wait until their American and Canadian allies had swept down from the north coast and attacked the enemy from the rear.

Friday, 23rd July 1943

Rome bombed for [the] first time,
by "picked crews" in Fortresses.
A daylight sortie, preceded some
4 hours before by a shower of
leaflets announcing our intention!
Palermo, the largest town of Sicily
and an excellent port, falls to us intact.

An attack was carried out by specially selected crews of the U.S.A.F., on 19th July, against the railway marshaling yards in Rome

Whilst General Montgomery was heading for Messina, on the north east corner of the island, General Patton Commanding the American forces raced towards Palermo, which his men took with little resistance.

Saturday, 24th July 1943

[The] Pope announces he deplores
the bombing of Rome – he considers that
it should have been declared as open city.

Sunday, 25th July 1943

MUSSOLINI RESIGNS.

Report that at the recent conference
Hitler and Mussolini, the latter asked
for 20 to 30 Divisions of Troops to
withstand the threatened invasion of ITALY.
Hitler refused, demanded a delaying action
by Italian troops alone, fighting a rearguard
action northwards from the toe of Italy and
abandoning Rome in the process. Mussolini's
Cabinet refused to take the responsibility, and
Mussolini is reported to have been captured by
Italian officers when about to fly to Germany for refuge.
He, with all his Cabinet, is under house arrest.
Marshal Badoglio takes over and peace
proposals are under discussion at the Vatican.

Monday, 26th July 1943

Attacks on Crete by light bombers,
Beaufighters and 3 Wings of Hurricanes,
including the Greek Squadron strafing in daylight.
Seventeen aircraft [were] lost, of which five were Greek.
At Flights this morning, I was demonstrating
to three Egyptian pupils the theory of shadow firing
before taking-off, when F/O "Spy" Hands appeared.

Flight Sergeant Marsh was quite amazed to see his old Squadron pal, "Spy" Hands appear at Ismailia. The last time Bill saw him was during a visit to Tripoli.

It transpired that the Intelligence Officer had been posted to a Baltimore equipped Operational Training Unit at Shandur, approximately twenty-five miles south of Ismailia.

Tuesday, 27th July 1943

Martial law proclaimed through Italy by Marshal Badoglio.
Rumor that S/L Young, C.F.I. is posted to England,
and that Major J.R. Wells, D.F.C. is coming down to replace him!

It seemed as though most of the pilots from No.274 Squadron had been posted to No.71 O.T.U. so why shouldn't the C.O. be posted there too.

It transpired later that Major Wells had in fact been sent home to England for a month's leave, which is something Bill had always hoped he personally would get. However, the rumors that Major Wells was destined to take over the C.F.I's job still persisted.

Sunday, 1st August 1943

News from Sweden says that only fifty
houses are still standing in Hamburg,
after a week of bombing – 8,000 tons of bombs!

The 24th July 1943 saw the start of a ten day concentrated battle against Hamburg, during which the Royal Air Force made four heavy night raids and the American Eighth Air Force made two daylight raids. It was also to be the first occasion that the RAF dropped "Window" (Chaff), the anti-radar strips of aluminum foil which confused the enemy radar.

No.XV (Bomber) Squadron, RAF, at their base in Mildenhall, England, detailed eighteen aircraft for the first attack on 24th July. The first aircraft to take-off was Short Stirling bomber, BK816, coded "X", piloted by Sergeant Gil Marsh, Bill's kid brother.

Regarding the attack on Hamburg, Gil wrote to his brother on 4th August. . .

> *". . .did you ready about Hamburg – it aint' what*
> *it used to be. We gave the remains of Essen a hell of a*
> *packet as well – "happy valley" still lives up to its*
> *name, its no ride down that way – Blackpool illumi-*
> *nations, Guy Fawkes display and Richtofen's [Fly-*
> *ing] Circus all in one, numerous breath taking side-*
> *shows, in fact the only thing we missed was a close-*
> *up of the fatman Goering. The newspapers reckon that*
> *in another three weeks the RAF will "Hamburgise"*
> *Berlin – that remains to be seen. . ."*

Thursday, 5th August 1943

Commission through this morning.
Spent most of the day filling up forms, but had
lunch in Officer's Mess and moved my kit
to share a room with Harry Crompton.

Pilot Officer Bill Marsh. It sounded good and he had waited a long while for his commission to officer rank. There were times when Bill wondered whether he would ever receive it, as he saw many of his colleagues on No.274 Squadron rise in rank above him.

He wasted no time in settling in to his new environment, as he moved from the Sergeant's Mess to the Officer's Mess, where he shared a room with the man who first welcomed him to No.71 O.T.U., and with whom he had become good friends.

Saturday, 7th August 1943

To Cairo by lorry – a 2 hour ride, a
bit rough but quite pleasant.

Following a long drive into Cairo, Bill checked in to the National Hotel, which was not too his liking and he described as lousy.

However, his feelings towards his accommodation were soon forgotten when he went out on a celebration binge with Chick McElhanny, Dinger Bell and Jack Neil.

Sunday, 8th August 1943

Moved into Junior Officers' Club.

Gil's Stirling bomber, BK816, coded LS-X, from a painting owned by Gil.

Being in a fit state the following morning to still worry about his accommodation, Bill chose to move to the Junior Officers' Club. As he was checking in, he recognized a voice asking to see a member of the N.A.A.F.I. staff, it belonged to yet another old face from No.274, that of Guy "Shotgun" Bickford-Smith. The latter had just arrived from Tripoli.

Bill was also handed a note which informed him that Austen Clough-Camm, the M.O., was in town having flown in from Derna, where the Squadron was now based.

To add to his pleasure, the following day Bill was able to visit Suds Sutherland, who had discarded his crutches and was able to get about with the use of sticks.

On 10th August 1943, "C" Flight of No. XV Squadron was formed into No.622 Squadron RAF. Being a member of "C" Flight, Gil automatically transferred to the new Unit. As yet, his brother, the desert flyer, was unaware of this move.

Wednesday, 11th August 1943

Got measured for a blue uniform at £15.
To be ready Saturday.

The real reason for Bill's trip to Cairo became apparent on Wednesday, 11th August, when he visited a tailors shop and was measured for an Officer's uniform, which he was informed would be ready for collection on the following Saturday.

It is not known how Bill filled in his time over the Thursday and Friday, as nothing is recorded in his journal. However, when he collected his new uniform he confided in his journal that it seemed quite good.

Sunday, 15th August 1943

Back to Ismailia.

F/O Bill Marsh, F/L Austen Clough-Camm and P/O Guy Bickford-Smith.

On Sunday, 15th August, Pilot Officer William "Bill" Marsh took the 06.30 train from Cairo to Ismailia, where he reported back for duty.

Over the next week, Bill neglected his journal, but he did receive a letter from his brother. The content of the letter dated 23rd August 1943 may well have tempted fate, but it brought home to both Gilbert and Bill the fact that one never knows what the new dawn may bring.

Of his recent experiences Gil wrote. . .

> "*. . .Have bunged in a few more hours since I last wrote you, included are two eight and a bit hour trips to Turin, on both of which by the way we got a wizard photo of the spot marked X.*
>
> *These long trips aren't too bad as regards flak etc., but flying for such a long period without a break of any sort gets very boring, makes one very tired and sleepy.*
>
> *Up to now we have coped very nicely and have only had one small hole thro' the tailplane so far, of course we have had some near do's but we have always spotted the E.A. in time to take action. . ."*

That night Gil Marsh took his bomber to Berlin, and the German nightfighter saw him first.

Monday, 23rd August 1943

*Gil in hospital with leg wounds, after
getting back to base. O.K. Condition not serious.*

It is obvious from the entry in his journal that Bill was not fully aware of the seriousness of his brother's injuries, or the circumstances that created them, until he received a letter from Gil, early in September.

Although seriously injured, Gil's sense of humor had not failed him, as he started his letter with the old RAF "line shoot" of "There we were upside down, with zero on the clock. . ."

*. . ."There we were upside down" – No! – I'll make
it different! – We had dropped our "cookies" (bombs)
and had weaved through three-quarters of the search-
light belt when the rear gunner suddenly shouted Ju
88 coming in [from the] port quarter down. Five very*

Gil Marsh, the bomber pilot (right), pictured with his rear gunner, "Art" Hynam.

quick attacks followed. I was hit in the second of these, but managed to keep up evasive action by pushing and pulling the rudder with my left leg; the right one become u/s immediately because the shell splinter in my starboard buttock (butt) partially severed the sciatic nerve – very painful will take months to heal!

After breaking the fifth attack and also telling the boys I had been hit, I lost consciousness for a short period. We were at 14,000' then – the next I remember was pulling the kite (aircraft) out of a hell-dive with the assistance of the navigator, who was in the second pilot's seat by then. We had a hell of a job to get her out and no wonder, the bloody Hun had blown the whole tailplane to pieces, he didn't touch the rear turret though which protrudes slightly beyond.

We came out of that lot at 3,400 feet. The only hit up front we sustained in the P.I. (port·inner) engine – Engineer said she was over heating and had best be feathered, feeling very dazed I leaned forward and pressed the P.O. (port outer) button by mistake – this engine went too cold to be restarted before I realized the mistake (starting a cold engine at night makes you look like a Roman candle) so had to leave it till out over the sea, however P.I. kept running – good old Hercs (Bristol Hercules engines) – and with the aid of Nav got her back up to 5,000 feet.

By this time Bailey, the bomb aimer, came back and took up second pilot, shortly afterwards however I became very faint, sitting in a pool of blood and the pain in my foot and leg became so unbearable in the sitting position, so Nav helped me from seat [on] to a bed of 'chutes etc. between the back of the first pilot's seat and Nav's [plotting] table; from here I could see all the instruments and controls and managed to instruct Bailey accordingly.

The Navigator gave me two shots of morphine, but it didn't deaden the pain. Eventually we arrived at base, and Bailey made a good landing (he nearly completed a pilots course before being scrubbed for a crash). . .

*. . . We had 75 gallons of fuel left when we landed.
I am still flat on my back, the largest of my wounds
still bleeds – bled 1/2 pint last Wednesday – but am
improving, will have an operation on the nerve after
my second transfusion. [I] will be in dock (hospital-
ized) for months yet, a very long business these nerves
– Don't worry old boy I'll pull through O.K., and Bill
I'm in dear old England which means a lot.*

A new chapter was about to begin in Gil Marsh's life, as it had recently for brother Bill.

CHAPTER SIXTEEN

Italy Surrenders

Friday, 3rd September 1943

Anniversary of outbreak of WAR

*At 04.30, British and Canadian troops in large numbers
landed on the south west tip of Italy, presumably
around Reggio di Calabrio, opposite Messina.*

Having successfully completed their objective of capturing Sicily, the Allies turned their sights to the mainland of Italy.

They wasted no time in crossing the narrow strip of sea, known as the Straits of Messina, which divided the mainland from the island.

Little opposition was encountered, and the Allies initial objectives were soon taken.

Saturday, 4th September 1943

*To Cairo by 2.10 train, arriving at 5.30.
Met Ron Dunfold at Junior Officers Club
and had dinner. Went to see show.*

The three hour train journey took Bill Marsh away for a while, from the arduous task of training new fighter pilots. Being able to relax with friends was as good a tonic as anything.

Ron Dunfold, whom Bill met at the Junior Officers' Club, was a Lieutenant, in the 2nd Battalion of the Royal Tank Regiment.

They spent much of the weekend enjoying each other's company, and taking in a show and a film. The latter being the famous film, "Gone With The Wind", which Bill recorded in his journal as "four hours of drama in Technicolor!"

Monday, 6th September 1943

*Letter from Mum and Lilian – who have just
been to see Gil in hospital.
Seems an [Ju]88 caught them coming back
from a show (mission). Gil has shrapnel wounds
in thighs and legs, and one foot.
Also a nerve severed in small of his back.
So he will be in hospital for some considerable time*

The letter from his mother and Lilian was the first indication that Bill had received of the seriousness of his brother's injuries. At this period of time, Bill had still not received Gil's letter giving the full story of events, but at least he was not totally unaware.

For his action, in bringing the crippled bomber home to RAF Station Mildenhall, Sergeant Jack Bailey, RCAF, received an immediate award of the Conspicuous Gallantry Medal; the highest decoration awarded to a member of the Squadron.

On 21st September 1943, Sergeant Jack Bailey, CGM, received a commission and was posted home to Canada, for pilot training.

Thursday, 9th September 1943

*News flash at 7 p.m. – ITALY unconditionally
surrendered on Sept. 3rd, was forced to conceal news
until Allies' chosen time for announcement.*

Although the Italians had surrendered, the Allies continued their advance further into the Italian mainland, meeting some resistance from the Germans who after all had not surrendered.

The Italians signed the document of surrender, in triplicate, at 17.15 hours on 3rd September 1943, but the American and British Governments chose to withhold announcing the news for a few days.

Bill neglected his journal for the reminder of September, and his Log didn't give any clues as to the reasons for this. The lack of entries in his journal could have been due to pressure of work, as on 12th September, a number of pupils arrived to form No.49 Course and No.8 Conversion Course.

The fact that there was not a single person amongst them who could speak proper

Jack Bailey, RCAF (left) photographed at RAF Mildenhall, with George Wright, the crew's wireless operator.

English, not only added to the Unit's workload, it also added to it's already cosmopolitan character.

It is known however that Bill undertook shadow firing instruction, led battle formation practices and air to air and air to ground firing exercises.

On 15th September 1943, Bill flew as a passenger on a twin-engined Bristol Blenheim, piloted by Wing Commander Shipley, to Kilo 40, otherwise known as Landing Ground 237. Here he collected a Hawker Hurricane MkIIC, BN127, and flew it back to No.71 O.T.U., at Ismailia, forty-five minutes flying time away.

During September, Bill's old Squadron, No.274, relocated to Cyprus, where it completed its re-equipment with Supermarine Spitfires, which created a pang of jealousy in Bill.

Changes were also occurring at No.71 O.T.U. On Monday 27th September 1943, the Chief Flying Instructor, Squadron Leader Young departed for the Air Headquarters, Air Defenses Eastern Mediterranean, where he was to undertake a Junior Commanders' Course. The Chief Ground Instructor, Squadron Leader Wilfred M. Sizer took over as C.F.I. The latter's former position was to be taken over, during October, by a face familiar to Bill

A letter written by Austen Clough-Camm, on 5th October 1943, whilst on leave with Guy Bickford-Smith, had Bill yearning for something other than desert sand, when the desert flyer read the following extract. . .

Solo take-off by a Hurricane coded "E."

> *. . .Guy and I have been up into some mountains*
> *for a spell and found the air very fine, and the view*
> *beyond description. Pines and firs abound to give the*
> *air a scent and fruits are of such variety and quantity*
> *as to astonish me – even strawberries to pick!. . .*

In reply to the letter he received from Gil, which explained in detail the events over Berlin on 23rd August, Bill wrote back to his brother on 7th October. . .

> *. . .I have now a much clearer picture of what hap-*
> *pened, and am even more amazed at the miracle of*
> *your safe return from that shambles. As you so wisely*
> *say, you are in England; and are visited by those you*
> *care for, surrounded with an atmosphere of humanity*
> *and kindness. Remember when you suggested volun-*
> *teering for over here – and my reply!*
> *How I wish that I could get home to see you! But*
> *prospects are dim indeed "Overseas" is a system*
> *which is little understood by those who haven't been*
> *out [here]. There's many a chap, aircrew or ground,*
> *who came out on a 3 month job (or so he thought)*
> *and remains the prescribed 4 years!. . .*

Making comment about the award to Jack Bailey, the bomb aimer, Bill continued. . .

> . . .*Well I am most disappointed that you got no recognition for the show. Perhaps it will come through yet. But your B/A type, I feel, certainly deserves his award.*
>
> *One is apt to think lightly of the feat of flying an aircraft, when one is accustomed to it. To handle, and land a huge, damaged aircraft at night is a responsibility that would give me the jumps (frights). And for a chap with very little flying (or rather, piloting, experience), I think its enough to merit a gong (medal). . .*

Friday, 8th October 1943

> *A Typhoon, flown by one of Stimpson's old friends landed here from Daba.*
> *[It is] one of only five in the Middle East.*
> *Stimpson flew it for a short time and demonstrated the terrific speed and climb.*

The Hawker Typhoon, a single seat fighter/bomber and ground attack aircraft, was the backbone of the 2nd Tactical Air Force in Northern Europe, following the invasion in 1944.

The visit to No.71 O.T.U. of this single-engined brute of an aircraft, and the aerial display it gave, photographically went unrecorded by Bill who was without his camera on this occasion.

Monday, 11th October 1943

> *To Kasfareet in a Harvard. Dinger Bell first pilot, self in back seat.*

Flying Officer Bell, piloting North American Harvard, Mk. IIA, EX111, took-off from Ismailia, with Bill Marsh as his passenger. The purpose of the flight was one of a ferry nature, where Bill had to make the return journey, from Kasfareet, piloting a fragile Miles Magister training aircraft.

He did not relish the idea of making the flight, especially as he had not flown this type of aircraft since August 1941, when he was with No.605 Squadron at Baginton!

Wednesday, 13th October 1943

Harry Crompton, my room mate, is posted.
[He] hopes to go to 417 Squadron in Italy;
but may go home!
ITALY (represented by [Marshal] Badoglio)
declares war on GERMANY!!!

Warrant Officer Harry Crompton had completed his "rest" tour of teaching rookie pilots to become desert flyers and was to be posted. He hoped to join No.417 Squadron RCAF, who were flying Spitfires in the Italian campaign but, in the light of recent events was not sure if he would finish up back in England.

Following the recent signing of the unconditional surrender, the government of Marshal Badoglio, who had taken over after the overthrow of the Fascist dictator Benito Mussolini, declared war on their former allies, the German Third Reich.

On Friday, 15th October 1943, Major John Wells arrived at the Unit, not to take over as C.F.I. as rumor had indicated, but to take over as Chief Ground Instructor.

Saturday, 16th October 1943

Going on seven days leave -
hope to see Ron Dunfold.

Bill's leave was to be taken at Alexandria, where he hoped to meet up with his army friend Ron Dunfold. Hoping to catch the Cairo Express as it passed through a nearby junction, Bill left Ismailia at 09.40 hours and was at the appropriate junction in good time, but when the express train came through it did not slow down enough for him to jump on board.

Thinking he was stranded, the airman was fortunate to be able to hitch a ride in a truck full of Greek Navy types, which happened to pass by shortly after the train had failed to stop.

Bill rode with the seamen as far as Tanta, from where he caught a train to Alexandria; finally arriving there at 16.30 hours.

Tired and hungry, Bill was perturbed to find that he could not secure accommodation for himself and Ron at the Union Club, which was full. Fortunately the army officer had had the foresight to realize this situation might happen and had written to Bill, via the Union Club, to say he would meet him at the Piccadilly Hotel.

Bill made his way to the hotel and booked two rooms, prior to setting off for the railway station, where he was to meet his friend. Due to the train being delayed, the latter arrived one hour late.

Desert Flyer

Sunday, 17th October 1943

Got rooms at the Union Club and moved in.

The accommodation being cheaper at the Union Club, Bill and Ron did not hesitate to relocate from the Piccadilly, when they heard that rooms were available at the former.

Apart from anything else, it made Bill feel more at home when he met a group of No.274 groundcrew (maintenance) on leave.

Unbeknown to Bill, whilst he was away on leave, Headley Lyle from No.274 Squadron arrived at No.71 O.T.U. having been posted there as a flying instructor!

Monday, 18th October 1943

Met more of 274 Squadron, now [based] at Idku.

The conditions under which Bill, and many like him, had lived, flown, and fought during the desert campaign had made him very close to his colleagues. He knew well their likes and dislikes and how and where they were likely to spend their respective leave. With the latter in mind, Bill and Ron ventured off to a particular nightclub where, as he thought, Bill found a group of No.274 pilots.

Lt. Ron Dunfold.

The Squadron was still based in Cyprus, but Sergeant Pretlove, Warrant Officer Westcott and Flight Sergeant Ross had all been posted back to North Africa.

Wednesday, 20th October 1943

Doctor Austen Clough-Camm came in to see us
- went for dinner.

No.274 Squadron personnel seemed to be everywhere, as Doc Clough-Camm called in at the Union Club to see Bill and Ron. Following a superb dinner at a French restaurant, the trio returned to the Union Club where, over drinks, they talked the night away.

The following night, Guy "Shotgun" Bickford-Smith about whom the trio had been talking the previous evening, arrived at the Club to see Bill and Ron!

Bill did not know who was going to turn up next.

Saturday, 23rd October 1943

Saw Ron off to Cairo by 12.30 train.

Ron Dunfold's leave expired the day before Bill's and therefore had to return to his unit. Bill saw him off at the railway station, before going into town on a shopping expedition.

Having purchased some silk stockings for his mother and sister Lilian, and a tobacco pouch, Bill returned to the Union Club where he had arranged to meet Austen and Guy Bickford-Smith. Upon their arrival, Bill returned to the town center with his two friends in order to search for a cigarette case as a 21st birthday present for Bickford-Smith.

The sought after item was located in a decent jewelers and, after some haggling by Doc, it was purchased for a reasonable sum.

The cigarette case, together with the tobacco pouch purchased earlier, were duly presented to Bickford-Smith over dinner at Athineos Restaurant, during the course of the evening.

This being Bill's last night in town, the trio also took in a show, which Bill recorded as being "not bad", followed by coffee at the Anglo-Hellenic Club.

It was at this club that Doc Clough-Camm imparted the news that he had requested a special posting to the North African Air Force Headquarters, which probably meant him going to Naples!

Sunday, 24th October 1943

Finished off shopping, had an excellent
lunch at the Union Bar and then back to pack
and catch the 3.15 to Ismailia.

Upon his arrival back at base later that day, Bill found a number of letters waiting for him. One of them was from his brother Gil, who imparted the news that apart from feeling much better he was now sitting up. Good news indeed, for both of them.

Monday, 25th October 1943

Back to the old grind (work) – saw
Major Wells, newly installed as C.G.I.

The rumors that had been circulating since the end of July, concerning Major Wells' possible appointment to No.71 O.T.U., Bill found had proved correct. On his return to the unit, he was surprised to see John Wells newly installed as C.G.I.

On his first day back at No.71 O.T.U., Bill got straight on with the routine of instructing. His first flight consisted of leading a combat and formation flying exercise.

Tuesday, 27th October 1943

My new room mate, since Harry Crompton
was posted to No.80 Squadron, is F.Lt Henshaw-White.

The end of October and beginning of November were rather routine, with Bill teaching and leading Vic formations, flying line astern formations and air to air firing exercises.

On 7th November he took time out to write to his brother. The letter showed however that life on an operational training unit was not all work; he wrote. . .

> . . .Yesterday, Ron Dunfold came over for the evening with a couple of friends in a jeep, and of course I was booked for a soccer match against the Sergeants' Mess. However, he watched that, not seeming too cheesed-off (bored), and fortunately we won, which created a good impression, I hope.
>
> Then we went down to the Officers' Club nearby and had a mild [drinking] session – there was beer there for once – and then dinner and another beer, with much joviality of course by this time
>
> I count myself quite a marvel to have found my way back to camp, alone and unaided, and even in my own bed; pyjama clad too.
>
> Only too often one finds oneself, after such evenings, lying on the ruins of the mosquito net and natterley clad in a pair of flying boots only. . .

Bill Marsh with some colleagues from No.71 OTU. The officer with the walking stick is thought to be F/L Henshaw-White.

The letter went on to contain some news about Bill's old friend Ray Woodcraft. . .

> *. . .Ray Woodcraft writes to say that his new (and first) daughter is to be named Hillary Christine. . . . . .I am to be an Honorary Godfather. . .*

Accidents were a regular part of life on a training unit, some were due to a lack of vigilance, but others were assisted by other factors.

One such accident occurred at 09.25 hours, on the morning of 4th November 1943, whilst two aircraft were carrying out a dog-fighting exercise, at 4,000' in cloudy conditions.

An Australian pupil, Flight Sergeant Shipway piloting Hawker Hurricane Mk.I, V4863, was "attacking" Hurricane Mk.I, V6757, flown by fellow pupil Sergeant Clements.

On seeing the "enemy" Hurricane coming in for the attack, Clements took evasive action by flying into the cloud. A few minutes later on emerging from his place of concealment, Clements saw Shipway's Hurricane below him, and immediately carried out an attack. Shipway saw Clements diving down from above and took the necessary avoiding action, whilst Clements again concealed himself by flying back into the cloud.

On emerging from the cloud for a second time, Clements was horrified to see Shipway's Hurricane converging on him and, although the former tried to take evasive action, he realized a collision was inevitable.

Clements wasted no time and baled out. As he floated down under his parachute, he saw the other aircraft, minus its starboard wing, flutter down and burst into flame upon impact. Flight Sergeant Shipway, who fell with his Hurricane, was killed.

Austen Clough-Camm who, whilst dining with Bill, expressed his desire to be posted got his wish. He was not posted to Naples as he had hoped, but Sicily. However, he had nothing to complain about, although he was a little sad, as was revealed in a letter he wrote to Bill on 10th November, in which he stated. . .

> *. . .I am superbly housed in a marvelous flat with painted ceilings, chandeliers, damask chairs and marble floors. . .*
>
> *. . .My office is beautiful/impressive with a black glass topped desk, red damask chairs, lovely paintings and an easy chair. Apparently I have everything I could wish for – but there is something sadly missing. I miss you and Guy very much and the old Squadron not a little. . .*
>
> *. . .I have been looking at an atlas this evening and felt quite nostalgic for the Libyan days of a year ago. . .*

Another accident, which occurred on Thursday, 11th November 1943, had an almost humorous touch to it.

A pupil, a flight sergeant with the Royal Yugoslav Air Force, who was experiencing problems with the brake pressure, decided to seek advice on the problem. He was taxiing towards the Duty Instructor when, to his great consternation, the undercarriage of his Hurricane collapsed!!

It later transpired that the undercarriage collapsed due to the strain placed upon it, when the pupil "ground looped" his aircraft whilst landing.

Wednesday, 1st December 1943

F/O came through.

December started on a good note for Bill who, on the first day of the month, learned that not only had he been promoted to the rank of Flying Officer, but that his promotion had been back-dated to 25th August.

F/O William Marsh

Wednesday 8th December 1943

Mess meeting this evening; Group Captain being away Wing Commander Shipley is Officer Commanding Station.

Wing Commander Shipley, in the absence of the Station Commander, assumed command and as such acted as President of the Mess Committee.

On completion of the official Mess business, Wing Commander Shipley issued an ultimatum in order to find a transgressor. He called upon the officer who had written "Bull" under one of his notices to reveal his identity and collect the reward for his insolence and temerity!

If this was not forthcoming, as President of the Mess Committee he ordered the Mess Bar be closed until the culprit revealed himself.

After dinner that evening, there were about seven people sitting in the Mess, the rest had gone into town or to the cinema!

Gilbert Marsh, in England, was still undergoing treatment for the injuries his received in the aerial attack on 23rd August.

On 10th December he wrote to brother Bill. . .

> *. . .On Tuesday last (7th Dec) I went to Wingfield and had the old plaster cut off, quite an unpleasant experience. The cutters are like a pair of "dog-grips" and one part goes down the inside of the plaster, consequently around the knee and ankle where the plaster is very tight, it feels very much as tho' ones bones are passing through a very efficient stone crusher.*
>
> *Next came the removal of the stitches – as most of my leg is still numb I felt very little pain, in fact the only ones that really hurt were the first dozen at the butt end.*
>
> *You can imagine how surprised I was when informed I had 119 stitches, I previously thought that 80 would be the maximum.*
>
> *To put the new plaster and turn-buckle on, the body is placed in a big iron frame which supports only the head, shoulders, base of [the] spine and heels. When they first fix the body up on this contraption it isn't too bad, but after supporting the mass of plaster for about half an hour (until it hardens off) one doesn't*

> *feel so good – to be quite candid, its the nearest I have ever been or want to be, to being crucified. . .I shall be in bed during the [Christmas] festivities but don't you worry we'll make a "go" of it. . .*

The rest of the letter went on to inform Bill about what was happening on No.XV Squadron, with particular reference to Gil's old crew who still had a tour of operations to complete!

As the year began to draw to a close, the entries in Bill's journal began to diminished in quantity, his Log giving the only indication of how he was spending the time

Obviously his promotion to Flying Officer brought a little more responsibility, but in the main it was his instructional duties which were taken up the time

On the other hand, brother Gilbert had plenty of time lying in bed all day and, although he had found things to keep him occupied, he still wrote letters on a regular basis. Bill received another letter from him date 18th December, in which Gil wrote. . .

> *. . .Last weekend mum came down (from Ormskirk) to see me – first [visit] since my operation at Ely. I felt and must have looked pretty deadly then, however seeing me back in good health and feeling very lively, bucked her up no end.*
>
> *Yesterday I was amazed at receiving a letter from, now, Mr Hewlett, he was our Flight Commander at No.5 I.T.W. Torquay and was a Pilot Officer in those days – he has packed up the R.A.F. and returned to his collieries (coal mines) at Wigan to improve production.*
>
> *You may remember him from your visit; what a grand chap. I'll never forget him, he really was a father figure to us all. . .By the way old boy, congrats on your F/O and I hope further promotion will be yours in the near future. . .*

The future was only a few days aware with the start of the New Year, but as though in a prophetic gesture Flying Officer Bill Marsh stopped writing his journal at the end of 1943.

The final entry in the journal was a Christmas menu, for the Officers Mess, R.A.F. Station Ismailia, the back cover of which boasted numerous autographs.

CHAPTER SEVENTEEN

Fall of the Desert Flyer

Weatherwise, the new year started as the old one ended with rain and low cloud precluding all forms of aerial exercises.

To the pupils of No.52 Course this did not create a problem, as on New Years Day they completed their training program and were granted seven days leave.

Two days later a new course, No.54, commenced with the arrival of the now usual cosmopolitan group of pupils. This particular group consisted of nine officers and thirty-one N.C.O.s of the Royal Australian Air Force, two Free French Air Force officers and two N.C.O.s from the Royal Hellenic Air Force. No language problems with this group!

The weather continued to interrupt the various training programs at RAF Ismailia, causing flying on 4th January to be curtailed at 14.00 hours.

However, when flying did resume, it was not always due to the weather that incidents occurred, as was the case on the 5th January 1944.

A pupil from No.53 Course, whilst flying Hurricane P2640, crash-landed some eight miles east of Ismailia, sustaining slight injuries. It later transpired that the engine problem the pilot had reported was due to the fact that he had run out of fuel in his reserve tank!

Wednesday, 5th January 1944

Ismailia to Kilo 40

On Wednesday, 5th January Bill flew to Landing Ground Kilo 40, as a passenger in Defiant, AA347, with Flying Officer Bellerby as pilot.

The purpose of the flight was to allow Bill to collect a new Hurricane, MkIIC, serial HV303, and ferry it back to Ismailia.

Chapter 17: Fall of the Desert Flyer

Two days later, Bill flew as a passenger in the rear seat of a North American Harvard, when he flew to the firing ranges, again with Flying Officer Bellerby as pilot.

Monday, 10th January 1944

Letter to Mother and sister Lilian

. . .We are getting busier and busier, more to do all the time, and in between, jaunts of a few hours or a day or two ferrying aircraft. . .

. . .Last week I was up near Nazareth and stayed a night. . .It's nearly two years since I was last in Palestine, and it brought back memories of those days there with Ray [Woodcraft] and Yves Tedesco.

Another bunch of memories were stirred by the arrival (after months of tracing) of a kit bag and suitcase which I had put in stores before I went into the desert. . .Glad to hear that Gil had a pleasant Xmas, and hope to hear that he is up soon.

At the rate the pupils on the courses at RAF Ismailia were crashing and damaging the aircraft, it was not surprising that Bill and his fellow instructors spent so much time ferrying-in replacement machines.

Five days after a pupil on No.53 Course had force-landed an aircraft due to failing to register his fuel consumption, another pupil on the same course made a wheels up forced landing, on 10th January, due to a similar reason.

The weather seemed determined to interrupt the flying program as much as possible, and when the pilots ignored the conditions the elements retaliated.

On 11th January, two inexperienced sergeant pilots were reminded of the forces of nature whilst landing their respective Hurricane aircraft in fierce crosswinds. Both Hurricanes swung on landing, although no damage was reported to either machine or its pilot.

Wednesday, 12th January 1944

Drogue towing.

The winds subsided enough to allow flying training to continue on 12th January, Bill piloted Hurricane, Mk.IIA, Z3672, a drogue towing aircraft.

However, the exercise was not without its element of drama, which occurred when an officer pupil on No.11 Course flew so low that he struck the ground with the aircraft's propeller!

Needless to say, on landing, he was required to explain his actions to the Station Commander.

Two days later another pupil pilot was facing the Station Commander.

Sergeant J.M. Shearer, a member of No.54 Course, whilst attempting his first landing in a Hawker Hurricane, bounced the aircraft so hard it went into a violent swing and crabbed across the runway causing the undercarriage to collapse.

However, due to Sergeant Shearer's inexperience on this type of aircraft, the Station Commander decided to take no further action.

During the last two weeks of January, Bill continued to teach the never-ending stream of pupils the battle tactics they would need to ensure they could be classified as combat ready.

Formation flying, battle formations, shadow firing and aerial gunnery being, as always, the order of the day.

During this period, Flying Officer Bill Marsh added two "new" aircraft to his log-book. On 26th January, he flew himself to the firing range piloting a Fairchild Argus, a single-engined American aircraft. Three days later he piloted a Boulton Paul Defiant drogue towing aircraft, during air to air firing exercises; as though life were not dangerous enough!

The penultimate day of January was to prove to be a sad one for both Bill Marsh and Jackie Neil. The latter was being posted to No.21 Personnel Transit Camp prior to returning to the United Kingdom.

Bill so wanted to go home and see his family, especially his younger brother. The fact he had completed a six month "rest" period at the operation training unit, together with the fact his friend was going home, gave Bill hope for the immediate future.

The parting of the ways came hard, but as they had spent most of their service lives together, both Bill and Jackie hoped they would be together soon. The inevitable promises of meeting at a particular "watering hole" in England were made, but neither was to appreciate that fate would very soon intervene and prevent that meeting from ever taking place.

Monday, 31st January 1944

Drogue Towing.

On the last day of the month Bill Marsh flew two separate missions as pilot of the drogue towing Defiant aircraft.

During the course of the days program, a pupil from No.54 Course struck an army lorry whilst carrying out a low flying exercise! The incident occurred on the Palestine Road, approximately thirty miles east of Ismailia. The fate of the aircraft is unknown, but the pilot was admitted to the Station Sick Quarters with slight head injuries.

Since the cessation of hostilities in North Africa, a number of dignitaries and high ranking air force officers had visited the various squadrons and training units in that theater.

No.71 O.T.U. received such a visit on 1st February, when Air Marshal Sir Keith Park, Air Officer Commanding-in-Chief, Middle East, accompanied by Air Vice-Marshal Malcolm Taylor, Air Officer Commanding No.203 Group arrived and carried out an inspection of the unit.

Another "accident" occurred the day after the visit of the A.O.C. in C. and A.O.C., but on this occasion the aircraft was not flying.

An officer pupil, whilst carrying-out a cockpit check on Hurricane BN173, prior to take-off, selected "undercarriage up" causing the aircraft to collapse to the ground with a resounding crash and damage to the airframe; another red face paraded before the Station Commander.

Friday, 4th February 1944

Wrote to Gil

In a most prophetic (and final) letter to his brother, Bill wrote. . .

> *. . .every day a new revelation of our pupils' crass stupidity arises, until now I know that nothing is secure, nothing permanent, on the face of this earth. As for mental and ocular alertness, they are the stone end. [I] took a drogue aircraft up yesterday, within 200 yards of the five aircraft detailed to fire at it; and though I flew past them three times and informed the fourth aircraft that his wheels were down, they didn't see me till I fired a Very (flare). Afterwards I asked them about their eyes, and speculated on whether I am psychic and use my reflector sight bowl as a magic crystal. They improved today, apart from two colliding and baling out and another flying into the deck (ground) when trying to force land minus engine!*
>
> *Well, you'll be out of plaster now, no doubt, and able to hobble around leering at the fair but susceptible feminine talent.*
>
> *And in that, may I say, you are far better placed than we. The fables of the East are, now at least, moonshine on the water of a silent creek. . .*

The mid-air collision to which Bill referred in his letter involved two Hurricane aircraft flown by the two Free French Air Force pilots.

Both Lieutenant Nouvel and Sergeant Hans managed to bale-out and escape uninjured by parachute, but the two stricken aircraft Hawker Hurricanes, HV302 and HV559, were completely destroyed.

Sunday, 6th February 1944, dawned like any other day, with no indication of the impending tragedy that was to unfold so early in the morning.

By the time two new instructors, Pilot Officer D. Jackson and Pilot Officer W. Tye, both of the Royal New Zealand Air Force, reported for duty, No.71 O.T.U. was trying to come to terms with the Unit's 30th fatal flying accident.

It was a sharp reminder to the two new instructors, on their first day as Ismailia, that the risk of instructional/training duties could be as hazardous as combat flying.

Flying Officer William Marsh, piloting Hawker Hurricane Mk.IIB, serial BD926, was leading a large formation of aircraft on an early morning practice battle flight.

A few seconds before 08.30 hours, he radioed an instruction to the flight that the formation was to turn ninety degrees to starboard. As Bill inaugurated the turn, there was a terrifying wrenching of metal and two Hurricanes fell to earth.

Epilogue

Bill Marsh's Hurricane aircraft had been struck by a similar machine, piloted by 2nd/ Lieutenant J.V. Peters, a pupil pilot from the South African Air Force.

As the two aircraft made their final descents, Peters took to his parachute and baled out of Hurricane, HL699, landing without injury. Bill Marsh's Hurricane fell to earth, and crashed one mile south of Fayid railway station, at 08.30 hours.

The funeral of Flying Officer William "Bill" Ernest Marsh, RAFVR, took place at the British War Cemetery, Moascar, Egypt, on Monday, 7th February 1944. In attendance, apart from his friends and fellow officers, were the Commanding Officer, Chief Flying Instructor and Instructors, of No.71 Operational Training Unit.

William "Bill" Marsh, the Desert Flyer, could have no better epitaph than the content of a letter received by his mother from Flight Lieutenant Austen Clough-Camm, who was now serving with No.283 Squadron, RAF, on Malta. The letter read:

> . . .*When I came to 274 Squadron in 1942, as its Medical Officer, "Bill" was one of the first who attracted me by his unfailing courtesy, and a diffidence which was most refreshing.*
>
> *Very soon it became apparent that he was a most useful member of the Squadron, "nursing" the new pilots (alas all too frequently they came) through their first few operational flights, and preserving throughout the most trying times, a cheerful and encouraging spirit. . .*

Moascar War Cemetery. The headstone marking Bill's grave is extreme left center of the picture. Courtesy of the C.W.G.C, Publicity Department.

> *. . .Later on, I knew him better and learned to respect him even more. From early in 1943, three of us – "Bill", Guy (Bickford-Smith) and myself used, almost invariably, to spend pleasant evenings together. . .*
>
> *. . .Since he left the old Squadron he has written fortnightly to me until early in February, when I received no reply to my letters.*
>
> *I was very moved to hear of his death, he was a real friend to me and I shall miss him a great deal with his good cheer and extreme kindliness.*
>
> *He would hurt no one willingly and was one of the kindest men I have ever met.*

Making comment about the incident, Flight Lieutenant Clough-Camm's letter continued. . .

> *His piloting was extremely sound and "steady" and the accident which caused his passing was not*

Gil Marsh, looks at a photograph, shown to him by Martyn R. Ford-Jones, of his brother's last resting place at Moascar War Cemetery. It was the first time Gil had seen where Bill was laid to rest and the occasion, which took place at Gil's home, on 8th February 1997, was recorded by the Ormskirk Advertiser; Bill's favourite paper. Courtesy of Ormskirk Advertiser Series Newspapers.

his fault. He was instructing in a "battle formation" Balbo (RAF slang for a large formation) when some-one flew into him. This news I had from one of his pupils who was posted here a few days ago. The pupil praised him highly as an instructor – such praise is praise indeed.

. . .It was a good job, well done and you have cause to be very proud of him, and to treasure his memory, as I shall.

The Moascar burial ground, in which Bill Marsh lies, is a desert cemetery, situated four miles west of Ismailia.

Eucalyptus and Casurrina trees form a screen around the cemetery, preventing the intrusion of wind blown sand, whilst plants, flowers and mown grass give the impression of a garden in the desert. A fitting location to lay to rest the man who was both a gardener and a Desert Flyer.

APPENDIX I

SERVICE RECORD
for
FLYING OFFICER WILLIAM E. "BILL" MARSH
Pilot, Royal Air Force

1940

To	Receiving Center, Padgate	17 Apr – 17 May 1940
To	Marham, Station Headquarters	18 May – 20 June 1940
To	No.1 Squadron	
	No.3 Initial Training Wing, Hastings	20 Jun – 3 July 1940
To	No.1 Squadron,	
	No.3 Initial Training Wing, Torquay	4 Jul – 28 Oct 1940
To	No.11 Elementary Flying Training School,	
	Perth,	30 Oct – 31 Dec 1940

1941

To	Personnel Despatch Center, Wilmslow,	
	Cheshire.	1 Jan – 7 Jan 1941
To	No.33 Service Flying School,	
	Carberry, Manitoba, Canada	27 Jan – 16 May 1941
To	No.1 Manning Depot, Halifax	
	Nova Scottia, Canada	21 May – 30 May 1941
To	Transit Camp, Iceland	16 Jun – 24 Jun 1941
To	Personnel Reception Center, Bournemouth	29 Jun – 9 Jul 1941
To	No.55 Operational Conversion Unit,	
	Usworth, Durham	10 Jul – 16 Aug 1941
To	No.605 (County of Warwick) Squadron,	
	Baginton, Warwickshire	
	(Flying Hawker Hurricane Mk.IIAs)	20 Aug – 6 Aug 1941
To	No.605 (County of Warwick) Squadron	
	Honily, Warwickshire.	6 Nov – 30 Oct 1941

(Converted to Hawker Hurricane Mk.IIB, during August 1941).

To	No.605 Squadron	
	(En route to Far East via HMS Argus)	1 Nov -
To	Transit Camp – Gibraltar	14 Nov – 23 Dec 1941

1942

To	Transit Camp – Takoradi, Gold Coast	3 Jan – 6 Jan 1942
To	Transit Camp – Khartoum, Sudan	8 Jan – 12 Jan 1942
To	Transit Camp – Port Sudan, Sudan	14 Jan – 27 Jan 1942
To	Transit Camp – Almaza, Cairo, Egypt	1 Feb – 15 Feb 1942
To	Advanced Flying School, Bilbeis, Egypt	15 Feb – 22 Feb 1942
To	Transit Camp – Almaza, Cairo, Egypt	22 Feb – 25 Feb 1942
To	Transit Camp – Sidi Haneish, Egypt	26 Feb – 28 Feb 1942

WESTERN DESERT

To   No.274 Squadron, Gambut, Egypt   3 Mar – 17 Jun 1942
(Converted to Hawker Hurricane Mk.IIC, during May 1942)

To   No.274 Squadron, Masheifa, Egypt
(Landing Ground No.76)   17 Jun – 23 Jun 1942

To   No.274 Squadron, Matruh West, Egypt
(Landing Ground No.07)   24 Jun – 25 Jun 1942

THE RETREAT

To   No.274 Squadron, Sidi Haneish, Egypt
(Landing Ground No.88)   25 Jun – 1 Jul 1942

To   No.274 Squadron, Amiriya, Egypt
(Landing Ground No.92, Amiriya and
Landing Ground No.173)*   1 Jul – 9 Sep 1942
*Landing Ground No.92 and No.173 were also referred to as Amiriya

THE ADVANCE

To   No.274 Squadron, Idkou (Edku) Egypt
(Landing Ground No.229)   9 Sep – 10 Oct 1942

To   No.274 Squadron, Egypt
(Landing Ground No.89,
Landing Ground No.37, Hamman South   10 Oct – 21 Dec 1942
Landing Ground No.104, Qotafiyah II.
Landing Ground No.13, Sidi Haneish South)

To   No.274 Squadron, Bu Amud*, Martuba, Benina
Misurata, Libya. (*Landing Ground No.147)   23 Dec – 26 Jan 1943

1943

TRIPOLI FELL   23 Jan 1943

To   No.274 Squadron, Castel Benito, Mellaha
Libya (Defense of Tripoli)   26 Jan – 29 May 1943

POSTED

To   No.71 Operational Training Unit, Ismailia
Egypt. (Posted as Instructor on Hawker
Hurricane aircraft).   17 Jun – Feb 1944

Killed 6th February 1944.

APPENDIX II

COMBAT CLAIMS OF WILLIAM "BILL" MARSH
March 1942 - May 1943

Date	Type	Result	Remarks
03.04.42	M.202	Damaged	Diversion sweep over Gazala. Piloting Hurricane, MKIIB, BD820, "D"
12.06.42	Me 109F	Probable	Fighter Sweep over El Adem. Piloting Hurricane, "Z"
13.07.42	Me 109F	Damaged	Bombing of Motor Transport and Infantry concentrations near El Alamein. Piloting Hurricane, Mk.IIB, BE699, "G"
17.07.42	M.202	Damaged	Patrol over El Alamein. Piloting Hurricane, Mk.IIB, BE487, "F"
12.04.43	Ju 88	Damaged	Harbor patrol. Piloting Hurricane, HW659, "H"

APPENDIX III

AIRCRAFT FLOWN BY BILL MARSH
March 1942 - May 1943

Type	Mk.	Serial	Code	Remarks
Hawker Hurricane	IIA	Z4844	"L"	To. No.74 Squadron
Hawker Hurricane	IIB	Z5064		To No.134 Squadron
Hawker Hurricane	IIB	Z5313		Shot down by flak, whilst being flown by Sgt. Mullis
Hawker Hurricane	IIB	Z5443		To No.134 Squadron
Hawker Hurricane	IIB	BD820	"D"	
Hawker Hurricane	IIB	BD827		Struck off charge on 23rd September 1942, as having been lost to enemy action
Hawker Hurricane	IIB	BD880		To No.1566 Flight.
Hawker Hurricane	IIB	BD926	NH-X	Struck off charge 06.02.44
Hawker Hurricane	IIB	BE204		
Hawker Hurricane	IIB	BE231		
Hawker Hurricane	IIB	BE281	NH-T	Crashed and exploded during fighter affiliation practice, after aircraft piloted by Sgt Caldwell, collided with Hurricane, HL738, piloted by F/Sgt Sutherland of the same Squadron. Caldwell was killed, whilst Sutherland force-landed, wheels up.
Hawker Hurricane	II	BE397	NH-K	Lost 01.09.43
Hawker Hurricane	IIC	BE487	NH-F	Struck off charge 31.06.45
Hawker Hurricane	IIB	BE490	NH-W	To No.1555 Flight
Hawker Hurricane	IIC	BE491	NH-W	To Turkey on 1st September 1943
Hawker Hurricane	II	BE669	NH-G	To No.1414 Flight
Hawker Hurricane	IIB	BE699	NH-C	To No.335 Squadron
Hawker Hurricane	IIB	BG700		
Hawker Hurricane	IIB	BG706	NH-G	
Hawker Hurricane	IIB	BG750	"W"	To Turkey 01.07.43
Hawker Hurricane	IIB	BH287	NH-X	Shot down into sea, by enemy fighters, during a bombing operation on 5th November 1942. Aircraft piloted by W/O Jack Neil.

Hawker Hurricane	IIB	BN109	H-B	Belly-landed in desert by Sgt Macfarlane, after being attacked and damaged by Me 109s, on 25.09.45
Hawker Hurricane	IIB	BN113	NH-J	To Turkey on 1st August 1943
Hawker Hurricane	IIB	BN162	"G"	
Hawker Hurricane	IIC	BN173	NH-R	Struck-off charge on 31st May 1945
Hawker Hurricane	IIC	BN183		
Hawker Hurricane	IIC	BP334		Struck-off charge on 27th October 1944
Hawker Hurricane	IIB	BP443	NH-F	To South African Air Force, on 29 June 1943
Hawker Hurricane	II	BP693	NH-P	Shot down by Me 109s, whilst attacking enemy armored convoy on 25th August 1942
Hawker Hurricane	IIB	BP763	NH-N	To No.1415 Flight
Hawker Hurricane		HL547	NH-	
Hawker Hurricane	IIA	HL794	NH-	Fighter Bomber
Hawker Hurricane	II	HV484	NH-Z	

APPENDIX IV

No.274 SQUADRON COMBAT CLAIMS
March 1942 - May 1943

Date	Pilot	Claim	Remarks
02/03/42	Sgt Dodds	M.202	Shot down in flames
13/03/42	Sgt Dodds	M.200	Crashed on beach, 20 miles west of Trobuk
17/03/42	Sgt Eagle	Me 110	Last seen going down with port engine on fire
27/03/42	P/O Conrad	M.202	Damaged. Observed pieces falling off
27/03/42	Sgt Barwick	M.202	Damaged. Last seen going down emitting black smoke
03/04/42	P/O Hunter	Me 109	Probable
03/04/42	Sgt Garwood	Me 109	Probable
03/04/42	Sgt Marsh	M.202	Damaged
06/04/42	Sgt Eagle	Me 109	Destroyed
06/04/42	Sgt Dodds	M.200	Probable
		Me 109	Damaged
25/04/42	P/O Keefer	Me 109	Probable
25/05/42	P/O Browne	Me 109	Damaged
25/05/42	P/O Samuels	Me 109	Damaged
27/05/42	F/S Neil	Ju 87	Destroyed
27/05/42	Sgt Walsh	Me 109	Damaged
27/05/42	Sgt Dodds	Me 109	Damaged
27/05/42	P/O Samuels	Ju 87	Damaged
29/05/42	Sgt Dodds	Me 109	Damaged
31/05/42	Sgt Bruckshaw	Ju 87	Damaged
01/06/42	Sgt Eagle	Me 109	Damaged
05/06/42	Sgt Dodds	Me 109F	Damaged
05/06/42	F/S Neil	Me 109F	Damaged
08/06/42	P/O Keefer	M.202	Destroyed
08/06/42	Sgt Craggs	M.202	Damaged
09/06/42	Sgt Eagle	Me 109	Probable. Observed pieces falling off wings and fuselage, as e/a went into dive emitting black smoke.
09/06/42	Sgt Eagle	Me 109	Damaged
09/06/42	Sgt Henderson	Me 109	Damaged. Observed glycol stream
11/06/42	P/O Walsh	Me 109	Destroyed. Burst into flames
11/06/42	P/O Walsh	Me 109	Damaged

11/06/42	F/S Neil	Me 109	Destroyed
12/06/42	P/O Browne	Me 109	Probable. Observed strikes on fuselage, emitted black smoke and went into dive.
12/06/42	Sgt Henderson	Me 109	Probable. Pieces flew off, aircraft went into dive streaming glycol.
12/06/42	Sgt Henderson	Me 109	Damaged
12/06/42	Sgt Thompson	Me 109	Probable. Aircraft dived streaming glycol.
12/06/42	Sgt Marsh	Me 109	Probable. Sprayed e/a, pieces flew off and a/c went into dive. Recovered 20' above ground and then undercarriage dropped
12/06/42	P/O Hunter	M.202	Probable
12/06/42	P/O Buckley	M.202	Damaged
12/06/42	P/O ?	Me 109F	Destroyed
12/06/42	Sgt Dodds	Me 109F	Destroyed
		Me 109F	Damaged
12/06/42	F/S Parbury	Me 109F	Probable
15/06/42	W/C Fenton	CR.42	Destroyed
		M.202	Probable
15/06/42	Sgt Dodds	CR.42	Probable
15/06/42	F/L Darwin	Me 109E	Damaged
16/06/42	P/O Conrad	Me 109	Probable
16/06/42	P/O Keefer	Me 109	Destroyed
16/06/42	Sgt Dodds	Me 109	Destroyed
		Me 109E	Destroyed
17/06/42	P/O Keefer	M.202	Damaged
17/06/42	Sgt Lerche	M.202	Damaged
17/06/42	Sgt Dodds	M.202	Destroyed
		M.202	Destroyed
23/06/42	P/O Samuels	Me 109	Damaged
03/07/42	Sgt Garwood	M.202	Destroyed
03/07/42	Sgt Lerche	M.202	Damaged
03/07/42	F/S Neil	Me 109F	Damaged
10/07/42	S/L Hayter	M.202	Probable
10/07/42	F/O Keefer	M.202	Damaged
		M.202	Damaged
10/07/42	F/S Garwood	Me 109	Damaged
		Me 109	Probable
10/07/42	F/L Conrad	M.202	Damaged
10/07/42	Sgt Henderson	M.202	Damaged
10/07/42	Sgt Ott	Me 109	Damaged

17/07/42	F/L Keefer	Me 109F	Damaged
17/07/42	Sgt Henderson	Ju 87	Destroyed
17/07/42	Sgt Marsh	M.202	Damaged
18/07/42	S/L Hayter	Me 109E	Damaged
18/07/42	F/O Hunter	M.202	Damaged
18/07/42	Sgt Lerche	Me 109	Damaged
22/07/42	F/S Neil	Me 109	Probable
22/07/42	P/O Mitchell	Me 109	Probable (Shared with P/O Bell)
22/07/42	P/O Bell	Me 109	Probable (Shared with P/O Mitchell)
22/07/42	P/O Bell	Ju 87	Probable
22/07/42	F/L Darwin	Me 109	Damaged
22/07/42	P/O Browne	Ju 87	Damaged
08/08/42	F/S Gordon	Me 109F	Destroyed
09/08/42	F/S Neil	M.202	Damaged
25/08/42	Sgt Marfarlane	M.109F	Damaged
02/09/42	F/S Neil	Ju 87	Destroyed
		Ju 87	Probable
		Me 109	Damaged
02/09/42	Sgt Carter	Me 109	Destroyed
		Ju 87	Probable
		Ju 87	Damaged
02/09/42	P/O Henderson	Ju 87	Damaged
02/09/42	Col Loftus	Ju 87	Damaged
		Me 109F	Damaged
02/09/42	F/O Graves	Me 109F	Damaged
02/09/42	Sgt Ott	Me 109	Destroyed
03/09/42	P/O Mitchell	Me 109E	Damaged
21/09/42	P/O Mitchell	Ju 88	Probable (Shared with Sgt Carter)
21/09/42	Sgt Carter	Ju 88	Probable (Shared with P/O Mitchell)
24/10/42	Sgt Bruckshaw	Me 109	Probable
02/11/42	W/O Neil	Me 109	Damaged
02/11/42	P/O Brickhill	Me 109	Damaged
02/11/42	Sgt Bruckshaw	Me 109	Probable
05/11/42	Sgt Burman	Fi.156	Destroyed. One wing broke off, aircraft crashed into sea.
01/12/42	Sgt Gordon	Ju 88	Damaged (Shared). Fragments seen to detach during attack. Aircraft bounced off sea, but continued to fly.

01/12/42	Sgt Aron	Ju 88	Damaged (Shared). Fragments seen to detach during attack. Aircraft bounced of sea, but continued to fly.
07/02/43	Sgt Meldrum	Ju 88	Damaged. (Shared). Attacked and registered strikes against fuselage and tailplane. Enemy aircraft escaped into cloud
07/02/43	Sgt Matthews	Ju 88	Damaged. (Shared). Attacked and registered strikes against fuselage and tailplane. Enemy aircraft escaped into cloud
20/03/43	F/L Graves	Ju 88	Damaged (Shared). Attacked Ju 88. Black smoke seen to emit from port engine. Last seen entering cloud.
20/03/43	Sgt Bickford-Smith	Ju 88	Damaged (Shared). Attacked Ju 88. Black smoke seen to emit from port engine. Last seen entering cloud.
12/04/43	F/S Marsh	Ju 88	Damaged. Black smoke seen to emit from one engine. E/A escaped.
19/05/43	P/O Neil	Ju 88	Damaged. Fragments seen to detach during attack. Aircraft went down with an engine on fire.

APPENDIX V

No.274 SQUADRON CASUALTIES
March 1942 - May 1943

Date	Name	Remarks	Condition
02/03/42	Sgt Wildy	Shot down by Me 109, Tobruk area. Baled out.	Wounded
02/03/42	Sgt MacDonnell	Shot down by Me 109, Tobruk area. Baled out.	Wounded.
02/03/42	Sgt Eagle	Crash-landed, 25 kms west Gambut	Wounded in shoulder
08/03/42	Sgt Persse	Attacked by Me 109s whilst landing. Force landed.	Wounded in leg
21/03/42	Sgt Mullis	Shot down by ground fire, on return from patrol south of Bir Hackeim. Aircraft burst into flames.	Killed
03/04/42	Sgt Howell	Shot down during sweep over Gazala	Wounded
25/05/42	F/L Playford	Shot-up in dogfight over Gazala area	Wounded.
31/05/42	P/O Ismay	Shot down by Me 109s, during a patrol over El Adem-Bir Hacheim	Killed.
02/06/42	F/Lt Moriarty	Shot down by three Me 109s over Gazala area.	Killed
11/06/42	P/O Persse	Shot down in dog-fight	Killed.
17/06/42	P/O Conrad	Shot down in combat. Force landed in desert. Straffed by Me 109s before he could get out of the cockpit.	Wounded in both legs and left arm by cannon shell fragments
26/06/42	Sgt Thompson	Shot down during attack against enemy columns	Killed
10/07/42	Sgt Craggs	Shot down in dog-fight, over El Alamein.	Killed
16/07/42	Sgt Hemmer	Dogfight with Me 109s and M.202s west of El Alamein	Wounded.

16/07/42	Sgt Presland	Aircraft shot down in flames	Killed
07/08/42	F/L Darwin	Shot down by Me 109.	Killed.
07/08/42	Sgt Hemmer	Shot down into sea	Drowned
08/08/42	Sgt Hamilton	Shot down by Me 109	Killed
25/08/42	P/O Simpson	Aircraft damaged by machine gun fire	Wounded.
13/10/42	F/S Beckett	Collided with another Hurricane from same Squadron, during air to ground firing exercise.	Killed
13/10/42	Sgt Lyle	Aircraft struck by Hurricane flown by F/S Beckett during air to ground firing exercise.	Crash-landed with Cat.II. damage.
25/10/42	Sgt Ott	Landed at high speed at night. Wrenched off undercarriage.	
25/10/42	Sgt Everington	Crash-landed at night.	Minor injuries
02/11/42	F/S Howie	Shot down during bombing attack	Captured
02/11/42	Sgt Robertson	Shot down during bombing attack	Returned to unit
12/01/43		Hurricane HN-N struck by over-shooting Wellington bomber whilst parked at dispersal	
23/01/43	Sgt Lyle	Crash landed ten miles west of Misurata, having run out of fuel.	Returned to unit.
03/02/43	Sgt Eaglen	Aircraft overturned, having burst a tyre on landing.	Died of a broken neck
04/02/43	W/O Neil	Burst tyre on landing, undercarriage written-off in subsequent crash.	Twisted shoulder
12/02/43	Sgt Lyle	Landed with broken undercarriage strut. Made wheels-up landing.	
25/02/43	Sgt Caldwell	Touched down with drift on and broke starboard oleo undercarriage leg.	
26/02/43	Sgt Caldwell	Hurricane struck by aircraft flown by F/S Sutherland	Killed

26/02/43	F/S Sutherland	Hurricane struck by aircraft flown by Sgt Caldwell	Severe back injuries
23/04/43	LAC Holme	Hurricane damaged by member of groundcrew who attempted to fly it.	
27/04/43	F/L Thompson	Hurricane destroyed after hitting windsock during take-off.	Memory loss

Appendices

APPENDIX VI

EQUIVALENT RANKS

United States Army Air Force   Royal Air Force

Rank	Abbr	Rank	Abbr
General (Five Star)	Gen	Marshal of the Royal Air Force	MRAF
General (Four Star)	Gen	Air Chief Marshal	ACM
Lieutenant General	Lt.Gen	Air Marshal	AM
Major General	Maj.Gen	Air Vice-Marshal	AVM
Brigadier General	Brig-Gen	Air Commodore	Air Cdre
Colonel	Col	Group Captain	Gp.Capt or G/C
Lieutenant Colonel	Lt.Col	Wing Commander	Wing Co or W/C
Major	Maj	Squadron Leader	Sqd/Ldr or S/L
Captain	Cap	Flight Lieutenant	Flt/Lt or F/L
First Lieutenant	1st. Lt	Flying Officer	Flg/Off or F/O
Second Lieutenant	2nd.Lt	Pilot Officer	Pil/Off or P/O
Flight Officer	Flt.Off	Warrant Officer	W/O
Master Sergeant	MSgt	Flight Sergeant	F/S
Technical Sergeant	TSgt	Sergeant	Sgt
Sergeant	Sgt		
Corporal	Cpl	Corporal	Cpl
		Leading Aircraftman	LAC
Private 1st Class	PFC	Aircraftman 1st Class	AC1
Private	Pvt	Aircraftman 2nd Class	AC2

BIBLIOGRAPHY

Ford-Jones, Martyn R. *Bomber Squadron: Men Who Flew with XV*.
London, England: Kimber William & Co Ltd. 1987

Form 540/541 *No.274 Squadron*: London, England:
Public Record Office. 1942- 1943

Form 540/541 *No.605 Squadron*: London, England:
Public Record Office. 1941

Moore, John. *The Fleet Air Arm*: London, England:
Chapman & Hall Ltd. 1943.

The War In Pictures, Third Year: London, England.
Oldhams Press Limited